The Poem of the Cid

IN THIS SERIES

Sir Gawain and the Green Knight
edited by W. R. J. Barron

Further titles in preparation

MANCHESTER MEDIEVAL CLASSICS   *general editor* G. L. Brook

El Cid Campéador.

The Poem
of the Cid

A new critical edition of the Spanish text

WITH AN INTRODUCTION AND NOTES
by Ian Michael
TOGETHER WITH A NEW PROSE TRANSLATION
by Rita Hamilton *and* Janet Perry

MANCHESTER UNIVERSITY PRESS

BARNES & NOBLE BOOKS · NEW YORK

EDITION OF SPANISH TEXT, INTRODUCTION, NOTES AND MAP
© 1975 Ian Michael

TRANSLATION
© 1975 Rita Hamilton

Published by MANCHESTER UNIVERSITY PRESS
Oxford Road, Manchester M13 9PL

UK ISBN 0 7190 0578 7

USA HARPER & ROW PUBLISHERS INC
BARNES & NOBLE IMPORT DIVISION

US ISBN 0 06 494799 8

Printed in Great Britain by T. & A. CONSTABLE LTD
Hopetoun Street, Edinburgh EH7 4NF

Contents

Editor's preface

Although work on the present edition of the Spanish text was formally begun only towards the end of 1967, the undergraduates who had earlier studied the text with me in my classes given at the University of Manchester provided some idea of the kind of edition they would have liked to have; while the work was in progress I was able to try out my ideas on later years of undergraduates there and, more recently, at the University of Southampton. Part of my aim was to produce a fully annotated yet low-priced edition for the 'Spanish Texts' series, but the escalating costs of modern publishing have, most unhappily, caused that project to be abandoned. I am nevertheless delighted to fulfil here the other part of the aim: to print the critical text, together with a small selection from the complete notes, alongside the prose translation so carefully prepared by Rita Hamilton and the late Janet Perry. Considerations of space in the present edition permit the inclusion of only a very small part of the textual notes, and I crave the indulgence of scholars for being unable to include the whole *apparatus criticus*, which I hope to publish in a future Spanish edition.

In addition to my gratitude to J. W. Rees, J. M. Blecua and the greatly missed Frederick Whitehead, which I express on p. 17 of the Introduction, I wish to acknowledge my debt to Rita Hamilton, F. W. Hodcroft and H. M. Ettinghausen, who read the typescript of the full edition and saved me from a number of errors. P. E. Russell most kindly read the introduction and notes in the original edition, and A. D. Deyermond those in the present edition; both made helpful suggestions for improvement. The General Editor, G. L. Brook, has given us most valuable advice on matters of presentation and has been indulgent to us in the difficulties we have faced. I am indebted to Diane Rankin for her careful preparation of a substantial part of the typescript and to the Cartographic Unit of the Department of Geography, University of Southampton, for their skilful drawing of the map to my instructions.

My hope is that at least some of my former undergraduate students will recollect their youthful enthusiasm and return to these *versos bárbaros notables*, accompanied as they are here with a better 'crib' than they could possibly have imagined and than I would have allowed them to use.

I. M.

Translator's preface

I willingly and eagerly take this opportunity of paying very warm tribute to my collaborator Miss Janet Perry, whose death in 1958 left in the lives of all who knew and loved her a gap that can never be filled. Hers was the inspiration that led to our undertaking the rewarding task of making an English prose version of the *Poema*, although she flattered me by insisting that she would not embark upon it without my collaboration.

From the outset we decided on prose rather than verse, not only because other translations in verse had recently appeared, but because we thought that prose was more suited to the forthright, rugged metre of the original. We first of all intended it to be read independently of the Spanish text. This did not at all weaken our respect for accuracy but it did mean that we allowed ourselves sometimes to suppress repetitions, notably those of the epic epithets and phrases where in modern English the name of the hero or other personage would produce the same effect. Our method was that of true collaboration in that we each took portions of the text and worked on our own at the translation. Then, in our weekly meetings, we each read aloud to the other our translation for criticism, comment and emendation. Two of our colleagues in the English Department of King's College who overheard our reading sessions became greatly interested in the project and offered themselves as a critical audience, listening carefully for departures from current English usage. Their encouragement and enthusiasm helped us greatly in our wholly absorbing but exacting task. We were able to discuss with them the problems involved in dealing with the use of tenses (e.g. the effectiveness or otherwise of using the historic present in English) and we were happy to be guided by their advice.

If readers obtain in reading even a small amount of the pleasure which we had in preparing the translation, we shall be richly rewarded.

R. H.

Introduction

Few medieval outlaws made such a success of their banishment as Rodrigo Díaz de Vivar, and none has matched him in posthumous literary fame. Born into the rank of *infanzón* (or baronet) in the small village of Vivar, near Burgos, *c.* 1043, by his exploits he became known as 'The Battler'—*Campidoctor* in Latin chronicles and *El Campeador* in vernacular accounts; but the most enduring title he won was *Mio Cid*—from the Arabic *Sayyidī*, 'My lord'. He served as standard-bearer to Sancho II of Castile, who was assassinated at the siege of Zamora in 1072. That event marked the beginning of the Cid's political vicissitudes, for Sancho's brother and bitter enemy, Alfonso VI, King of León, not only recovered his own kingdom but now added Castile to his domains, thereafter having the uneasiest of relations with the Cid: he banished him from 1081 to 1087 and again from 1089 to 1092. Rodrigo spent most of his first exile in the service of the Moorish Emir Mu'taman of Saragossa, aiding him in his wars against his younger brother al-Hāyyib, Emir of Lérida, and Berenguer Ramón II the Fratricide, Count of Barcelona. During his second exile the Cid at first continued his earlier campaigns, taking the Count of Barcelona prisoner for the second time in 1090, but in 1092 he began the siege of the Moorish city of Valencia, which fell to him at last in 1094, after he had fought off an Almoravid attempt to save the city. Rodrigo died there in July 1099. In May 1102 his widow, Jimena Díaz, brought his embalmed remains to Castile for interment in the monastery of San Pedro de Cardeña near Burgos, and Valencia was abandoned to the Muslims once more.[1]

Even before his death the Cid was celebrated in a panegyrical Latin poem known as the *Carmen Campidoctoris* (1093-94?) and soon after it in a brief Latin chronicle, the *Historia Roderici* (*c.* 1110?)—both works written in the east of the peninsula, where he achieved his greatest

---

[1] The best account of the Cid's life and contemporary events, though it is sometimes fanciful, is still Ramón Menéndez Pidal's *La España del Cid*, 7th edn. (vols. VI and VII of the author's *Obras completas*) (Madrid, 1969), which contains transcriptions of the most important documents. English translation of the abridged form by H. Sutherland, *The Cid and his Spain* (London, 1934).

military success. The interment of the Cid's body at Cardeña and Doña Jimena's gifts to the monastery gave rise during the thirteenth century to a legendary tradition connected with the development of a tomb cult there;[2] it is possible that the cult attracted *jongleurs* who would have recited poems about the Cid's exploits. There is some evidence, as will be seen, to connect the extant *Poema de Mio Cid* (sometimes called *Cantar de Mio Cid, c.* 1201-07?) with Cardeña, Vivar and Burgos itself. With the possible exception of Corneille's *Le Cid, The Poem of the Cid* is the best and most successful literary treatment of Rodrigo Díaz's career, yet it left almost no echoes in contemporary or later medieval poetry and had no effect on later literary elaborations until the modern period. It was the ballads of the fifteenth and sixteenth centuries, with their wild fantasies about the Cid's exploits, which were to have the chief influence on later developments. The poem is also remarkable in that it is the only survivor in near-complete form of medieval Spanish epic poems; the only other extensive text that has come down to us is the incomplete *Mocedades de Rodrigo*, which is late and full of fictitious material.[3]

History and fiction in the poem

As we might expect from a poem composed probably over a hundred years after the events it purports to describe, *The Poem of the Cid* exhibits a considerable haziness on some historical points and contains fictitious material, yet, unlike most medieval heroic poems, it contains much historical fact and some surprisingly accurate references to real personages. P. E. Russell has suggested that 'The one explanation of the partial "historicity" of the *Cantar* which seems to have escaped consideration is that it could be the product of a certain amount of historical investigation by its author.'[4]

It is clear that the historical basis of the poem was the Cid's second banishment, which began in December 1089, but the poet was out of his historical depth in most of the Cid's alliances and battles in the *Levante*, and his orientation was towards the politics of Castile and its eastern border. Thus there is a very detailed account of the Cid's

[2] See P. E. Russell, 'San Pedro de Cardeña and the heroic history of the Cid', *Medium Aevum*, XXVII (1958), 57-79, and W. J. Entwistle, 'La Estoria del noble varón el Cid Ruy Díaz', *Hispanic Review*, XV (1947), 206-11.

[3] For a full account and edition of this poem, and an excellent study of the Cidian epic cycle, see A. D. Deyermond, *Epic Poetry and the Clergy: Studies on the 'Mocedades de Rodrigo'* (London, 1969).

[4] 'Some problems of diplomatic in the *Cantar de Mio Cid* and their implications', *Modern Language Review*, XLVII (1952), 340-49, at 348.

campaigns along the Henares and the Jalón, which are not well documented at all, especially his capture of Castejón and Alcocer, while the account of the campaigns in the east is confused. The treatment of the defeat of the Count of Barcelona becomes little more than 'a comic interlude',[5] while his handling of the capture of Valencia and the lengthy siege that led up to it does less than justice to that shattering event. Given this tendency to contain the Cid's affairs within the context of home politics, it was therefore a most ingenious step to choose two fairly obscure Leonese nobles to take the villainous roles; they had the artistic advantage of forming a feuding faction with the Cid's longstanding enemy, Count García Ordóñez, a favourite of Alfonso VI, and were capable of being presented as greedy spendthrifts, ambitious cowards, haughty weaklings and, at last, disgraced and defeated traitors. The poet could hardly have taken such a line with personages better known to history.

The poet's daring in the invention of the marriages of the Cid's daughters with the Infantes of Carrión shows us how vital this departure from history was to the overall structure of his poem. Other inventions also have some importance: the poem basically describes the Cid's second banishment, but gives as the reason for it the false accusations made by 'meddlers at court' (the Vanigómez faction) which led to his first banishment in 1081. The poet has Doña Jimena and the children taking refuge at Cardeña, though there is no historical evidence for that; it has the effect, however, of giving the abbey an important position in the poem which it did not have in the historical sequence of events. Alfonso's *mandato real* or decree and the resultant lack of hospitality at Burgos are also quite unattested, and the nine-year-old girl's speech has the ring of pure fiction.[6] The invention of Martín Antolínez and his importance as the one inhabitant of Burgos who saves the day for the Cid,[7] the fictitious episode of the Jewish moneylenders, the highly improbable defiance of the *mandato real* by the unknown abbot of Cardeña,[8] all these inventions fulfil the artistic needs of the poet. It is a distortion to imagine that the poem only becomes more fictitious as it proceeds—it is in many essentials fictitious from the outset. The immediate introduction of Álvar Fáñez as the Cid's right-hand man and his continuance in that role have no historical foundation at all. The Cid's campaigns are presented geographically as

---

[5] See Thomas Montgomery, 'The Cid and the Count of Barcelona', *Hispanic Review*, XXX (1962), 1-11.

[6] See Russell, 'Some problems of diplomatic . . .', 342 and n. 4.

[7] See Rita Hamilton, 'Epic epithets in the *Poema de Mio Cid*', *Revue de Littérature Comparée*, XXXVI (1962), 162-78, especially 163-66.

[8] See Russell, 'San Pedro de Cardeña . . .', 72.

a progression or journey from Vivar towards Valencia, never as the historically somewhat haphazard raids stemming for the most part from Saragossa. The space allotted to Castejón and Alcocer, and the role accorded to San Esteban de Gormaz and Medinaceli in the itineraries, are due primarily to the proximity of those towns to Old Castile and their comparative familiarity to the poet and his audience, rather than to their importance, or even their occurrence, in the Cid's career.[9]

Yet what has made the poem seem so historical in comparison with other medieval epics is the occurrence of details, unimportant to the poem, which nevertheless have turned out to be historically accurate. It is surprising to find that minor characters such as Diego Téllez, Mal Anda and Galind García had a solid historical existence, even if their deeds in the poem cannot be attested. This provides some evidence that the poet may have done some historical research, as Russell has suggested, in order to give the whole the appearance of history.

The Cid as poetic hero

The basic aim of the poem is to present the Cid as a hero, that is, as a man who proves himself in action to be superior to his fellow men. This superiority is not only shown to be physical and combative, it is also seen to include excellence in generalship, religious devotion, family obligation, vassalage, knowledge and observance of legal procedure, generosity, courtesy, wiliness and discretion. These are the qualities which the Cid is shown to possess in high degree, and which go to make him *valer más*, to be worth more than other men. This inner superiority is represented outwardly by his honour, which depends on his *nuevas*, or renown of his deeds. The banishment, and later the outrage at Corpes, touch his honour, which he must therefore be seen to vindicate.

The Cid also represents and idealises the restless, hardy ethos of Castile in an outward-looking moment, when there were lands to conquer and fortunes to be made. This exhilarating air of opportunity and territorial expansion foreshadows that of the *conquistadores* in Spanish America, of the pioneers in the American west, or of the colonisers of the British empire in their headier moments. Whether or not these feelings were shared by the historical Cid and his followers, what matters is the effect on early thirteenth-century audiences: it was once again a propitious moment for the adventurously minded. We

[9] See Ian Michael, 'Geographical problems in the *Poema de Mio Cid: I*. The Exile route', in *Medieval Hispanic Studies presented to Rita Hamilton* (forthcoming), and '. . . II. The Corpes route', in *Mio Cid Studies* (London, forthcoming).

may in fact regard the poem as the earliest production in what A. D. Deyermond has called 'The literature of the thirteenth-century expansion'.[10] The defeat of the Spanish Christians at Alarcos in 1195 had been crushing, but by 1212 they avenged it at Las Navas de Tolosa, where the armies of Castile, León and Aragon, with French help, broke the Almohad power. It may not be too fanciful to see a poem which exalted the Cid as a man who succeeds by his own efforts in Moorish territory being used as part of a recruiting drive during the lull before the new and unstoppable Christian advance that began in 1212.

The Cid of the poem is unusual among medieval literary heroes because of his practical aims and his down-to-earth humanity. Much more unusual is his age: the poet chose to present only the last ten years of his life, and he is shown to possess an august gravity. None the less, we are afforded glimpses of his wilder youthful exploits: his imprisonment of Count García Ordóñez at the castle of Cabra, where he pulled the count's beard (lines 3285-90), and his striking of the Count of Barcelona's nephew at the Catalan court (lines 962-63). In a curious way, the Cid's poetic character is an amalgam of the poetic Roland's youthful boldness and Charlemagne's elderly caution. Yet the difference in tone between the French and Spanish poems is striking: the *Roland* has an air of sadness and inevitability, and an emphasis on protocol, dissension and death, which provide a marked contrast with the optimism and joy of the Spanish poem, in which the Cid and his men are in easy accord, ready for all comers in their resolve to 'earn their bread'. By rounding the Cid's character and giving us a detailed account of his private life, the poet has diminished his impact as a heroic warrior, and in this sense the poem is less 'epic' than other medieval heroic poems, as C. M. Bowra observed.[11] On the other hand, he has achieved a stronger literary personage, who seems to be the product of an age of writing, rather than of oral formulaic composition.

The literary form and the poetic language

The poem has certain formal features in common with other heroic poems of the kind C. M. Bowra has called 'primitive' or 'folk'.[12] Its unit is (a) the single line of verse which has a caesura, or (b) the half-line; the lines are grouped in strophes or *laisses* of varying size;

[10] See his *A Literary History of Spain* (ed. R. O. Jones) [vol. 1]: *The Middle Ages* (London, 1971), pp. 55-58.

[11] *Heroic Poetry* (London, 1952), p. 249.

[12] *Heroic Poetry* (London, 1952) and *From Virgil to Milton* (London, 1945); in his last book Bowra rejected the term 'epic' for the Homeric poems; see *Homer* (London, 1972), pp. 2-3.

the lines within each *laisse* usually have the same assonating ending. Furthermore, this kind of poetry was composed only for oral performance before an audience, and may well have been sung in its entirety.[13] The most important feature is the formula, which is normally of the length of a half-line or a full line and which Parry defined as 'a group of words which is regularly employed under the same metrical conditions to express a given essential idea'.[14]

In contrast to the quite strict metres of French epic poems, the Spanish poem has an irregular metre in which each hemistich may have as few as four syllables or as many as fourteen. The commonest lines, however, consist of $7+7, 6+7, 7+8, 6+8, 8+7$ and $8+8$ (in that order of frequency), and according to the calculations of Menéndez Pidal, *ed. crít.* pp. 92-103, all such lines account for almost 62 per cent of the total. It is difficult to imagine that this amount of irregularity could be due simply to faulty copying from dictation, especially since the epic formulae themselves give rise to some of the irregularity, and they are very likely to have come from the poet unchanged, cf. *la missa dicha* 320 and 1703, against *La oración fecha, la missa acabada la an* 366 and *La oración fecha* 54. As F. Whitehead said, 'There is no theoretical reason why epic poets should not have written lines containing an irregular number of syllables . . . what we condemn as corruptions may in some cases be quite legitimate licences of scansion.'[15] It must be stated, however, that the licences of scansion are so many in the Spanish poem that we have little idea of whether the 'normal' line consisted of thirteen, fourteen, fifteen or sixteen syllables, nor do we know what criteria governed hiatus, synaloepha and synaeresis. Robert A. Hall has claimed that the poem has a stress-timed verse derived from Germanic poetry, in which the unstressed syllables might vary in number in singing or recitation; this theory is similar to the older theory of Pidal and others that the line length was controlled not by the number of syllables but by the number of musical beats.[16]

[13] See Jean Rychner, *La Chanson de geste. Essai sur l'art épique des jongleurs* (Geneva and Lille, 1955), especially pp. 10-25.

[14] See Milman Parry, *Serbocroatian Heroic Songs*, ed. A. B. Lord (Cambridge, Mass. and Belgrade, 1954), vol. I, and Albert B. Lord, *The Singer of Tales* (Cambridge, Mass., 1960).

[15] *La Chanson de Roland*, 2nd edn. (Oxford, 1946), p. xii.

[16] Hall, 'Old Spanish stress-timed verse and Germanic superstratum', *Romance Philology*, XIX (1965-66), 227-34. Jules Horrent, *Roncesvalles. Etude sur le fragment de cantar de gesta conservé à l'Archivo de Navarra (Pampelune)* (Paris, 1951), gives the best account of discussions up to that date and criticises Pidal's method of calculation, by which he excluded lines where there was doubt about hiatus and synaloepha (pp. 68-69). For a lucid account of later studies see Deyermond, *Epic Poetry and the Clergy . . .* , pp. 55-57.

Whatever the merits of these theories, the debate has been narrowed by the general assumption that, if the verse was syllable-timed, all the lines must have had the same number of syllables; one might suggest that the metre may have been only semi-strict, with no single 'normal' line length, and that we ought rather to address ourselves to the amount of toleration it permitted in individual lines where there is no other reason to suspect error.

The assonances are also less strictly observed than in the French poems. Whitehead, like Bédier before him, pointed out that 'many Old French epic poets introduce impure assonances into their *laisses* and . . . consequently an imperfect assonance is not *prima facie* evidence of scribal corruption.'[17] The Spanish poem again exhibits much greater irregularities, and some of them may well be the result of scribal error; but we should be unwise to take upon ourselves, as Pidal and earlier editors did, the dubious task of 'correcting' them all. Many of them occur at the beginning or end of the *laisses* and they seem to mark a change of gear in the process of composition; they may have had some relation to the music that is hidden from us; sometimes they appear to serve a poetic function by heightening a moment of particular emotion or excitement, cf. lines 412, 897-98, 1010, 1885, 2155, 2428, etc.

The poem is composed in a kind of *Kunstsprache* or 'art language', not dissimilar to that which we find in ballads. The use of archaic forms lends an antique patina to the lines. The range of verb tenses is extraordinarily varied and there are frequent and striking changes of tense, cf. lines 35-40, where almost all the verbs could, more monotonously, have been rendered by preterites. There is also a great deal of periphrastic construction, principally by the use of modal auxiliaries, which is perhaps the most striking feature of the language of the poem, but it need not be regarded as evidence of oral composition; these forms also occur in the thirteenth-century narrative poems, though not with the same frequency, and in both cases they may be the result of what F. Whitehead, apropos Old French epic style, called 'la contrainte métrique' (i.e. restrictions imposed by the metrical form).[18]

The lexicon of the poem also has certain characteristic features. There are phrases of legal or ecclesiastical origin, and others may be derived from Latin chronicles.[19] The absolute constructions ('La missa dicha',

[17] *La Chanson de Roland*, 2nd edn., p. xi, and cf. Joseph Bédier, *La Chanson de Roland* (Paris, 1927), II (Commentaires), pp. 270-97.

[18] In an unpublished paper entitled 'Le style épique et la contrainte métrique', read to the IVe Congrès de la Société Rencesvals, Heidelberg, August-September 1967 (summary in *Bulletin Bibliographique de la Société Rencesvals*, No. 5, Paris, 1970, p. 111).

[19] Colin Smith, 'Latin histories and vernacular epic in twelfth-century Spain: similarities of spirit and style', *Bulletin of Hispanic Studies*, XLVIII (1971), 1-19.

etc.) may also stem from the poet's familiarity with Latin. There are many phrases with a 'kindred' or 'internal' complement ('weeping from the eyes', 'saying with the mouth'), but they appear to be popular and traditional, and it is noteworthy that they are principally 'physical' in range.[20] One of the most consistent features is the epic epithet ('he who girt on his sword in a good hour', 'the excellent Battler', etc.), which serves a number of functions: as a *leitmotif*, a reminder of the past, for dramatic or ironic effect.[21] Other features of the style include synecdoche, metonymy, enumeration, meiosis, litotes and hyperbaton. The examples of ellipsis, parataxis and anacoluthon should not be regarded as 'mistakes'; where the poet has only loose juxtapositions we should destroy the effect by making them conform to our notions of syntactical correctness.

The structure and interrelation of the 'laisses'

The poem has 3730 lines scattered unevenly among 152 *laisses*—an average of just over twenty-four lines per *laisse*, though this figure rarely occurs in practice. Some *laisses* contain well over a hundred lines, others have as few as three. The brief *laisses* occur sometimes, but not always, when the action is swift, or simply when the narration is broken into small units. One structure to be found in the *laisses* has been analysed by H. Ramsden;[22] this is in fact a dual arrangement of a basic structure (exposition, recapitulation and development, conclusion), which can be found elsewhere in the poem singly, or in an even more complex arrangement, cf. the battle descriptions, with preparations, attack, rout, pursuit, stripping of the battlefield and division of the booty. The amount of complexity is obviously determined by the material to be narrated. A complex structure also occurs in the possible cases of 'double narration', which resembles within a composite *laisse* the procedure of *laisses similaires* between *laisses* (see below); for this repeated view of the same event, see lines 394-95, 2121-25 and 3678-79.

The *laisses* are interrelated in a number of ways: (1) they may be connected by a consecutive narration of events, and this is the commonest connexion, cf. *laisses* 4-5, 9-10, etc.; (2) the second may take up

---

[20] See C. C. Smith and J. Morris, 'On physical phrases in Old Spanish epic and other texts', *Proceedings of the Leeds Philosophical and Literary Society: Literary and Historical Section*, XII (1966-68), 129-90.

[21] See Rita Hamilton, 'Epic epithets . . .'; Edmund de Chasca, *El arte juglaresco en el Cantar de Mio Cid* (Madrid, 1967), ch. IX, pp. 173-93; and Ian Michael, 'A comparison of the use of epic epithets in the *Poema de Mio Cid* and the *Libro de Alexandre*', *Bulletin of Hispanic Studies*, XXXVIII (1961), 32-41.

[22] 'The taking of Alcocer . . .', *Bulletin of Hispanic Studies*, XXXVI (1959), 129-34.

anew the narration at the end of a discourse in the first, and this is also very common, cf. *laisses* 1-2, 3-4, etc.; (3) the connexion may be an interchange of speakers, or a change of subject or direction within a single discourse, cf. *laisses* 5-6, 6-7, 10-11, etc.; (4) where there is bifurcation of the narration, the last lines of the first *laisse* or the first line of the second *laisse* will dismiss one of the chains of events for the time being and concentrate upon the other, cf. *laisses* 43-44, 46-47, 48-49, etc.; (5) when two separated narrations are being linked together, the first line of the second *laisse* will mark the link, cf. *laisses* 84-85, 88-89, though this may occur within a composite *laisse*, cf. lines 915-16 in *laisse* 49, lines 1914-16 in *laisse* 102; (6) the second *laisse* may be a *reprise* of the end of the first *laisse* with additional material, cf. *laisses* 6-7, 28-29, 55-56, etc.; (7) the second *laisse* may be a *laisse similaire*, i.e. it may do no more than repeat the previous *laisse* in an exclamatory tone, cf. *laisses* 45, 51, or fill it out, cf. *laisses* 73, 129, or it may provide a different view of an event described in the previous *laisse*, cf. *laisses* 120, 130. The Spanish poem offers only one example of *laisses parallèles*,[23] in the description of the duels (*laisses* 150-52); here we have represented three separate but similar acts in three separate but similar *laisses*, yet the three combats are taking place simultaneously (the third combat is made more complex still by the use of double narration within it).

I have by no means included all the possible ways by which the poet interrelates his *laisses* in the above rather roughly drawn categories, but I present them to draw the readers' attention to the fact that they are not dealing with a work that necessarily follows modern conceptions of temporal or rational progression in narrative, and to provide at least a possible starting-point for a more comprehensive study of the poet's complex narrative technique.

The structure of the poem

The poem has an overlapping bipartite structure. The first part consists of the Cid's moral and political dishonour brought about by his unjust banishment and of his gradual rehabilitation by his own efforts, culminating in the complete vindication of his honour, in his capture

[23] This term, used by Jean Rychner, *La Chanson de geste* . . . , ch. IV, makes a valuable distinction; it corresponds to what the pioneer in the study called her first type of *laisse similaire*; see Mildred K. Pope, 'Four chansons de geste: a study in Old French versification', *Modern Language Review*, VIII (1913), 352-67, IX (1914), 41-52, and X (1915), 310-19; see also Angelo Monteverdi, 'La laisse épique', in *La Technique littéraire des chansons de geste. Actes du Colloque de Liège (septembre 1957)* (Paris, 1959), pp. 127-40, and Eugène Vinaver, *The Rise of Romance* (Oxford, 1971), pp. 1-14.

of Valencia, and in his receipt of the royal pardon (lines 2034-35). This 'plot' accounts for just over 54 per cent of the extant poem. The second part of the structure is set in train before the first part is completed: in *laisse* 82 the Infantes of Carrión decide that it would be advantageous to marry the Cid's daughters (lines 1372-76). This is the decision that begins the second 'plot', in which the Cid will suffer family dishonour by the outrage committed upon his daughters; but the king shares in the dishonour by his insistence on the marriages between the Infantes and the Cid's daughters, and he has to put it to rights by convoking a judicial court at which the Cid successfully wins redress. The Cid's career is crowned, and his daughters' position heightened, by the new marriages, which make them, according to the poem, Queens of Navarre and Aragon. The poet skilfully connects the two 'plots' in lines 1345-49, just before the Infantes make their fateful decision: their adviser and the chief ally of the Carrión faction at court, Count García Ordóñez, is there reproached by the king for his scornful remark about the ease with which the Cid seems to be winning battles; yet he, an old enemy of the Cid, was, we can assume, one of the 'evil meddlers' who maliciously persuaded the king to banish the Cid, before the poem opens. If that was the case, it is the same court faction which instigates each of the two parts of the poem's structure; the king on both occasions follows their advice and brings about dishonour for the Cid, and on both occasions has to set it to rights—once by a royal pardon, the second time by judicial intervention. Into the two parts of the basic structure the poet incorporates a number of interrelated episodes. Both parts may be analysed in broad divisions, each with subdivisions, but the rough scheme outlined below is not intended to suggest either that I think the poet planned it out in this way, or that he necessarily thought in tripartite subdivisions; the reader may prefer to include episodes that I have omitted, or exclude ones that I have inserted.

It will be seen that the traditional division of the poem into three *Cantares* does not correspond well to the overall bipartite structure:

Poema de Mio Cid   *possible analysis of structure*

First Cantar

A   I   Preparations for exile (*laisses* 1-18)

(a) Vivar	(b) Burgos	(c) Cardeña

II   Campaign along the Henares (*laisses* 18-26)

(a) A vision at Figueruela	(b) Castejón	(c) Sale of the booty and the Cid's generosity

III Campaign along the Jalón (*laisses* 26-46)

   (*a*) Alcocer   (*b*) Defeat of Fáriz   (*c*) First gift to
                               and Galve   Alfonso

IV Campaign along the Jiloca (*laisses* 46-63)

   (*a*) El Poyo   (*b*) Alfonso pardons   (*c*) Defeat of the
                              Alvar Fáñez   Count of
                                                       Barcelona

Second Cantar

V Campaign in the Levante (*laisses* 64-71)

   (*a*) Murviedro   (*b*) Cebolla   (*c*) Peña Cadiella

VI Valencian campaign (*laisses* 72-77)

   (*a*) Siege and capture   (*b*) Defeat of the emir   (*c*) Second gift to
         of Valencia   of Seville   Alfonso

VII The Cid established in Valencia (*laisses* 78-95)

   (*a*) Jerónimo made   (*b*) The Cid's family   (*c*) Defeat of Yúsuf
         bishop   arrives

VIII The Cid vindicated (*laisses* 96-104)

   (*a*) Third gift to   (*b*) The Infantes of   (*c*) Alfonso pardons
         Alfonso   Carrión take   the Cid
                                            counsel

B   I The weddings (*laisses* 104-11)

   (*a*) Marriage   (*b*) Betrothals   (*c*) Wedding
         negotiations   ceremonies

Third Cantar

II The Infantes in Valencia (*laisses* 112-23)

   (*a*) The lion episode   (*b*) Defeat of King   (*c*) The Infantes
                              Búcar   praised, and
                                                  mocked

III The Infantes' revenge (*laisses* 123-30)

   (*a*) The Infantes and   (*b*) A vain plot to kill   (*c*) The outrage at
         the daughters   Avengalvón   Corpes
         depart

IV The Cid plans to seek redress (*laisses* 131-35)

   (*a*) The daughters are   (*b*) The Cid asks   (*c*) Alfonso pro-
         rescued   Alfonso for justice   claims a court in
                                                  Toledo

v   The Cid vindicated once more (*laisses* 135-52)

   (*a*) The lawsuit   (*b*) The duels   (*c*) The second
                                                              marriages

[v (*a*) and (*b*), like some of the other sections outlined above, may be analysed in further subdivisions, i.e. the three challenges, and the three duels.]

The only reason for dividing the first and second *Cantares* is the presence of line 1085: lit. 'Here begin the deeds of My Cid of Vivar'—a curious statement when we consider that the poet has already described three of the Cid's campaigns; nor are the immediately preceding lines composed so as to produce a tone of conclusion. The line may well have been an interpolation into the MS from which the extant MS was copied—an interpolation perhaps made by a minstrel to make a break in an actual performance. The division of the second and third *Cantares* depends on lines 2276-77: lit. 'The verses of this song are ending here. May the Creator avail you, with all His saints!' Here there is a much better effort to introduce a break in the narrative: 2271-73 inform us that after the weddings the Infantes stayed in Valencia for nearly two years, that they were affectionately treated and that the Cid was content. Then a note of warning that things will go wrong in the future is introduced by the pious hope in 2274-75. The third *Cantar* begins very abruptly, as though it were a separate poem, yet much that is in it will not be understood by anyone unfamiliar with what has gone before, nor does the division correspond particularly well to the overall structure, which would be better divided, if it had to be, before the marriage negotiations rather than after the wedding ceremonies.

The division into *Cantares* corresponds approximately to the following proportions of the extant poem: first *Cantar*, 29 per cent; second *Cantar*, 32 per cent; third *Cantar*, 39 per cent. Each section may well coincide with the amount sung at a single performance, and the minstrels may quite deliberately have chosen to make their breaks at forward-looking moments before the exciting action of that part of the 'plot' had reached completion, in order to entice the audience back to the next performance.[24] Thus the adjustments required for performance appear to have overridden the artistic structure shaped by the poet.

---

[24] See Jean Rychner, *La Chanson de geste* . . . , pp. 49-50; he suggests that between 1000 and 2000 lines might have been sung in a two-hour performance, but this does not seem to allow sufficient time to recite the longer lines of the Spanish poem, and would appear even more inadequate if they were sung, especially to a tune with as slow a tempo as is suggested by the uniquely surviving *Audigier* melody, printed by Rychner, p. 18.

The poet and his background

Menéndez Pidal, *ed. crít.*, p. 68, took the view that the poem was written in the extreme south-east of Old Castile and that the author was from Medinaceli, having received only part of his 'inspiration' in San Esteban de Gormaz; late in his life he was to talk of two poets, the earlier writing *c.* 1110 in San Esteban and the later *c.* 1140 in Medinaceli.[25] Recently T. Riaño Rodríguez has claimed that the poet was a cleric of Fresno de Caracena, not far from San Esteban.[26] These hypotheses are based principally on geographical and eulogistic references in the text, and partially on linguistic grounds. Even if we accept the hypothesis that the author had special knowledge of the areas around San Esteban and Medinaceli, it does not prove that he composed the poem there; the two occasions on which his knowledge appears to be faulty suggest that at most he had only travelled in the region.[27] With regard to the linguistic argument, it may be possible to make a case for linguistic forms influenced by the eastern dialects in the poem, but it seems to me impossible to prove that the poet came from this particular part of Castile's eastern border. There is, on the other hand, some evidence to connect the poem with the Burgos area: the connexion with the Cardeña legends of the Cid, the invention of Martín Antolínez, the attempt to place the abbey at Cardeña into the essential narrative, the fact that the MS turned up at Vivar. We cannot know whether the poem was at one time performed for pilgrims at the abbey, travellers at Vivar, or the people in Burgos, but the clerical knowledge possessed by the poet may suggest the abbey as the place of composition.

We might envisage the poet as the abbot's notary, perhaps, familiar with legal documents and disputes, having access to chronicles and knowledge of political affairs and the behaviour of the monarchs, nobles and knights who would visit the abbey from time to time. He must also have had the opportunity of hearing heroic poems (perhaps brought in from France along the pilgrim road to St James of Compostela), for thus would he have learned the techniques of the epic form and style. In his handling of historical material and his generally skilful intertwining of it with fictitious material, in his command of the shaping principle of his work, his abilities went well beyond a mere *jongleuresque* flair. Although the connexions between the Cid and

---

[25] See 'Dos poetas en el *Cantar de Mio Cid*', *Romania*, LXXXII (1961), 145–200, reprinted in his *En torno al Poema de Mio Cid* (Barcelona, 1963).

[26] 'Del autor y fecha del Poema de Mio Cid', *Prohemio*, II (1971), 467–500; Riaño assumes that Per Abbat was the author, but the use of the word *escrivió* in the *explicit* clearly suggests that he was a copyist (see note to line 3731).

[27] See I. Michael, *art. cit.* in n. 9 above.

Cardeña were established early, Russell has shown that the wilder
claims of the Cardeña monks apparent in the *Estoria del Cid* (now lost)
were not formulated until the period 1238-60 (see his 'San Pedro de
Cardeña . . .', 62). Thus we might hazard that the greater exaggeration
in the *Primera crónica general* version of the Cid legend (*c.* 1260) than in
our poem is not necessarily the result of more re-workings by successive
minstrels as Menéndez Pidal believed, but rather the consequence of
the acceleration of the tomb cult at Cardeña during the intervening
years (see Russell, 'San Pedro de Cardeña . . .', 67-68).

The manuscript and the date of the poem

The single extant MS now preserved in the Biblioteca Nacional, Madrid,
as MS Vitr. 7-17, is in a disastrous condition which seems to have come
about more from the attentions of nineteenth-century editors than
from the ravages of the five preceding centuries. It was found in the
archive of the Concejo de Vivar in the sixteenth century and there
Juan Ruiz de Ulibarri y Leyba copied it in 1596; his often faulty
transcription, preserved as B.N., Madrid, MS 6328 (*olim* R-200), none
the less provides evidence for those parts of the text damaged later.
The MS was still in the Vivar archive in 1601, but it then passed to a
nunnery in Vivar, the Convento de Santa Clara. In the 1770's Eugenio
Llaguno y Amírola, Secretary of the Council of State, removed the MS
from Vivar so that T. A. Sánchez could prepare his edition. Llaguno
kept the MS and from his heirs it passed to Pascual de Gayangos, during
whose possession of it Damas Hinard was allowed to consult it, and it
was even sent to Boston for Ticknor to see.

By 1863 the MS had been purchased by the first Marqués de Pidal (no
relation to Menéndez Pidal), and it was soon afterwards consulted by
Florencio Janer for his edition. It passed by inheritance to Don
Alejandro Pidal, and was then used by Vollmöller, Baist, Huntington
and Menéndez Pidal. One suspects that it was during this period that it
was so damaged by the application of reagents. It was obviously in a
bad condition when Menéndez Pidal saw it, with clear signs that
reagents had been used, and he may well have been correct in his
assertion that this had first been done as early as the sixteenth century.[28]

[28] Dr R. W. Hunt, Keeper of Western Manuscripts in the Bodleian Library,
Oxford, very kindly discussed this problem with me, and was able to point to
examples of oakgall being used on faded ink as early as the 1630's; he did not
think it altogether unlikely that it may have been used as early as, say, 1596, when
Ulibarri transcribed the MS. Dr Hunt recalled that some palaeographers would use
ammonic sulphydrate (the least harmful of the chemical reagents) as late as the
early 1920's, but he was surprised to learn that the more powerful acids had been
used in Spain as late as the 1890's.

There were also many places where the original ink had faded and had been gone over with fresh ink, sometimes with alteration of letters (some of these re-inkings had been done before 1596). Menéndez Pidal erased many of these re-inkings with an india-rubber, in most of these cases without trace. As he himself tells us (*ed. crít.*, p. 11), he also used ammonic sulphydrate in numerous places and on three occasions applied yellow potassium prussiate and hydrochloric acid. The erasures apart, it would not have been at that time abnormal practice to use ammonic sulphydrate on ordinary historical documents, but the use of the stronger chemicals on passages where the milder reagents had probably been applied more than once previously was open to serious question. It is difficult to think of any other important literary MS that has received such treatment as this, and it was unlucky that the poem was the subject of so much interest a few decades before the development of ultra-violet lamps and infra-red photography (the latter still not available in the Biblioteca Nacional), which, together with the very recent introduction of direct infra-red devices, provide much safer methods of reading faded ink and, of course, obviate the need either to erase or to place chemicals upon the parchment, assuming that anyone were now to be permitted to do such things.

In the fragile autumn of its years the MS passed to the Spanish State through the generous intervention of the Juan March Foundation in 1960, since when it has been kept in the Biblioteca Nacional. In the summer of 1968, through the kindness of Don Luis Vázquez de Parga and with the assistance of Sr. Magallón Antón, I was able to consult it and examine some of the more difficult passages under the ultra-violet lamp. The binding is now much looser than when Menéndez Pidal described it, and the reagents have not only blackened the folios where they were applied but also appear to have eaten through the parchment in the worst affected places; they have also left a fluorescence which greatly reduces the effectiveness of ultra-violet light.

The MS is in quarto, and consists of seventy-four folios of quite low-grade parchment, unevenly distributed into eleven gatherings, plus two guard-folios. The folios measure 198 × 140-153 mm, and the text is written on both sides with twenty-four or twenty-five lines per side (most have twenty-five lines), from 1r to line 22 of 74r. The MS was rebound on at least two occasions (for the last time in the fifteenth century) and the binders trimmed off parts of the text, sometimes writing in the missing letters. The handwriting is the same throughout and is considered by palaeographers to date from the fourteenth century. There are capital letters with rough decoration at fourteen points, but they do not correspond to obvious divisions of the poem; there are also two rough drawings which will be mentioned in the note to 1486. The MS appears to have been corrected by the copyist himself, and soon afterwards in lighter ink by another person, whom Pidal has termed 'the first corrector'. Later hands introduced other additions and alterations.

The *explicit* of the MS claims that it was copied out by a certain Per Abbat in May 1207 (see notes to 3731-33); if we assume that the date has not been altered or tampered with, it clearly cannot refer to the extant MS, and it might rather be the *explicit* of the MS from which the extant copy was made; thus, logically, Per Abbat would have been the scribe of that earlier copy, now lost. This hypothesis would put the *terminus ante quem* of the composition of the poem at 1207, and internal evidence might suggest a *terminus a quo* of 1201 (see note to 3724-25).

The reasons for the earliest possible date to be 1140, so long and vigorously put forward by Menéndez Pidal, can nowadays be seen to rest principally on the archaic language of the poem. This can in fact be explained by the use of a *Kunstsprache* for heroic poetry, as Russell was the first to suggest ('San Pedro de Cardeña . . .', 70). All the most recent researches—linguistic, historical and literary—have tended to put the date of composition much later, probably towards the end of the twelfth century or the beginning of the thirteenth, and possibly within the years 1201-07.[29]

The present edition of the Spanish text

This new critical edition has been made by carefully checking Menéndez Pidal's palaeographic editions against the photographic copy specially prepared by Hauser y Menet S.A., now preserved in the Sala de Lectura, Armario del Poema, in the Biblioteca Nacional (this company published the facsimile in a limited edition of 638 copies in 1946, but had published photographs of some of the folios of the MS as long ago as 1911); this facsimile has more contrast and is consequently at times easier to read than the *Edición facsímil del Códice de Per Abat* published by the Dirección General de Archivos y Bibliotecas in 1961 (which was also printed by Hauser y Menet). In addition, as has been explained, I was fortunate in being permitted to consult the MS itself. I have taken into account the readings of previous editors of the text;

[29] See A. Ubieto Arteta, 'Observaciones sobre el *Cantar de Mio Cid*', *Arbor*, XXXVII (1957), 745-70; Jules Horrent, 'Tradition poétique du *Cantar de Mio Cid* au XIIe siècle', *Cahiers de Civilisation Médiévale*, VII (1964), 451-77, at 472; D. G. Pattison, 'The date of the *Cantar de Mio Cid*: a linguistic approach', *Modern Language Review*, LXII (1967), 443-50; Colin Smith, 'The personages of the *Poema de Mio Cid* and the date of the poem', *Modern Language Review*, LXVI (1971), 580-98.

the best palaeographic notes are Menéndez Pidal's, though Huntington's comments are of great interest throughout. Menéndez Pidal's
palaeographic edition is, for the most part, a faithful transcription, but
in his critical editions he tried to reconstruct the primitive text. This
nineteenth-century method has long been discarded in European
editorial practice, yet it is still undertaken at times in medieval Spanish
studies. The reconstructive method goes far beyond correction of
scribal error and it will supply missing hemistichs, lines, even a whole
folio, usually on the basis of some other work (the chronicles, in the
case of our poem), but sometimes quite arbitrarily; it will also 'archaize'
the language and 'correct' the syllables to conform to the editors'
notions of metrical rules. The net result of the method is to provide us
with texts we have not got. In his recent edition of the *Poema de Mio Cid*
(Oxford, 1972) Colin Smith has completely eschewed the old reconstructive method and has produced an edition very close to the MS
readings; in matters of orthography he is usually ultra-conservative,
as he is also in his decision not to insert accent marks. We have worked
completely independently of each other, but I have included in the notes
the principal differences between his and my interpretations of the text.

In general I have followed the principles of the late Frederick Whitehead as he applied them in his edition of the *Chanson de Roland* (second
edition, Oxford, 1946) and I benefited too from the many happy
conversations we had on these complex problems. I have been fortunate indeed in having the constant advice of J. W. Rees, who has freely
placed at my disposal his knowledge of medieval texts and his great
skill in solving textual mysteries; as a result I have incorporated a
number of his suggested emendations and new readings. I was also
able to discuss certain editorial problems with Don José Manuel
Blecua in Jaca in the summer of 1968, and he gave me much valuable
advice. Nevertheless I may have been less conservative in some respects
than some or all three of these experienced scholars would have
expected, particularly with regard to rearranging word or line order,
the use of accent marks and the standardisation (but not modernisation)
of the orthography. I have borne in mind that scholars in other fields
and students often begin their study of Old Spanish with this text, while
advanced scholars have available to them a good palaeographic edition
as well as a facsimile of the MS.

All the text printed in roman type is from the hand of the scribe or the
first corrector, and all abbreviations have been resolved (I have
indicated the examples of missing nasal abbreviations throughout).
Letters or words printed in roman and placed within square brackets
either (1) were written in the MS in a later hand, or (2) were once
read in the MS by an earlier editor but cannot now be read. Letters or

words printed in italics and not enclosed within square brackets are my editorial alterations or my resolutions of numerals, and letters or words in italics placed within square brackets are my editorial additions. The orthography of the MS is chaotic in certain respects and often may reflect the practices of the fourteenth-century scribe rather than those of the time of composition; because of this, little is gained by preserving them, except where, in my opinion, there may be a rare phonological feature. I have therefore reduced otiose double letters, and standardised the confusion of *l* and *ll*, *n* and *ñ*, *c* and *ch*, and *s* and *ss* (reserving the latter for the intervocalic position of voiceless *s* only). I have altered all the cases of *th* to *t*, and *r*, *R* and *rr* representing the multiple vibrant have been given as *rr* throughout. The *ç* and *z* have been retained as in the MS, except that when *ç* precedes *i* or *e* the cedilla is not printed. The pleonastic *h* has been suppressed, but has been inserted before the diphthong *ue*; the silent *h* derived from Latin is preserved where it occurs. I have resolved long and short *i*, *j*, and *g* (except before *i* and *e*), representing $/ʒ/$, to *j*; and *i* and *y*, representing $/ĵ/$, to *y*. The *g* and *gu* representing $/g/$ or $/γ/$ have been standardised to conform with modern practice. The *u* and *v* are standardised as *u* for the vowel and *v* for the consonant, but the scribe's *b*'s are preserved.

Accent marks, which are generally much more of a help than a hindrance, have been introduced to conform to modern Spanish practice, and they are inserted in addition to the inverted comma to warn the reader of apocope of a weak object pronoun, but the inverted comma should not be taken to mean that the missing vowel was sounded. In the case of the Old Spanish imperfect indicative and conditional endings in *-ía*, *-ies*, *-ie*, *-iemos*, *-iedes*, *-ien*, accent marks are always placed (except in the separated forms) on the *e* of *-iés*, *-ié*, *-ién*, so that the reader not very familiar with Old Spanish should recognise the forms easily, but this is done without prejudice to a possible stressing *-íe*, *-íen*, etc.[30] Accent marks are also introduced to mark distinctions between homonymic forms; thus *só* = mod. Sp. 'soy', *so* = either the m. sg. possessive (= mod. Sp. 'su'), or the preposition < Latin SUB; *ál* is the pronoun = 'the other', 'the remainder', while *al* is the contraction of *a + el* (m. sg. def. art.), etc. The O. Sp. subject pronouns *nós*, *vós* are distinguished from the weak object pronouns *nos*, *vos*.[31] The Tironian sign (τ) has been transcribed as *e* throughout.

[30] For a thorough examination of the problem see Yakov Malkiel, 'Towards a reconsideration of the Old Spanish imperfect in *-ía~-ié*', *Hispanic Review*, XXVI (1959), 435-81.

[31] See Yakov Malkiel, 'Stressed *nós*, *vós* vs. weak *nos*, *vos* in Old Spanish', *Romance Philology*, XVI (1962-63), 137, and 'Old Spanish *ý*, *ó* vs. *y*, *o*', *ibid.*, XVII (1963-64), 667.

The punctuation follows modern practice, but I have lightened the use of the comma wherever possible. I have marked the caesura with a clear space. Lacunae are noted, and apparently missing hemistichs are marked by suspension points. At a few points I have rearranged the line order when it seemed essential for the sense, and these changes are clearly indicated in the line numeration and in the notes. In a very small number of lines I have inverted the hemistich order and in others I have rearranged the word order, where it seemed possible that the scribe had either been confused by a marginal or interlinear insertion in the MS from which he was copying or that he had put the line in more prosaic, or less poetic, order, thereby destroying the assonance; these are the rare occasions on which I have made a change to achieve 'correct' assonance. The lines with faulty assonance at the beginning or end of *laisses* are placed in the *laisse* to which their sense takes them. Where two lines or parts of lines have been joined together I have inserted a thin rule to indicate the line division in the MS. I have adhered to Menéndez Pidal's *laisse* numeration and to the division into three *Cantares*, but readers should bear in mind that the MS has no punctuation, caesura marks or indication of *laisse* division.

My aim has been, as far as was practicable, to allow the poem to be read in the faulty state in which it has survived, with its difficulties exposed to view; few of us are likely to resolve more than a fraction of the remaining problems, and none will achieve as much as Don Ramón Menéndez Pidal, whose vast and prolonged researches have put all later editors and readers in his debt.

The Poem of the Cid

El Poema de Mio Cid

Cantar primero

[*Possible lacuna of up to fifty lines (first folio missing)*]

1

　De los sos ojos　tan fuertemientre llorando,
tornava la cabeça　e estávalos catando;
vio puertas abiertas　e uços sin cañados,
alcándaras vazías,　sin pielles e sin mantos
e sin falcones　e sin adtores mudados.　　　　　　　　[*5*
Sospiró Mio Cid,　ca mucho avié grandes cuidados;
fabló Mio Cid　bien e tan mesurado:
'¡Grado a ti, Señor,　Padre que estás en alto!
Esto me an buelto　mios enemigos malos.'

2

　Allí piensan de aguijar,　allí sueltan las rriendas;　　[*10*
a la exida de Bivar　ovieron la corneja diestra
e entrando a Burgos　oviéronla siniestra.
Meció Mio Cid los ombros　e engrameó la tiesta:
'¡Albricia, Álbar Fáñez,　ca echados somos de tierra!'

3

　Mio Cid Rruy Díaz　por Burgos entrava,　　　　　　[*15*
en su conpaña　*sessaenta* pendones.
Exiénlo ver　mugieres e varones,　　　　　　　　　　[*16b*
burgeses e burgesas　por las finiestras son,
plorando de los ojos,　tanto avién el dolor;
de las sus bocas　todos dizían una rrazón:
'¡Dios, qué buen vassallo,　si oviesse buen señor!'　　[*20*

4

　Conbidar le ien de grado,　mas ninguno non osava,
el rrey don Alfonso　tanto avié la grand saña;

The Poem of the Cid

First Cantar

1

Tears streamed from his eyes as he turned his head and stood looking at them. He saw doors left open and gates unlocked, empty pegs without fur tunics or cloaks, perches without falcons or moulted hawks. The Cid sighed, for he was weighed down with heavy cares. Then he said, with dignity and restraint: 'I give Thee thanks, O God, our Father in Heaven. My wicked enemies have contrived this plot against me.'

2

They made ready for the journey and slackened their reins. As they left Vivar a crow flew on the right, and as they entered Burgos they saw it on the left. The Cid shrugged his shoulders and nodded his head: 'Good cheer, Álvar Fáñez, for we are banished from this land.'

3

Ruy Díaz entered Burgos with his company of sixty knights. Men and women came out to see him pass, while the burghers and their wives stood at their windows, sorrowfully weeping. With one accord they all said, 'What a good vassal. If only he had a good lord!'

4

They would have offered him hospitality, but no one dared to do so for fear of the King's anger. The King's despatch had

antes de la noche   en Burgos d'él entró su carta
con grand rrecabdo   e fuertemientre sellada:
que a Mio Cid Rruy Díaz   que nadi nol' diessen posada   [25

1v   e aquel que ge la diesse   sopiesse vera palabra
que perderié los averes   e más los ojos de la cara
e aun demás   los cuerpos e las almas.
Grande duelo avién   las yentes cristianas,
ascóndense de Mio Cid,   ca nol' osan dezir nada.   [30
El Campeador   adeliñó a su posada,
assí como llegó a la puerta,   fallóla bien cerrada
por miedo del rrey Alfonso,   que assí lo avién parado
que si non la quebrantás por fuerça,   que non ge la abriesse nadi.
Los de Mio Cid   a altas vozes llaman,   [35
los de dentro   non les querién tornar palabra.
Aguijó Mio Cid,   a la puerta se llegava,
sacó el pie del estribera,   una ferídal' dava;
non se abre la puerta,   ca bien era cerrada.
Una niña de nuef años   a ojo se parava: [40
'¡Ya Campeador,   en buen ora cinxiestes espada!
El rrey lo ha vedado,   anoch d'él e[n]tró su carta
con grant rrecabdo   e fuertemientre sellada.
Non vos osariemos   abrir nin coger por nada;
si non, perderiemos   los averes e las casas   [45
e demás   los ojos de las caras.
Cid, en el nuestro mal   vós non ganades nada,
mas el Criador vos vala   con todas sus vertudes sanctas.'
Esto la niña dixo   e tornós' pora su casa.

2r   Ya lo vee el Cid   que del rrey non avié gr[aci]a;   [50
partiós' de la puerta,   por Burgos aguijava,
llegó a Sancta María,   luego descavalga,
fincó los inojos,   de coraçón rrogava.
La oración fecha,   luego cavalgava,
salió por la puerta   e Arlançón p[a[s]]sava,   [55
cabo essa villa   en la glera posava,
fincava la tienda   e luego descavalgava.
Mio Cid Rruy Díaz,   el que en buen ora cinxo espada,
posó en la glera   quando nol' coge nadi en casa,
derredor d'él   una buena conpaña;   [60
assí posó Mio Cid   como si fuesse en montaña.
Vedádal' an conpra   dentro en Burgos la casa
de todas cosas   quantas son de vianda;
non le osarién vender   al menos dinarada.

arrived the night before, laying down severe conditions and heavily sealed: no one was to give lodging to the Cid, and anyone who received him into his house should know for a certainty that he would forfeit his wealth and would lose his eyes and furthermore his body and soul as well. All these Christian people were overcome with grief; they hid from the Cid and dared not speak to him. The Campeador made his way to the house where he hoped to lodge, but when he arrived there he found the door locked fast. They had all agreed on this: for fear of King Alfonso, if the Cid did not break in the door, nobody would open it to him. His followers called loudly, but those within returned no answer. The Cid spurred his horse, rode up to the door and, drawing his foot from the stirrup, gave it a kick, but the door did not open, for it was securely locked. A little nine-year-old girl appeared (and said): 'Campeador, you were knighted in a fortunate hour. The King has forbidden us (to receive you); his letter came last night, with harsh conditions and heavy seals. We could not possibly dare to open the door or ask you to come in. If we did, we should lose our money and our houses and even the sight of our eyes. Cid, you have nothing to gain by our misfortune. May the Creator protect you with all his holy powers.' When the little girl had finished speaking she turned and went back into her house. Then the Cid saw that he had lost the King's favour. He turned away from the door and rode through Burgos. When he came to the Church of Santa María he alighted from his horse, knelt down and prayed from his heart. When his prayer was ended the Cid remounted, rode out by the city gate and crossed the river Arlanzón. Beside the town (of Burgos) he had his tent pitched on the sandy shore and then dismounted. The Cid Ruy Díaz, knighted in a fortunate hour, encamped on the river bank, since no one would give him lodging in his house; with his good band of followers around him he settled there as if he were out in the woods. He had been forbidden to buy any food at all in the town of Burgos, and they did not dare to sell him as much as a pennyworth.

B

5

Martín Antolínez,   el burgalés conplido,   [65
a Mio Cid e a los suyos   abástales de pan e de vino,
non lo conpra,   ca él se lo avié consigo,
de todo conducho   bien los ovo bastidos;
pagós' Mio Cid e todos los otros   que van a so cervicio.
Fabló Martín A[n]tolínez,   odredes lo que á dicho: [70
'¡Ya Canpeador,   en buen ora fuestes nacido!
Esta noch y[a]gamos   e vay[á]mosnos al matino,
ca acusado seré   de lo que vos he servido,
en ira del rrey Alfonso   yo seré metido.
Si convusco escapo   sano o bivo,   [75
aún cerca o tarde   el rrey querer me ha por amigo,
si non, quanto dexo   no lo precio un figo.'

6

Fabló Mio Cid,   el que en buen ora cinxo espada:
'¡Martín Antolínez,   sodes ardida lança!
Si yo bivo,   doblar vos he la soldada.   [80
Espeso é el oro   e toda la plata,
bien lo vedes   que yo non trayo aver
e huebos me serié | pora toda mi compaña.   [82b-83
Fer lo he amidos,   de grado non avrié nada:
con vuestro consejo   bastir quiero dos arcas,   [85
inchámoslas d'arena,   ca bien serán pesadas,
cubiertas de guadalmecí   e bien enclaveadas.

7

Los guadamecís vermejos   e los clavos bien dorados.
Por Rrachel e Vidas   vayádesme privado:
quando en Burgos me vedaron conpra   e el rrey me á airado, [90
non puedo traer el aver,   ca mucho es pesado,
enpeñar ge lo he   por lo que fuere guisado,
de noche lo lieven   que non lo vean cristianos.
Véalo el Criador   con todos los sos sanctos,
yo más non puedo   e amidos lo fago.'   [95

8

Martín Antolínez   non lo detarda,
por Rrachel e Vidas   apriessa demandava;
passó por Burgos,   al castiello entrava,
por Rrachel e Vidas   apriessa demandava.

5

Martín Antolínez, worthy citizen of Burgos, provided the Cid and his companions with bread and wine; he did not buy them, for he had them already. He supplied them lavishly with provisions for the journey, and the Cid and all those who served him were very well satisfied. Martín Antolínez spoke, and you will hear what he said: 'Campeador, born in a fortunate hour, let us rest here tonight and take our departure in the morning, for I shall be accused of having helped you and shall incur the King's anger. If I escape safe and sound with you, sooner or later the King will want me for a friend. Whether or not, I don't care a fig for all that I am leaving behind.'

6

The Cid spoke: 'Martín Antolínez, you are a brave and daring fighter. If I survive, I shall double your pay. I have spent the gold and all the silver. As you can very well see, I have no money with me and I shall need some to pay all my followers. I shall do this reluctantly, but otherwise I should have nothing. With your help I shall provide two chests: let us fill them with sand to make them very heavy; they shall be covered with figured leather and finely studded.

7

The leather will be red and the studs will be fine golden ones. You must go in secret to Rachel and Vidas. (Say) that I am forbidden to trade in Burgos and that the King has banished me; I cannot carry my wealth about with me as it is too heavy, so I intend to pawn it for a reasonable sum. Let them take it away by night so that no one may see it. May the Creator and all His saints see it (and know) there is nothing else I can do, and I do it reluctantly.'

8

Martín Antolínez set off at once, enquiring in haste for Rachel and Vidas; he rode through Burgos and entered the fortifications of the town, making hasty enquiries for Rachel and Vidas.

9

3r   Rrachel e Vidas   en uno estavan amos   [100
en cuenta de sus averes,   de los que avién ganados.
Llegó Martín Antolínez   a guisa de menbrado:
'¿Ó sodes, Rrachel e Vidas,   los mios amigos caros?
En poridad fablar   querría con amos.'
Non lo detardan,   todos tres se apartaron: [105
'Rrachel e Vidas,   amos me dat las manos
que non me descubrades   a moros nin a cristianos;
por siempre vos faré rricos   que non seades menguados.
El Campeador   por las parias fue entrado,
grandes averes priso   e mucho sobejanos,   [110
rretovo d'ellos   quanto que fue algo,
por én vino a aquesto   por que fue acusado.
Tiene dos arcas   llenas de oro esmerado,
ya lo vedes   que el rrey le á airado,
dexado ha heredades   e casas e palacios;   [115
aquéllas non las puede levar,   si non, serién ventadas,
el Campeador   dexar las ha en vuestra mano
e prestalde de aver   lo que sea guisado.
Prended las arcas   e metedlas en vuestro salvo,
con grand jura   meted í las fes amos   [120
que non las catedes   en todo aqueste año.'
Rrachel e Vidas   seyénse consejando:
'Nós huebos avemos   en todo de ganar algo;
3v bien lo sabemos   que él algo gañó,
quando a tierra de moros entró,   que grant aver sacó;   [125
non duerme sin sospecha   qui aver trae monedado.
Estas arcas   prendámoslas amas,
en logar las metamos   que non sean ventadas.
Mas dezidnos del Cid,   ¿de qué será pagado,
o qué ganancia nos dará   por todo aqueste año?'   [130
Rrespuso Martín Antolínez   a guisa de menbrado:
'Mio Cid querrá   lo que sea aguisado,
pedir vos á poco   por dexar so aver en salvo.
Acógensele omnes   de todas partes me[n]guados,
á menester   seiscientos marcos.'   [135
Dixo Rrachel e Vidas: 'Dar ge los [emos] de grado.'
'Ya vedes que entra la noch,   el Cid es pressurado,
huebos avemos   que nos dedes los marcos.'
Dixo Rrachel e Vidas: 'Non se faze assí el mercado,
sinon primero prendiendo   e después dando.'   [140
Dixo Martín Antolínez: 'Yo d'esso me pago;

9

Rachel and Vidas were sitting together, counting the money they had made. Martín Antolínez, like the shrewd fellow he was, came up and greeted them: 'Is that you, my good friends, Rachel and Vidas? I should like a word with you two in private.' All three of them went aside at once. 'Both of you give me your hands and promise to keep this secret from everyone, Moors and Christians alike, and I shall make your fortune so that you will be rich for life. When the Campeador went to collect the tribute, he received vast sums of money and kept the best part of it. For this reason accusations were brought against him. He has in his possession two chests full of pure gold. The King, as you know, has banished him and he has left his properties, holdings and manors. He cannot carry the chests away with him, for then their existence would be revealed. The Campeador will entrust them to you and you must lend him a suitable amount of money. Take the chests and keep them in a safe place, and both of you swear a solemn oath not to look into them for a whole year from now.' Rachel and Vidas took counsel together, saying: 'We are obliged to make a profit on all our transactions. We know very well that the Cid made his fortune when he went to the land of the Moors and brought back great wealth. A man who carries a large amount of coin about with him cannot sleep without anxiety. Let us take these chests and hide them in a secret place. But tell us, how much will satisfy the Cid and what interest will he give us for the whole of this year?' The shrewd Martín Antolínez replied: 'The Cid will ask what is right and just; he will require little of you for the sake of leaving his property in good hands. Needy men are flocking to him from all sides and he will want six hundred marks.' Rachel and Vidas answered: 'We are quite willing to give them to him.' 'You see that night is coming on and the Cid is in a hurry. We are in pressing need of these marks.' Rachel and Vidas replied: 'That is not the way to do business, for taking comes first and then comes giving.' Martín Antolínez said: 'I am content.

amos tred al Campeador contado
e nós vos ayudaremos, que assí es aguisado,
por aduzir las arcas e meterlas en vuestro salvo
que non lo sepan moros nin cristianos.'   [145
Dixo Rrachel e Vidas: 'Nós d'esto nos pagamos;
las arcas aduchas, prendet seyescientos marcos.'
4r Martín Antolínez cavalgó privado
con Rrachel e Vidas de volu[n]tad e de grado.
Non viene a la puent, ca por el agua á passado,   [150
que ge lo non ventassen de Burgos omne nado.
Afévoslos a la tienda del Campeador contado,
assí como entraron, al Cid besáronle las manos.
Sonrrisós' Mio Cid, estávalos fablando:
'¡Ya don Rrachel e Vidas, avédesme olbidado!   [155
Ya me exco de tierra ca del rrey só airado.
A lo quem' semeja, de lo mío avredes algo,
mientra que vivades non seredes menguados.'
Don Rrachel e Vidas a Mio Cid besáronle las manos.
Martín Antolínez el pleito á parado   [160
que sobre aquellas arcas dar le ien *seis*cientos marcos
e bien ge las guardarién fasta cabo del año,
ca assil' dieran la fe e ge lo avién jurado
que si antes las catassen que fuessen perjurados,
non les diesse Mio Cid de la ganancia un dinero malo.   [165
Dixo Martín Antolínez: 'Carguen las arcas privado,
levaldas, Rrachel e Vidas, ponedlas en vuestro salvo;
yo iré convus[c]o que adugamos los marcos,
ca a mover á Mio Cid ante que cante el gallo.'
Al cargar de las arcas veriedes gozo tanto,   [170
non las podién poner en somo, maguer eran esforçados.
4v Grádanse Rrachel e Vidas con averes monedados,
ca mientra que visquiessen refechos eran amos.

    10
    Rrachel a Mio Cid la mánol' ba besar:
'¡Ya Canpeador, en buen ora cinxiestes espada!   [175
De Castiella vos ides pora las yentes estrañas,
assí es vuestra ventura, grandes son vuestras ganancias,
una piel vermeja, morisca e ondrada,
Cid, beso vuestra mano en don que la yo aya.'
'Plazme,' dixo el Cid, 'd'aquí sea mandada;   [180
si vos la aduxier d'allá; si non, contalda sobre las arcas.'
[*Brief lacuna*]

Come, both of you, to the illustrious Campeador and we shall help you, as is only right, to bring the chests here and place them, unknown to all, in your safe-keeping.' Rachel and Vidas answered: 'We are satisfied. Once the chests are here you may have the six hundred marks.' Martín Antolínez eagerly rode off at once with Rachel and Vidas. He did not cross over the bridge but forded the river so that no one in Burgos should get wind of what was happening. There they were, then, at the tent of the famous Campeador, and on entering they kissed his hands. The Cid smiled and addressed them: 'Well, my friends, Rachel and Vidas, you have forgotten me! Now I am going into banishment, for I have lost the King's favour. It seems to me that you are going to share in my wealth, and as long as you live you will never be the losers.' Rachel and Vidas now kissed the Cid's hands (in token of gratitude). Martín Antolínez arranged the conditions of the bargain—that, on the security of those chests, they should give the Cid six hundred marks and that they should keep the chests in safety for a year. They had given their promise and sworn to keep it, so that they would be guilty of perjury if they looked into them before then, and in that case the Cid would refuse to give them a single penny of the interest. Then Martín Antolínez said: 'Let the chests be loaded promptly. Take them away, Rachel and Vidas, and put them in your safe-keeping. I shall accompany you to bring back the marks, for the Cid has to set out before cock-crow.' How delighted they all were when the chests were loaded up! They could hardly hoist them into place, though they were hefty men. Rachel and Vidas were greatly pleased with the treasure, for they saw themselves rich for the rest of their lives.

10

Rachel then kissed the Cid's hand (to beg a favour of him). 'Campeador' (he said), 'you were knighted in a fortunate hour. You are leaving Castile to go among strangers. As you are sure of good fortune and great gains, I kiss your hand, Cid, (to ask you) for a fine red fur-lined Moorish tunic as a gift.' 'Agreed,' said the Cid. 'I promise it to you now if I can bring it back with me, and if not, you must deduct the value from the contents of the chests.'

[*Brief lacuna*]

En medio del palacio   tendieron un almofalla,
sobr'ella una sávana   de rrançal e muy blanca.
A tod' el primer colpe   *trezientos* marcos de plata echaron,
notólos don Martino,   sin peso los tomava;   [185
los otros *trezientos*   en oro ge los pagavan;
cinco escuderos tiene don Martino,   a todos los cargava.
Quando esto ovo fecho,   odredes lo que fablava:
'Ya don Rrachel e Vidas,   en vuestras manos son las arcas,
yo que esto vos gané   bien merecía calças.'   [190

II

Entre Rrachel e Vidas   aparte ixieron amos:
'Démosle buen don,   ca él no' lo ha buscado.
Martín Antolínez,   un burgalés contado,
vós lo merecedes,   darvos queremos buen dado
de que fagades calças   e rrica piel e buen manto,   [195
dámosvos en don   a vós *treínta* marcos,
merecer no' lo hedes,   ca esto es aguisado;
atorgar nos hedes esto   que avemos parado.'
Gradeciólo don Martino   e rrecibió los marcos,
gradó exir de la posada   e espidiós' de amos.   [200
Exido es de Burgos   e Arlançón á passado,
vino pora la tienda   del que en buen ora nasco.
Rrecibiólo el Cid   abiertos amos los braços:
'¡Venides, Martín Antolínez,   el mio fiel vassallo!
¡Aún vea el día   que de mí ayades algo!'   [205
'Vengo, Campeador,   con todo buen rrecabdo,
vós *seis*cientos   e yo *treínta* he ganados.
Mandad coger la tienda   e vayamos privado,
en San Pero de Cardeña   í nos cante el gallo,
veremos vuestra mugier,   menbrada fija d'algo.   [210
Mesuraremos la posada   e quitaremos el rreinado,
mucho es huebos   ca cerca viene el plazo.'

12

Estas palabras dichas,   la tienda es cogida,
Mio Cid e sus conpañas   cavalgan tan aína,
la cara del cavallo   tornó a Sancta María,   [215
alçó su mano diestra,   la cara se sanctigua:
'A ti lo gradesco, Dios,   que cielo e tierra guías,
¡válanme tus vertudes,   gloriosa Sancta María!
D'aquí quito Castiella,   pues que el rrey he en ira,
non sé si entraré í más   en todos los mios días.   [220
¡Vuestra vertud me vala,   Gloriosa, en mi exida

There in the middle of the room they spread out a rug and on it a sheet of white linen. To begin with, they poured three hundred silver marks into it. Don Martín counted them and accepted them without weighing, and the other three hundred were paid him in gold. With the money Don Martín loaded all the five squires who had accompanied him. When that was done, listen to what he said: 'Now, Rachel and Vidas, the chests are in your hands. Surely, since I got them for you, I deserve a present of hose.'

11

Rachel and Vidas went aside: 'Let us make him a good present for he has put this bit of business in our way.' 'Martín Antolínez, renowned citizen of Burgos, as you have well deserved it, we shall make you a substantial gift to buy yourself hose, a rich fur coat and a good cloak. We present you with thirty marks; you will certainly earn them by acting as guarantor in this agreement.' Don Martín thanked them and took the marks, and as he was eager to leave the house he bade them both farewell. He (then) left Burgos, crossed the river Arlanzón and arrived at the Cid's tent. The Cid welcomed him with open arms. 'Here you are, Martín Antolínez, my loyal vassal! May the time come when I can reward you!' 'Yes, here I am, Campeador, and I have concluded the deal successfully. You have gained six hundred marks, and I thirty. Give the order to strike camp. Let us start off quickly and let cock-crow find us at San Pedro de Cardeña, where we shall see your worthy and noble wife. We shall make a brief stay there and then leave the country. We must do this, as the term of grace has nearly come to an end.'

12

No sooner had he spoken than the tents were taken down. The Cid rode off quickly with his companions. Turning his horse's head towards the church of Santa María, he raised his right hand and made the sign of the cross on his forehead, saying: 'I thank Thee, O God, Ruler of Heaven and Earth! May the power of the Blessed Virgin protect me. Now I must leave Castile, for I have incurred the King's wrath. I do not know whether I shall return to it in all my life. O Glorious Virgin, protect me as I depart, and help and succour me night

5v   e me ayude | e me acorra   de noch e de día!   221b-22
      Si vós assí lo fiziéredes   e la ventura me fuere conplida,
      mando al vuestro altar   buenas donas e rricas,
      esto é yo en debdo   que faga í cantar mill missas.'   [225

      ### 13
      Spidiós' el caboso   de cuer e de veluntad,
      sueltan las rriendas   e piensan de aguijar;
      dixo Martín Antolínez: . . . .
      'Veré a la mugier   a todo mio solaz,   [228b
      castigar los he   cómo abrán a far.
      Si el rrey me lo quisiere tomar,   a mí non m'incal.   [230
      Antes seré convusco   que el sol quiera rrayar.'
      Tornavas' Martín Antolínez a Burgos   e Mio Cid a aguijar
      pora San Pero de Cardeña,   quanto pudo, a espolear.   [233

      ### 14
      Apriessa cantan los gallos   e quieren quebrar albores   [235
      quando llegó a San Pero   el buen Campeador   [236
      con estos cavalleros   quel' sirven a so sabor.   [234
      El abat don Sancho,   cristiano del Criador,   [237
      rrezava los matines   abuelta de los albores,
      í estava doña Ximena   con cinco dueñas de pro,
      rrogando a San Pero   e al Criador: [240
      '¡Tú que a todos guías   vál a Mio Cid el Canpeador!'

      ### 15
      Llamavan a la puerta,   í sopieron el mandado,
      ¡Dios, qué alegre fue   el abat don Sancho!
      Con lu[n]bres e con candelas   al corral dieron salto,
      con tan grant gozo rreciben   al que en buen ora nasco.   [245
      'Gradéscolo a Dios, Mio Cid,'   dixo el abat don Sancho,
6r   'pues que aquí vos veo,   prendet de mí ospedado.'
      'Gracias, don abat,   e só vuestro pagado,
      yo adobaré conducho   pora mí e pora mis vassallos;
      mas porque me vo de tierra,   dovos cinquaenta marcos,'   [250
      si yo algún día visquier,   ser vos han doblados.
      Non quiero fazer en el monesterio   un dinero de daño,
      evades aquí pora doña Ximena   dovos ciento marcos,
      a ella e a sus dueñas   sirvádeslas est año.
      Dues fijas dexo niñas   e prendetlas en los braços,   [255
      aquí vos llas acomiendo   a vós, abat don Sancho,
      d'ellas e de mi mugier   fagades todo rrecabdo.
      Si essa despensa vos falleciere   o vos menguare algo,

and day. If you will do this and my good fortune holds, I shall
endow your altar with rich gifts and I make a solemn promise
to have a thousand masses sung there.'

13

The gallant Cid thus took a devout farewell. The riders
slackened their reins and rode away. Martín Antolínez said:
'I shall go to see my beloved wife, and I must tell those of my
household how to behave. I care not a jot if the King wishes to
confiscate my property, and I shall rejoin you before the day
dawns.' Martín Antolínez returned to Burgos, and the Cid
spurred on towards San Pedro de Cardeña as speedily as possible.

14

The cocks crowed betimes and the dawn was about to break
when the good Campeador reached San Pedro with the knights
who had sworn to serve him faithfully. The Abbot, Don Sancho,
a worthy Christian, was saying matins as the day dawned.
Doña Jimena was there with five noble ladies, praying to St
Peter and to God the Creator: 'Thou who dost rule us all, help
(my husband), the Cid Campeador.'

15

They knocked at the gate, and those within learnt that the
party had arrived. Heavens, how delighted the Abbot was!
The monks poured out into the courtyard with torches and
candles, and joyfully received the fortunate Cid. 'Thanks be to
God,' said the Abbot Don Sancho, 'that I see you here. You are
welcome to stay in the monastery.' 'Thanks, my lord Abbot'
(said the Cid). 'I am greatly obliged to you. Here I shall be able
to prepare food for the journey for myself and my vassals.
As I am leaving the country I shall give you fifty marks, but if
I survive I shall double the amount. I do not wish the monastery
to be at any loss on my account. Here are one hundred marks
that I give you for Doña Jimena, so that you may look after her
and her ladies for this year. I am leaving behind my two little
daughters; take them under your care. I entrust them to you,
my lord Abbot; take care of them and of my wife. If this supply
of money should prove insufficient and you should run short,

bien las abastad,   yo assí vos lo mando,
por un marco que despendades,   al monesterio daré
yo [quatr]o.'   [260
Otorgado ge lo avié   el abat de grado.
Afevos doña Ximena   con sus fijas dó va llegando,
señas dueñas las traen   e adúzenlas adelant;
ant'el Campeador doña Ximena   fincó los inojos amos,
llorava de los ojos,   quísol' besar las manos: [<i>265</i>
'¡Merced, Canpeador,   en ora buena fuestes nado!
Por malos mestureros   de tierra sodes echado.

16

¡Merced, ya Cid,   barba tan conplida!
Fem' ante vós,   yo e vuestras fijas,
iffantes son   e de días chicas,   [<i>269b</i>
con aquestas mis dueñas   de quien só yo servida.   [<i>270</i>
6v Yo lo veo   que estades vós en ida
e nós de vós   partir nos hemos en vida.
¡Dadnos consejo,   por amor de Sancta María!'
Enclinó las manos   la barba vellida,
a las sus fijas   en braço' las prendía,   [<i>275</i>
llególas al coraçón,   ca mucho las quería;
llora de los ojos,   tan fuertemientre sospira:
'Ya doña Ximena   la mi mugier tan conplida,
como a la mi alma   yo tanto vos quería.
Ya lo vedes   que partir nos emos en vida,   [<i>280</i>
yo iré e vós   fincaredes rremanida.
¡Plega a Dios   e a Sancta María
que aún con mis manos   case estas mis fijas,   [<i>282b</i>
o que dé ventura   e algunos días vida
e vós, mugier ondrada,   de mí seades servida!'

17

Grand yantar le fazen   al buen Canpeador;   [<i>285</i>
tañen las campanas   en San Pero a clamor.
Por Castiella   oyendo van los pregones
cómo se va de tierra   Mio Cid el Canpeador,
unos dexan casas   e otros onores.
En aqués día   a la puent de Arla[n]çón,   [<i>290</i>
ciento quinze cavalleros   todos juntados son,
todos demandan   por Mio Cid el Canpeador,
Martín Antolínez   con ellos' cojó,
vanse pora San Pero   dó está el que en buen punto nació.

I bid you let them have what they need. For every mark you spend I shall give four to the monastery.' The Abbot willingly granted this request. Now here comes Doña Jimena, with her daughters carried along in the arms of two ladies. Doña Jimena knelt down in front of the Campeador, weeping and kissing his hands. 'I beg a favour of you, my fortunate Campeador,' she said. 'You have been driven out of Castile by the wiles of mischief-makers.

16

I ask a favour, Cid of the flowing beard. Here I am with your daughters, who are still of tender age, and these ladies who attend on me. I see that you are on the eve of departure and we shall be separated. Give us some words of advice, for the love of Holy Mary.' The Cid stretched out his hands, took his daughters in his arms and pressed them to his heart, for he loved them dearly. He wept and sighed heavily (saying): 'Doña Jimena, my excellent wife, I have always loved you with all my heart, but you see that we must part now, for I am going away while you remain behind. May it please God and Holy Mary that I may be able to give my daughters in marriage with my own hands. With good luck and time on my side I shall provide for you well, my noble wife.'

17

A great banquet was prepared for the worthy Campeador, and the bells rang loudly in San Pedro. The news was cried throughout Castile that the Cid was leaving the country. Some left their houses and others their lands. On that day one hundred and fifteen knights assembled at the bridge over the Arlanzón, all enquiring for the Cid Campeador. Martín Antolínez joined them and they set out for San Pedro, where he was staying.

18

Quando lo sopo Mio Cid el de Bivar   [*295*
quel' crece conpaña por que más valdrá,
apriessa cavalga, rrecebirlos salié,
7r   . . . .   tornós a sonrrisar;
lléganle todos, la mánol' ban besar,   [*298b*
fabló Mio Cid de toda voluntad:
'Yo rruego a Dios e al Padre spiritual   [*300*
vós que por mí dexades casas e heredades,
enantes que yo muera, algún bien vos pueda far,
lo que perdedes doblado vos lo cobrar.'
Plogo a Mio Cid porque creció en la yantar,
plogo a los otros omnes todos quantos con él están.   [*305*
Los *seis* días de plazo passados los an,
tres an por trocir, sepades que non más.
Mandó el rrey a Mio Cid a aguardar,
que, si después del plazo en su tiérral' pudiés tomar,
por oro nin por plata non podrié escapar.   [*310*
El día es exido, la noch querié entrar,
a sos cavalleros mandólos todos juntar:
'Oíd, varones, non vos caya en pesar,
poco aver trayo, darvos quiero vuestra part.
Sed me[n]brados como lo devedes far: [*315*
a la mañana quando los gallos cantarán,
non vos tardedes, mandedes ensellar;
en San Pero a matines tandrá el buen abat,
la missa nos dirá, ésta será de Sancta Trinidad;
la missa dicha, pensemos de cavalgar,   [*320*
ca el plazo viene acerca, mucho avemos de andar.'
Cuemo lo mandó Mio Cid, assí lo an todos a far.
Passando va la noch, viniendo la man,
a los mediados gallos piessan de *ensellar*.
7v   Tañen a matines a una priessa tan grand,   [*325*
Mio Cid e su mugier a la eglesia van,
echós' doña Ximena en los grados delant'el altar,
rrogando al Criador quanto ella mejor sabe
que a Mio Cid el Campeador que Dios le curiás de mal:
'Ya Señor glorioso, Padre que en cielo estás,   [*330*
fezist cielo e tierra, el tercero el mar,
fezist estrellas e luna e el sol pora escalentar;
prisist encarnación en Sancta María madre,
en Beleem aparecist como fue tu voluntad,
pastores te glorificaron, oviéronte a laudare,   [*335*

18

When the Cid, the man from Vivar, heard of the numbers who were crowding to join his band, he rode out in haste to welcome them. He smiled, and all approached to kiss his hand. The Cid gave them a hearty welcome (and said): 'I pray God our heavenly Father that I may be able to reward you before I die, you who have left houses and lands for my sake. What you lose I hope one day to repay you doubly.' The Cid was pleased that his company had increased during the meal, and all who were with him shared his pleasure. Six days of the term of grace had passed and only three remained, please note. The King had ordered a close watch to be kept to see if the Cid might be caught in his territory after the term had expired. If so, he would not escape for all the gold and silver in the world. Day was over and night was coming on when the Cid ordered his knights to assemble (and he addressed them in these words): 'Hear me, my brave men, do not let what I say discourage you. I have only a small amount of money, but I shall share it with you. Bear this in mind like sensible men. Tomorrow at cock-crow have your horses saddled without delay. The worthy Abbot will ring for matins in San Pedro and will say the Mass of the Holy Trinity for us. When mass has been said we must prepare to ride away, for the days of grace are coming to an end and we have a good distance to cover.' All were eager to obey the Cid's commands. The night went by and next morning, at cock-crow, they had their horses saddled. The bells were pealing out for matins as the Cid and his wife went to the church. Doña Jimena prostrated herself on the altar steps, praying earnestly to God to preserve the Cid from all harm. 'O Glorious Lord, our Father in Heaven. Thou didst create Heaven and Earth and after them the sea. Thou didst create the stars and the moon and the sun to give us warmth. Thou didst become incarnate in Thy mother, Holy Mary, and wast born in Bethlehem according to Thy will. The shepherds worshipped and praised Thee. Three kings from

tres rreyes de Arabia   te vinieron adorar,
Melchior   e Gaspar e Baltasar
oro e tus e mirra | te ofrecieron,   como fue tu veluntad; [337b-38
[salveste] | a Jonás   quando cayó en la mar,   [338b-39
salvest a Daniel con los leones   en la mala cárcel,   [340
salvest dentro en Rroma   al señor San Sabastián,
salvest a Sancta Susanna   del falso criminal;
por tierra andidiste   *treinta e dos* años, Señor spiritual,
mostrando los miráculos   por én avemos qué fablar:
del agua fezist vino   e de la piedra pan,   [345
rresucitest a Lázaro   ca fue tu voluntad;
a los judíos te dexeste prender;   dó dizen Monte Calvarie
pusiéronte en cruz   por nombre en Golgotá,
dos ladrones contigo,   éstos de señas partes,
el uno es en paraíso,   ca el otro non entró allá;   [350

8r   estando en la cruz   vertud fezist muy grant:
Longinos era ciego   que nu[n]quas vio alguandre,
diot' con la lança en el costado   dont ixió la sangre,
corrió por el astil ayuso,   las manos se ovo de untar,
alçólas arriba,   llególas a la faz,   [355
abrió sos ojos,   cató a todas partes,
en ti crovo al ora,   por end es salvo de mal;
en el monumento rresucitest,   fust a los infiernos | como
                             fue tu voluntad, [358-59
quebranteste las puertas   e saqueste los sanctos padres.   [360
Tú eres rrey de los rreyes   e de tod' el mundo padre,
a ti adoro e creo   de toda voluntad
e rruego a San Peidro   que me ayude a rrogar
por Mio Cid el Campeador   que Dios le curie de mal;
quando oy nos partimos,   en vida nos faz juntar.'   [365
La oración fecha,   la missa acabada la an,
salieron de la eglesia,   ya quieren cavalgar.
El Cid a doña Ximena   ívala abraçar,
doña Ximena al Cid   la mánol' va besar,
llorando de los ojos   que non sabe qué se far,   [370
e él a las niñas   tornólas a catar:
'A Dios vos acomiendo, fijas,   e al Padre spiritual,
agora nos partimos,   Dios sabe el ajuntar.'

8v   Llorando de los ojos   que non viestes atal,
assís' parten unos d'otros   como la uña de la carne.   [375
Mio Cid con los sos vassallos   pensó de cavalgar,
a todos esperando,   la cabeça tornando va;
a tan grand sabor   fabló Minaya Álbar Fáñez:

Arabia came to do Thee homage, Melchior, Caspar and Balthazar, who offered Thee gold, frankincense and myrrh, as was Thy holy will. Thou didst save Jonah when he fell into the sea and Daniel in the lions' evil den. In Rome Thou didst save St. Sebastian, and Thou didst save Susanna when she was falsely accused. Thou didst walk the earth for thirty-two years, our heavenly Lord, performing miracles, which will always be narrated. Thou didst change water into wine and a stone into bread. Thou didst raise Lazarus from the dead according to Thy will. Thou didst allow Thyself to be taken by the Jews, and on Mount Calvary in the place called Golgotha they put Thee on the cross. With Thee were crucified two thieves, one on either side; one of them is in Paradise but the other did not enter there. Whilst on the cross Thou didst work a great miracle. Longinus, who was blind from birth, pierced Thy side with his lance; the blood flowed out and, running down the shaft, it stained his hands. He raised them to his face, opened his eyes and looked around him. He believed in Thee from that moment and so was saved from damnation. Thou didst rise again in the tomb; Thou didst go down to hell, as was Thy holy will. Thou didst break down its gates and didst lead out the holy prophets. Thou art the King of Kings and Father of the world. I worship Thee and believe in Thee with all my heart and soul. I pray to St Peter to help me to intercede for the Cid Campeador that God may keep him from harm. Though we must part today, may He reunite us in life.' When her prayer was ended and mass had been said, they left the church and the knights prepared to mount their horses. The Cid embraced Doña Jimena and she kissed his hand, weeping and distracted with grief. Then he turned to look at his daughters and said: 'My daughters, I give you into the keeping of God our heavenly Father. We must part now and God knows when we shall meet again.' Weeping bitterly, they parted with such pain as when the finger-nail is torn from the flesh. The Cid prepared to ride away with his vassals, but as he waited for them he kept turning his head (to look behind). Minaya Álvar Fáñez spoke these timely words:

'Cid, ¿dó son vuestros esfuerços?   En buen ora
                   nasquiestes de madre;
pensemos de ir nuestra vía,   esto sea de vagar.   [380
Aún todos estos duelos   en gozo se tornarán,
Dios que nos dio las almas   consejo nos dará.'
Al abat don Sancho   tornan de castigar
cómo sirva a doña Ximena   e a la[s] fijas que ha
e a todas sus dueñas   que con ellas están;   [385
bien sepa el abat   que buen galardón d'ello prendrá.
Tornado es don Sancho   e fabló Álbar Fáñez:
'Si viéredes yentes venir   por connusco ir, | abat,   [388-89
dezildes que prendan el rrastro   e piessen de andar   [389b
ca en yermo o en poblado   poder nos [han] alcançar.' [390
Soltaron las rriendas,   piessan de andar,
cerca viene el plazo   por el rreino quitar.
Vino Mio Cid yazer   a Spinaz de Can,
grandes yentes se le acojen   essa noch de todas partes. [395
Otro día mañana   piensa de cavalgar,   [394
ixiendos' va de tierra   el Canpeador leal,   [396
de siniestro Sant Estevan,   una buena cipdad,
de diestro Alilón las torres   que moros las han,
passó por Alcobiella,   que de Castiella fin es ya,
la calçada de Quinea   ívala traspassar,   [400
sobre Navas de Palos   el Duero va passar,
a la Figueruela   Mio Cid iva posar;
vánsele acogiendo   yentes de todas partes.

19

Í se echava Mio Cid   después que fue cenado,
un suéñol' priso dulce,   tan bien se adurmió;   [405
el ángel Gabriel   a él vino en sueño:
'¡Cavalgad, Cid,   el buen Campeador!
Ca nunqua | en tan buen punto   cavalgó varón;   [407b-08
mientra que visquiéredes   bien se fará lo to.'
Quando despertó el Cid,   la cara se sanctigó,   [410
sinava la cara,   a Dios se acomendó,
mucho era pagado   del sueño que á soñado.

20

Otro día mañana   piensan de cavalgar,
és día á de plazo,   sepades que non más.
A la sierra de Miedes   ellos ivan posar.   [415

'Cid, where is your courage? Your mother bore you in a fortunate hour! Let us go on our way and not waste time like this.
All these sorrows will one day be turned to joy. God, who gave
us our souls, will give us counsel.' The Abbot Don Sancho was
again admonished to care for Doña Jimena, her daughters and
her ladies, and he was promised a substantial reward. As Don
Sancho turned to go, Álvar Fáñez said to him: 'If any men should
come looking for us, tell them to follow on in our tracks;
they will be able to overtake us in countryside or town.' Then,
slackening their reins, they rode away, for the time for them to
leave the country was nearly up. The Cid spent the night in
Spinaz de Can, where great numbers joined them, coming from
all parts. The next morning they started off again. The loyal
Campeador left Castile, with the town of San Esteban on the
left and on the right the fortifications of Ayllón, which belong
to the Moors. He went through Alcubilla, the last town in
Castile, crossed the Roman road called Quinea and the river
Douro at Navapalos and halted at Figueruela. (There) men
crowded in from all directions to go with him.

19

After having his supper, the Cid lay down and fell into a deep
and pleasant sleep. The angel Gabriel came to him in a dream and
said: 'Ride out, good Cid Campeador, for no man ever set forth
at so fortunate a moment. All your life you will meet with
success.' When the Cid awoke he made the sign of the cross on
his forehead and his lips. He crossed himself and commended
himself to God, greatly pleased with his dream.

20

Next morning they mounted and rode on their way, for note
that they had only one day left; they came to a halt at the Sierra
de Miedes.

21

Aún era de día, non era puesto el sol,
mandó ver sus yentes Mio Cid el Campeador,
sin las peonadas e omnes valientes que son,
notó trezientas lanças que todas tienen pendones.

22

9v 'Temprano dat cevada, ¡sí el Criador vos salve! [420
El qui quisiere comer; e qui no, cavalgue.
Passaremos la sierra que fiera es e grand,
la tierra del rrey Alfonso esta noch la podemos quitar;
después, qui nos buscare, fallarnos podrá.'
De noch passan la sierra, vinida es la man [425
e por la loma ayuso piensan de andar.
En medio d'una montaña maravillosa e grand
fizo Mio Cid posar e cevada dar,
díxoles a todos cómo querié trasnochar;
vassallos tan buenos por coraçón lo an, [430
mandado de so señor todo lo han a far.
Ante que anochesca piensan de cavalgar,
por tal lo faze Mio Cid que no [l]o ventasse nadi,
andidieron de noch, que vagar non se dan.
Ó dizen Castejón, el que es sobre Fenares, [435
Mio Cid se echó en celada con aquellos que él trae.
Toda la noche yaze en celada el que en buen ora nasco
como los consejava Minaya Álbar Fáñez.

23

'¡Ya Cid, en buen ora cinxiestes espada!
Vós con *ciento* de aquesta nuestra conpaña, [440
pues que a Castejón sacaremos a celada ...'
[*Brief lacuna*]
'Vós con los *dozientos* idvos en algara,
allá vaya Álbar Á[l]barez | e Álbar Salvadórez sin falla, [442b-43
e Galín García, una fardida | lança, [443b-44
cavalleros buenos que aconpañen a Minaya; [444b
10r a osadas corred, que por miedo non dexedes nada, [445
Fita ayuso e por Guadalfajara,
fata Alcalá lleguen las alg[a]ras] [446b
e bien acojan todas las ganancias
que por miedo de los moros non dexen nada;
e yo con lo[s] *ciento* aquí fincaré en la çaga,
terné yo Castejón dón abremos grand enpara. [450

21

It was still daylight and the sun had not set when the Cid ordered a review of his men. Not counting the valiant foot soldiers he reckoned three hundred horsemen, each with a pennon on his lance.

22

'(Do not fail to) rise early to give fodder to the horses, as you hope for salvation. Any man who wishes to eat may do so; the rest (must) mount and ride on. We shall cross this wild and lofty mountain range and leave the land of King Alfonso tonight. After that anyone who wishes to join us will be able to find us.' They crossed the mountains by night and when morning came they began the descent into the valley. In the middle of a vast wood the Cid ordered a halt to be made to feed the horses. He told his followers that he wished to continue marching by night, and like good vassals they wholeheartedly agreed to obey his commands. So they mounted again before nightfall, for the Cid wished to avoid discovery. They travelled all night without resting, and at the place called Castejón de Henares the Cid went into ambush with the whole of his troops. The Cid lay all night in ambush and listened to the advice of Álvar Fáñez (who said):

23

'Cid, as our plan is to entice the men of Castejón into an ambush, you with one hundred of our company . . .'
[Brief lacuna]
(The Campeador answered) 'You go on in advance with two hundred men, taking Álvar Álvarez, Álvar Salvadórez as well, and Galín Garcíaz, a bold fighter, all good men to support Minaya. All must ride out boldly and do the work thoroughly without fear of the Moors. The advance guard should go down to Hita and through Guadalajara as far as Alcalá to gather up the spoils. I shall remain in the rear with one hundred men and I shall take possession of Castejón, where we shall hold a strong

Si cueta vos fuere   alguna al algara,
fazedme mandado   muy privado a la çaga,
¡ d'aqueste acorro   fablará toda España!'
Nonbrados son   los que irán en el algara
e los que con Mio Cid   ficarán en la çaga.   [455
Ya quiebran los albores   e vinié la mañana,
ixié el sol,   ¡Dios, qué fermoso apuntava!
En Castejón   todos se levantavan,
abren las puertas,   de fuera salto davan
por ver sus lavores   e todas sus heredades;   [460
todos son exidos,   las puertas abiertas an dexadas
con pocas de gentes   que en Castejón fincaron;
las yentes de fuera   todas son derramadas.
El Campeador   salió de la celada,
corre a Castejón   sin falla.   [464b
Moros e moras   aviénlos de ganancia   [465
e essos gañados   quantos en derredor andan.
Mio Cid don Rrodrigo   a la puerta adeliñava,
los que la tienen,   quando vieron la rrebata,
1ov   ovieron miedo   e fue dese[m]parada.
Mio Cid Rruy Díaz   por las puertas entrava,   [470
en mano trae   desnuda el espada,
quinze moros matava   de los que alcançava.
Gañó a Castejón   e el oro e la plata,
sos cavalleros   llegan con la ganancia,
déxanla a Mio Cid,   todo esto non precia[n] nada.   [475
Afevos los *dozientos   e tres* en el algara
e sin dubda corren; . . . .
fasta Alcalá llegó   la seña de Minaya   [477b
e desí arriba   tórnanse con la ganancia,
Fenares arriba   e por Guadalfajara.
Tanto traen   las grandes gana[n]cias,   [480
muchos gañados | de ovejas e de vacas,   [480b-81
e de rropas   e de otras rriquizas largas;   [481b
derecha viene   la seña de Minaya,
non osa ninguno   dar salto a la çaga.
Con aqueste aver   tórnanse essa conpaña,
fellos en Castejón   ó el Campeador estava;   [485
el castiello dexó en so poder,   el Canpeador cavalga,
saliólos rrecebir   con esta su mesnada,
los braços abiertos   rrecibe a Minaya:
'¡Venides, Álbar Fáñez,   una fardida lança!
Dó yo vos enbiás   bien abría tal esperança;   [490

position. If you should run into any great danger in the van send me word quickly to the rear; all Spain will talk of the relief that I shall bring.' They named those who were to go with the raiding party and those who were to stay with the Cid in the rear. Dawn was breaking; it was morning, and what a lovely sunrise it was! In Castejón the inhabitants got up, opened the gates and went out to inspect their estates and the farm-work in progress there. Everyone went out, leaving the gates open. Only a few were left in Castejón, for most of them were scattered about in the fields. The Campeador issued from his hiding place and harried Castejón, capturing many Moorish men and women with the cattle and sheep that were in the fields. Don Rodrigo marched up to the gate, and when those on guard there saw the sudden attack they took fright and left it undefended. The Cid went through the gate and, carrying his sword unsheathed in his hand, he overtook and killed fifteen Moors. In the capture of Castejón he won much gold and silver. His knights then arrived with the loot they had collected and handed it over to the Cid as if it meant nothing to them. Here you have the two hundred and three knights of the raiding party going relentlessly into the attack. Minaya's banner reached Alcalá, and back upstream his men returned with the spoils, along the river Henares and through Guadalajara. They carried away great quantities of booty in sheep and cattle, garments and other rich gains. Minaya's banner went forward, borne high, and no one dared to disturb the rearguard. His troops returned with all this wealth and presented themselves in Castejón, where the Campeador was already in possession. He left the fortress well guarded and rode out with his men to welcome them. He received Minaya with open arms (saying): 'Here you come, Álvar Fáñez, (like the) daring fighter that you are! Wherever I send you I expect

esso con esto   sea ajuntado,
dovos la quinta,   si la quisiéredes, Minaya.'

24

11r 'Mucho vos lo gradesco,   Campeador contado;
d'aquesta quinta   que me avedes mand[ad]o
pagar se ía d'ella   Alfonso el castellano.   [495
Yo vos la suelto   e avello quitado;
a Dios lo prometo,   a Aquel que está en alto,
fata que yo me pague   sobre mio buen cavallo
lidiando con moros   en el campo,
que enpleye la lança   e al espada meta mano   [500
e por el cobdo ayuso   la sangre destellando
ante Rruy Díaz   el lidiador contado,
non prendré de vós   quanto vale un dinero malo.
Pues que por mí ganaredes   quesquier que sea d'algo,
todo lo otro   afelo en vuestra mano.'   [505

25

Estas ganancias   allí eran juntadas.
Comidiós' Mio Cid,   el que en buen ora fue nado,
el rrey Alfonso   que llegarién sus compañas,
quel' buscarié mal   con todas sus mesnadas.
Mandó partir   tod' aqueste aver,   [510
sos quiñoneros   que ge los diessen por carta.
Sos cavalleros   í an arribança,
a cada uno d'ellos   caen *ciento* marcos de plata
e a los peones   la meatad sin falla,
11v toda la quinta   a Mio Cid fincava.   [515
Aquí non lo puede vender   nin dar en presentaja,
nin cativos nin cativas   non quiso traer en su conpaña.
Fabló con los de Castejón   e envió a Fita e a Guadalfajara
esta quinta   por quánto serié conprada,
aun de lo que diessen   oviessen grand ganancia,   [520
asmaron los moros   *tres* mill marcos de plata;
plogo a Mio Cid   d'aquesta presentaja,
a tercer día   dados fueron sin falla.
Asmó Mio Cid   con toda su conpaña
que en el castiello   non í avrié morada,   [525
e que serié rretenedor   mas non í avrié agua:
'Moros en paz,   ca escripta es la carta,
buscar nos ie el rrey Alfonso   con toda su mesnada;
quitar quiero Castejón,   ¡oíd, escuelas e Minyaya!

to hear of victory. Putting the two lots of booty together I give you a fifth share of the whole, if you will accept it, Minaya.'

24

'I am most grateful to you, illustrious Campeador' (Minaya answered). 'King Alfonso of Castile would be well pleased with the fifth share you have assigned to me. I hand it back to you to have again freely, and I swear in God's name that until, on my good horse, fighting Moors in the field, I use my lance and my sword till the blood drips down to my elbow in the presence of the great warrior Ruy Díaz, I shall not take a penny piece from you. Until I have won on your behalf some really valuable prize, I leave everything in your hands.'

25

When all the booty had been collected together the fortunate Cid, reflecting that King Alfonso might arrive with his army and seek to harm him and his vassals, ordered those charged with the task to distribute all this wealth, writing down every man's share. The gains were great, one hundred marks falling to the share of each knight and half that amount to each foot soldier, the Cid receiving his customary fifth share. He could not sell or give it away, and as he did not wish to take the men and women prisoners with him, he parleyed with the inhabitants of Castejón and sent word to those of Hita and Guadalajara, asking how much they would offer for his share—even with what the Moors would give they would make a great gain. The Moors calculated the value of the property at three thousand silver marks, and the Cid was satisfied with this gift, which was paid in full on the third day. The Cid reckoned that he and his men should not remain in the fortress, for though he could indeed hold it, there would be no water there. 'The Moors' (he thought) 'are at peace, having a pact in writing, and King Alfonso might come after us with his entire army, so I shall leave Castejón.' (Then he said) 'Listen to me, my men, and Minaya Álvar Fáñez.

26

Lo que yo dixier   non lo tengades a mal,   [530
en Castejón   non podriemos fincar,
cerca es el rrey Alfonso   e buscarnos verná.
Mas el castiello   non lo quiero ermar,
ciento moros e ciento moras   quiero las quitar
porque lo pris d'ellos   que de mí non digan mal.   [535
Todos sodes pagados   e ninguno por pagar,
cras a la mañana   pensemos de cavalgar,
12r   con Alfonso mio señor   non querría lidiar.'
Lo que dixo el Cid   a todos los otros plaz.
Del castiello que prisieron   todos rricos se parten,   [540
los moros e las moras   bendiziéndol' están.
Vanse Fenares arriba   quanto pueden andar,
trocen las Alcarias   e ivan adelant,
por las Cuevas d'Anquita   ellos passando van,
passaron las aguas,   entraron al campo de Torancio,   [545
por essas tierras ayuso   quanto pueden andar.
Entre Fariza e Cetina   Mio Cid iva albergar,
grandes son las ganancias   que priso por la tierra dó va.
Non lo saben los moros   el ardiment que an.
Otro día moviós'   Mio Cid el de Bivar   [550
e passó a Alfama,   la Foz ayuso va,
passó a Bovierca   e a Teca que es adelant
e sobre Alcocer   Mio Cid iva posar
en un otero rredondo,   fuerte e grand,
acerca corre Salón,   agua nol' puedent vedar.   [555
Mio Cid don Rrodrigo   Alcocer cueda ganar.

27

Bien puebla el otero,   firme prende las posadas,
los unos contra la sierra   e los otros contra la agua.
El buen Canpeador   que en buen ora nasco
derredor del otero   bien cerca del agua   [560
12v   a todos sos varones   mandó fazer una cárcava
que de día nin de noch   non les diessen arrebata,
que sopiessen que Mio Cid   allí avié fincança.

28

Por todas essas tierras   ivan los mandados
que el Campeador Mio Cid   allí avié poblado,   [565
venido es a moros,   exido es de cristianos;
en la su vezindad   non se treven ganar tanto.

26

Do not take in bad part what I am about to say. We cannot
remain in Castejón, for King Alfonso is not far off and will
come in search of us. I do not wish to destroy the fortress, so I
shall set free one hundred Moorish men and their women, that
they may not blame me for taking it from them. You are all
well provided for and no one has been left unpaid. Let us ride
away tomorrow morning, for I should not like to fight against
my lord, King Alfonso.' The Cid's decision pleased them all.
They went away from the fortress which they had taken with a
rich booty and the blessings of the Moorish men and women.
They rode at full speed up the river Henares, traversed the
Alcarria and went past the caves of Anguita. There they crossed
the river (Tajuña) and entered Campo Taranz, riding down
through those lands as quickly as they could, taking great booty
as they went. At length the Cid pitched his camp between Ariza
and Cetina. The Moors were at a loss to know what his plan
might be. The next day the Cid, the man from Vivar, struck
camp, passed Alhama and went down the river bend and past
Bubierca and Ateca, which is farther on. Then he encamped near
Alcocer on a great rounded height. As the river Jalón ran past it
their water could not be cut off, so the Cid made up his mind to
take Alcocer.

27

He took firm possession of the slopes, placing some of his
men towards the mountain side and some by the river. The good
Campeador ordered his men to make a trench round the hill
quite close to the river bank to prevent attack by day or by night
and to let the Moors know that he meant to settle down there.

28

The news spread through the countryside that the Cid, having
left the land of the Christians to come among the Moors, had
established his camp there, and they did not dare to cultivate
their fields with him so near at hand. The Cid and his vassals

Aguardándose va Mio Cid   con todos sus vassallos,
el castiello de Alcocer   en paria va entrando.
Los de Alcocer a Mio Cid   yal' dan parias de grado   *[570*

29

   e los de Teca   e los de Ter*r*er la casa;
a los de Calataút,   sabet, ma[*l*] les pesava.
Allí yogo Mio Cid   complidas *quinze* semanas.
Quando vio Mio Cid   que Alcocer non se le dava,
él fizo un art   e non lo detardava: *[575*
dexa una tienda fita   e las otras levava,
cojó[*s*'] Salón ayuso,   la su seña alçada,
las lorigas vestidas   e cintas las espadas
a guisa de menbrado   por sacarlos a celada.
Veyénlo los de Alcocer,   ¡Dios, cómo se alabavan!   *[580*
'Fallido á a Mio Cid   el pan e la cevada;
las otras abés lieva,   una tienda á dexada,
13r de guisa va Mio Cid   como si escapasse de arrancada.
Demos salto a él   e feremos grant ganancia
antes quel' prendan los de Ter*r*er,   si non, non nos darán
                                   dent nada; *[585*
la paria qu'él á presa   tornar nos la ha doblada.'
Salieron de Alcocer   a una priessa much estraña,
Mio Cid, quando los vio fuera,   cogiós' como de arrancada,
cojós' Salón ayuso,   con los sos abuelta *anda*.
Dizen los de Alcocer: '¡Ya se nos va la ganancia!'   *[590*
Los grandes e los chicos   fuera salto dan,
al sabor del prender   de lo ál non piensan nada,
abiertas dexan las puertas   que ninguno non las guarda.
El buen Campeador   la su cara tornava,
vio que entr'ellos e el castiello   mucho avié grand plaça, *[595*
mandó tornar la seña,   apriessa espoloneavan:
'¡Firidlos, cavalleros,   todos sines dubdança!
¡Con la merced del Criador   nuestra es la ganancia!'
Bueltos son con ellos   por medio de la llana.
¡Dios, qué bueno es el gozo   por aquesta mañana!   *[600*
Mio Cid e Álbar Fáñez   adelant aguijavan,
tienen buenos cavallos,   sabet, a su guisa les andan,
entr'ellos e el castiello   en essora entravan.
Los vassallos de Mio Cid   sin piedad les davan,
en un ora e un poco de logar   *trezientos* moros matan.   *[605*
13v Dando grandes alaridos   los que están en la celada,
dexando van los delant,   por el castiello se tornavan,

were on the watch and they levied tribute from the fortress or Alcocer. The inhabitants of Alcocer, Ateca and Terrer all paid tribute to the Cid.

29

And you can understand that those of Calatayud felt their hearts sink. The Cid lay encamped there for fifteen weeks, and when he realised that Alcocer was unlikely to surrender he contrived a stratagem which he proceeded to put into practice at once. He left one tent standing and took the others away; he then made off down the Jalón with banner flying and the men in their coats of mail with swords at their belts. It was a wily move to draw them out by a trick. The men of Alcocer watched them go, and how delighted they were! (They thought) 'The Cid is short of bread and fodder, he has been forced to take up the tents against his will, leaving one behind. The Cid has gone off' (they thought) 'as if fleeing from defeat. Let us sally out to the attack and win great booty before the men of Terrer get at it. If they do they won't give us a penny. He shall pay us back double the tribute he has collected.' They rushed from Alcocer in the greatest haste. When the Cid saw them come out he made off as if in flight. Down the river Jalón he went, with all his men around him. The inhabitants of Alcocer said: 'Our prey is escaping!' Great and small, out they came, thinking of nothing but the loot they might get, leaving the gates wide open and unguarded. The worthy Campeador looked round and saw that there was a good distance between them and the fortress. Then he ordered his standard to turn back, and his knights spurred their horses to full speed. 'Strike them, my good knights' (he cried), 'all of you, fearlessly! With the help of God the victory is ours.' They came to grips with the Moors on the flat ground. What great joy they felt that morning! The Cid and Álvar Fáñez spurred ahead, for they had good horses that carried them as swiftly as heart could wish. They cut right into the space between the Moors and the fortress. The Cid's vassals dealt pitiless blows and in a short time they had killed three hundred Moors. While the Moors in the trap uttered loud cries, those who had gone ahead disengaged, reached the fortress

las espadas desnudas   a la puerta se paravan.
Luego llegavan los sos,   ca fecha es el arrancada.
Mio Cid gañó a Alcocer,   sabet, por esta maña.   [610

30
Vino Pero Vermúez,   que la seña tiene en mano,
metióla en somo,   en todo lo más alto.
Fabló Mio Cid Rruy Díaz,   el que en buen ora fue nado:
'Grado a Dios del cielo   e a todos los sos sanctos,
ya mejoraremos posadas   a dueños e a cavallos.   [615

31
¡Oíd a mí, Álbar Fáñez   e todos los cavalleros!
En este castiello   grand aver avemos preso,
los moros yazen muertos,   de bivos pocos veo;
los moros e la[s] moras   vender non los podremos,
que los descabecemos   nada non ganaremos,   [620
cojámoslos de dentro   ca el señorío tenemos,
posaremos en sus casas   e d'ellos nos serviremos.'

32
Mio Cid con esta ganancia   en Alcocer está,
fizo enbiar por la tienda   que dexara allá.
Mucho pesa a los de Teca   e a los de Terrer non plaze   [625
e a los de Calatayut   non plaze;
al rrey de Valencia   enbiaron con mensaje
que a uno que dizién   Mio Cid Rruy Díaz de Bivar:
14r   'Airólo el rrey Alfonso,   de tierra echado lo ha,
vino posar sobre Alcocer   en un tan fuerte logar,   [630
sacólos a celada,   el castiello ganado á.
Si non das consejo,   a Teca e a Terrer perderás,
perderás Calatayut,   que non puede escapar,
rribera de Salón   toda irá a mal,
assí ferá lo de Siloca,   que es del otra part.'   [635
Quando lo oyó el rrey Tamín   por cuer le pesó mal:
'Tres rreyes veo de moros   derredor de mí estar,
non lo detardedes,   los dos id pora allá,
tres mill moros levedes   con armas de lidiar,
con los de la frontera   que vos ayudarán   [640
prendétmelo a vida,   aduzídmelo deland,
porque se me entró en mi tierra   derecho me avrá a dar.'
Tres mill moros cavalgan   e piensan de andar,
ellos vinieron a la noch   en Sogorve posar.
Otro día mañana   piensan de cavalgar,   [645

and waited at the gate with drawn swords. The rest, victorious in the fight, came up soon after. Note that it was by this trick that the Cid took Alcocer.

30

Pedro Bermúdez arrived, bearing the standard, and planted it on the highest point. The ever fortunate Cid spoke these words: 'Thanks be to God in Heaven and to all his saints. Now we shall have better lodging for the horses and their masters.

31

Listen to me, Álvar Fáñez, and all my knights. We have gained great wealth in capturing this stronghold; many Moors lie dead and few remain alive. We shall not be able to sell our captives, whether men or women. We should gain nothing by cutting off their heads. Let us allow them to return to the town, for we are masters here. We shall occupy their houses and make them serve us.'

32

While the Cid was arranging the disposal of the booty in Alcocer, he sent for the tent he had left standing. The inhabitants of Ateca, Terrer and Calatayud were greatly perturbed by these events, and sent a message to the King of Valencia, saying: 'Someone called Ruy Díaz of Vivar, the Cid, has incurred the anger of King Alfonso, who has banished him. He encamped before the stronghold of Alcocer and he got them out by a trick and took the fortress. If you do not come to our aid you will lose Ateca, Terrer and Calatayud, which cannot escape—all will go from bad to worse along the river Jalón and the same thing will happen at the Jiloca on the other side.' When King Mu'taman received this message he was much distressed. 'I have three Moorish leaders here at my court' (he said). 'Two of you go without delay, taking with you three thousand fully armed Moors. With the help of the frontier Moors take him alive and bring him here to me. He will have to answer for his invasion of my land.' Three thousand Moors mounted and rode off. They arrived at Segorbe to spend the night there, and next morning they set off again and reached Cella at nightfall. They

vinieron a la noch   a Celfa posar;
por los de la frontera   piensan de enviar,
non lo detienen,   vienen de todas partes.
Ixieron de Celfa,   la que dizen de Canal,
andidieron todo'l día   que vagar non se dan,   [650
vinieron essa noche   en Calatayu[t] posar.
Por todas essas tierras   los pregones dan,
14v   gentes se ajuntaron   sobejanas de grandes
con aquestos dos rreyes   que dizen Fáriz e Galve;
al bueno de Mio Cid   en Alcocer le van cercar.   [655

33

Fincaron las tiendas   e prendend las posadas,
crecen estos virtos   ca yentes son sobejanas;
las arrobdas   que los moros sacan
de día | e de noch   enbueltos andan en armas;   [658b-59
muchas son las arrobdas   e grande es el almofalla,   [660
a los de Mio Cid   ya les tuellen el agua.
Mesnadas de Mio Cid   exir querién a la batalla,
el que en buen ora nasco   firme ge lo vedava.
Toviérongela en cerca   complidas tres semanas.

34

A cabo de tres semanas,   la quarta querié e[n]trar,   [665
Mio Cid con los sos   tornós' a acordar:
'El agua nos an vedada,   exir nos ha el pan,
que nos queramos ir de noch   no nos lo consintrán;
grandes son los poderes   por con ellos lidiar,
dezidme, cavalleros,   cómo vos plaze de far.'   [670
Primero fabló Minaya,   un cavallero de prestar:
'De Castiella la gentil   exidos somos acá,
si con moros non lidiáremos,   no nos darán del pan.
Bien somos nós seiscientos,   algunos ay de más,
15r   en el no[m]bre del Criador,   que non passe por ál;   [675
vayámoslos ferir   en aquel día de cras.'
Dixo el Campeador: 'A mi guisa fablastes;
ondrástesvos, Minaya,   ca aver vos lo iedes de far.'
Todos los moros e las moras   de fuera los manda echar
que non sopiesse ninguno   esta su poridad;   [680
el día e la noche   piénsanse de adobar.
Otro día mañana   el sol querié apuntar,
armado es Mio Cid   con quantos que él ha,
fablava Mio Cid   como odredes contar:

decided to send for the frontier Moors, who immediately
flocked in from all sides. They then left Cella, which people
call Cella de Canal, rode all day without rest and arrived at
Calatayud, where they lay encamped that night. Messengers
were sent throughout the whole region and men assembled
in vast numbers to join the two leaders, Fáriz and Galve, who
then proceeded to besiege the Cid in Alcocer.

33

They pitched their tents and took up their positions, and their
forces increased to enormous proportions. The scouts sent out
by the Moors kept watch day and night under arms—they were
many in number, for it was a large army. They found a way of
cutting off the water from the Cid's men. His troops were eager
to make a sortie, but the Cid firmly forbade it. The siege lasted
three full weeks.

34

At the end of the three weeks, at the beginning of the fourth,
the Cid took counsel with his followers: 'They have cut off our
water and we shall soon be short of food. They will not permit
our escape by night, and their forces are very strong for us to
attack. Tell me, my good knights, what do you wish to do?'
The valiant Minaya spoke first: 'We have left our homes in
fair Castile. If we do not fight the Moors they will starve us out.
We are a full six hundred men, and even more. God is my
witness, we have no choice but to attack them tomorrow.'
The Campeador replied: 'Your words are to my taste. They
do you credit, Minaya. I expected no less from you.' He then
ordered all the Moorish inhabitants, men and women, to be
turned out, so as to keep secret his preparations, which went on
day and night. Next day, when the sun was about to rise and the
Cid and his men were ready armed, he addressed them as you

C

'Todos iscamos fuera   que nadi non rraste   [685
sinon dos peones solos   por la puerta guardar,
si nós muriéremos en campo,   en castiello nos entrarán,
si venciéremos la batalla,   creçremos en rrictad;
e vós, Pero Vermúez,   la mi seña tomad,
como sodes muy bueno,   tener la edes sin art,   [690
mas non aguijedes con ella   si yo non vos lo mandar.'
Al Cid besó la mano,   la seña va tomar.
Abrieron las puertas,   fuera un salto dan,
viéronlo las arrobdas de los moros,   al almofalla se van tornar.
¡Qué priessa va en los moros!   e tornáronse a armar,   [695
ante rroído de atamores   la tierra querié quebrar;
veriedes armarse moros,   apriessa entrar en az.
De parte de los moros   dos señas ha cabdales,
15v e fizieron dos azes de peones mezclados,   ¿quí los podrié contar?
La[s] azes de los moros   yas' mueven adelant   [700
por a Mio Cid e a los sos   a manos los tomar.
'Quedas sed, me[s]nadas,   aquí en este logar,
non derranche ninguno   fata que yo lo mande.'
Aquel Pero Vermúez   non lo pudo endurar,
la seña tiene en mano,   conpeçó de espolonar: [705
'¡El Criador vos vala,   Cid, Campeador leal!
Vo meter la vuestra seña   en aquella mayor az;
los que el debdo avedes   veremos cómo la acorredes.'
Dixo el Campeador: '¡Non sea, por caridad!'
Rrespuso Pero Vermúez: '¡Non rrastará por ál!'   [710
Espolonó el çavallo   e metiól' en el mayor az.
Moros le rreciben   por la seña ganar,
danle grandes colpes   mas nol' pueden falsar.
Dixo el Campeador: '¡Valelde, por caridad!'

35
Enbraçan los escudos   delant los coraçones,   [715
abaxan las lanças   abueltas de los pendones,
enclinaron las caras   de suso de los arzones,
ívanlos ferir   de fuertes coraçones.
A grandes vozes llama   el que en buen ora nasco:
'¡Feridlos, cavalleros,   por amor de caridad!   [720
¡Yo só Rruy Díaz de Bivar,   el Cid Campeador!'
Todos fieren en el az   dó está Pero Vermúez,
16r trezientas lanças son,   todas tienen pendones;
seños moros mataron,   todos de seños colpes;
a la tornada que fazen   otros tantos [muertos] son.   [725

will now hear: 'Let us all go out and none remain behind but two foot soldiers to guard the gate. If we perish on the field our enemies will enter the fortress, but if we win the battle we shall be richer than ever. You, Pedro Bermúdez, take my standard; you will carry it loyally like the good soldier you are, but do not advance unless I give you the command.' Bermúdez kissed the Cid's hand and received the standard. They opened the gates and sallied out. The Moorish scouts saw this and returned to the camp to report it. What eagerness there was among the Moors to arm themselves! And they could be seen ranging themselves in battle order. The noise of the drums seemed to make the earth quake. There were two main banners on the Moorish side and they formed two battle lines of mixed infantry in countless numbers. The Moors advanced all along the line to attack the Cid and his followers. 'Stay where you are, my men' (said the Cid), 'and let none break ranks till I give the word of command.' But Pedro Bermúdez could hold out no longer; he held the standard and spurred on his horse, crying: 'God be on your side, loyal Campeador! I am going to plant your banner in the chief Moorish battle line. We shall see how all your true vassals rush to its defence.' The Cid cried, 'Stop, in Heaven's name!' Pedro Bermúdez answered: 'There is no going back now!' He set spurs to his horse and carried the standard into the main line of battle. The Moors, eager to capture the Cid's standard, dealt him mighty blows, but without piercing his armour. Then the Campeador spoke: 'To his aid, for pity's sake!'

35

The men clasped their shields to their hearts and lowered their lances, each with its pennon flying. With heads bent down over their saddle-bows, they dashed to the attack courageously. The Cid, sure of success, shouted his battle cry: 'Attack them, my knights, for the love of God! I am Ruy Díaz of Vivar, the Cid Campeador!' They assailed the Moorish ranks, where Pedro Bermúdez was already in the thick of the fight. There were three hundred knights with lance and pennon, and with every lance-thrust a Moor fell dead. On returning to the charge they killed as many more.

36

Veriedes tantas lanças   premer e alçar,
tanta adágara   foradar e passar,
tanta loriga   falsa[r] [e] desmanchar,
tantos pendones blancos   salir vermejos en sangre,
tantos buenos cavallos   sin sos dueños andar.   [730
Los moros llaman Mafómat   e los cristianos Sancti Yagü[e];
cayén en un poco de logar   moros muertos mill e [trezientos ya].

37

¡Quál lidia bien   sobre exorado arzón
Mio Cid Rruy Díaz,   el buen lidiador!
Minaya Álbar Fáñez,   que Çorita mandó,   [735
Martín Antolínez,   el burgalés de pro,
Muño Gustioz,   que fue so criado,
Martín Muñoz,   el que mandó a Mont Mayor,
Álbar Álbarez   e Álbar Salvadórez,
Galín García,   el bueno de Aragón,   [740
Félez Muñoz,   so sobrino del Campeador.
Desí adelante,   quantos que í son
acorren la seña   e a Mio Cid el Canpeador.

38

A Minaya Álbar Fáñez   matáronle el cavallo,
bien lo acorren   mesnadas de cristianos.   [745
La lança á quebrada,   al espada metió mano,
maguer de pie   buenos colpes va dando.
16v   Violo Mio Cid   Rruy Díaz el castellano,
acostós' a un aguazil   que tenié buen cavallo,
diol' tal espadada   con el so diestro braço   [750
cortól' por la cintura,   el medio echó en campo.
A Minaya Álbar Fáñez   íval' dar el cavallo:
'¡Cavalgad, Minaya,   vós sodes el mio diestro braço!
Oy en este día   de vós abré grand bando;
firme[s] son los moros,   aún nos' van del campo.'   [755
Cavalgó Minaya,   el espada en la mano,
por estas fuerças   fuertemientre lidiando,
a los que alcança   valos delibrando.
Mio Cid Rruy Díaz,   el que en buen ora nasco,
al rrey Fáriz   tres colpes le avié dado,   [760
los dos le fallen   e el únol' ha tomado;
por la loriga ayuso   la sangre destella[n]do

36

Who could say how many lances rose and fell, how many
shields were pierced, coats of mail torn asunder and white
pennons stained red with blood, how many riderless horses
ranged the field? The Moors called on Muhammad and the
Christians on St James. In a short time one thousand three
hundred Moors fell dead upon the field.

37

How well the Cid Ruy Díaz, that great soldier, fought,
bending down over his gilded saddle-bow! (Fighting there also
were) Minaya Álvar Fáñez, lord of Zorita, Martín Antolínez,
the worthy citizen of Burgos, Muño Gustioz, a member of the
Cid's household, Martín Muñoz, governor of Montemayor,
Álvar Álvarez and Álvar Salvadórez, Galín García, the worthy
Aragonese, and Félez Muñoz, the Cid's nephew. From this
moment onward the whole host rallied in support of the standard
and of the Cid Campeador.

38

Minaya's horse was killed under him and the Christian troops
dashed to his aid. His lance was broken, but he grasped his sword
and fought manfully on foot. The Cid Ruy Díaz of Castile
saw his plight; he approached a Moorish leader mounted on a
fine horse and dealt him such a blow with his sword that he cut
him through the waist and hurled the rest of him to the ground.
Then he rode up to Minaya and gave him the horse, saying:
'Mount him, Minaya, my good right arm! I shall have your
full support in the fight today. The Moors are making a firm
stand and still hold the field.' Minaya rode, sword in hand,
fighting hard to make his way through the Moorish troops,
dispatching all those his sword could reach. The Cid Ruy Díaz
had struck three blows at King Fáriz; two had missed but the
third went home. With blood dripping down his coat of mail,

bolvió la rrienda   por írsele del campo.
Por aquel colpe   rrancado es el fonsado.

39

 Martín Antolínez   un colpe dio a Galve,   [*765*
las carbonclas del yelmo   echógelas aparte,
cortól' el yelmo   que llegó a la carne;
sabet, el otro   non gel' osó esperar.
Arrancado es   el rrey Fáriz e Galve.
¡Tan buen día   por la cristiandad   [*770*
ca fuyen los moros   de la part!
Los de Mio Cid   firiendo en alcaz,
el rrey Fáriz   en Terrer se fue entrar
17r e a Galve   nol' cogieron allá,
para Calatayut,   quanto puede, se va;   [*775*
el Campeador   íval' en alcaz,
fata Calatayut   duró el segudar.

40

 A Minaya Álbar Fáñez   bien l'anda el cavallo,
d'aquestos moros   mató *treínta e quatro*,
espada tajador,   sangriento trae el braço,   [*780*
por el cobdo ayuso   la sangre destellando.
Dize Minaya: 'Agora só pagado,
que a Castiella   irán buenos mandados
que Mio Cid Rruy Díaz   lid campal á vencida.'
Tantos moros yazen muertos   que pocos bivos á dexados [*785*
ca en alcaz   sin dubda les fueron dando.
Yas' tornan   los del que en buen ora nasco;
andava Mio Cid   sobre so buen cavallo,
la cofia fronzida,   ¡Dios, cómo es bien barbado!
Almófar a cuestas,   la espada en la mano,   [*790*
vio los sos   cómos' van allegando:
'Grado a Dios,   [*a*] Aquel que está en alto,
quando tal batalla   avemos arrancado.'
Esta albergada los de Mio Cid   luego la an rrobada
de escudos e de armas   e de otros averes largos; [*795*
de los moriscos,   quando son llegados,
fallaron   *quinientos e diez* cavallos.   [*796b*
Grand alegreya va   entre essos cristianos,
más de quinze de los sos   menos non fallaron.
Traen oro e plata   que non saben rrecabdo,
17v rrefechos son todos essos cristianos   con aquesta ganancia. [*800*

Fáriz turned his horse to flee the field. The battle was decided by that blow.

39

Martín Antolínez struck one blow at Galve, hewed the garnets from his helmet and cut through it to the flesh. Galve dared not wait for another blow. The Moorish leaders, Fáriz and Galve, were defeated! What a great day it was for Christendom when the Moors fled from the place! The Cid's followers pursued the fleeing ranks. Fáriz took refuge in Terrer, but Galve fled farther and made at full speed for Calatayud. The Campeador and his men continued the pursuit as far as that town.

40

Riding swiftly, Minaya Álvar Fáñez killed thirty-four Moors with his sharp sword; his arm was stained with the blood dripping down to his elbow. (When he saw that) Minaya said: 'Now I am satisfied, for the good news will reach Castile that the Cid Ruy Díaz has been victorious in a pitched battle.' So many Moors lay dead that only a few were left alive, for even in the pursuit more were struck down relentlessly. Returning with his followers, the Cid rode on his good horse, sword in hand. His linen coif was creased as the mailed hood fell over his shoulders; his long, flowing beard was a wonderful sight! The Cid watched his men as they trooped up (and he said): 'Thanks be to God on high for the great victory we have gained!' The Cid's men despoiled the Moorish camp of shields and arms and other wealth in abundance. When those were collected they reckoned five hundred and ten Moorish horses. There was great rejoicing in the Christian host when they found they had lost only fifteen of their number. They brought in endless quantities of gold and silver, and all the Christians were enriched with the booty they

A so castiello a los moros   dentro los an tornados,
mandó Mio Cid aún   que les diessen algo.
Grant á el gozo Mio Cid   con todos sos vassallos,
dio a partir estos dineros   e estos averes largos;
en la su quinta al Cid   caen *ciento* cavallos.   [*805*
¡Dios, qué bien pagó   a todos sus vassallos,
a los peones   e a los encavalgados!
Bien lo aguisa   el que en buen ora nasco,
quantos él trae   todos son pagados.
'¡Oíd, Minaya,   sodes mio diestro braço!   [*810*
D'aquesta rriqueza   que el Criador nos á dado
a vuestra guisa   prended con vuestra mano.
Enbiarvos quiero   a Castiella con mandado
d'esta batalla   que avemos arrancada,
al rrey Alfonso   que me á airado   [*815*
quiérol' e[n]biar en don   *treínta* cavallos,
todos con siellas   e muy bien enfrenados,
señas espadas   de los arzones colgadas.'
Dixo Minaya Álbar Fáñez: 'Esto faré yo de grado.'

41
'Evades aquí   oro e plata,   [*820*
una huesa llena, | que nada nol' mingua;   [*820b-21*
en Sancta María de Burgos   quitedes mill missas,
lo que rromaneciere   daldo a mi mugier e a mis fijas
18r   que rrueguen por mí   las noches e los días;
si les yo visquier,   serán dueñas rricas.'   [*825*

42
Minaya Álbar Fáñez   d'esto es pagado;
por ir con él   omnes son [contados],   [*826b*
agora davan cevada,   ya la noch era entrada,
Mio Cid Rruy Díaz   con los sos se acordava.

43
'¡Ídesvos, Minaya,   a Castiella la gentil!
A nuestros amigos   bien les podedes dezir: [*830*
"Dios nos valió   e venciemos la lid."
A la tornada,   si nos falláredes aquí;
si non, dó sopiéredes que somos,   indos conseguir.
Por la[n]ças e por espadas   avemos de guarir,
si non, en esta tierra angosta   non podriemos [bivir].'   [*835*

had won. The Cid ordered that the Moors (of Alcocer), who were now allowed to return to the fortress, should receive their share. The Cid and all his vassals were highly delighted at the distribution of the money and the abundance of wealth of every kind. One hundred horses were included in the Cid's share. He paid all his men, foot soldiers and horsemen, very well indeed. The Cid arranged things so admirably that all were well satisfied with the booty assigned to them. 'Listen, Minaya, my good right arm' (said the Cid). 'Take what you will of all this treasure that God has given us. I wish to send a message to Castile telling of this battle we have won. To King Alfonso, whose wrath I have incurred, I wish to send as a gift, thirty horses with their saddles, fully harnessed, and each with a sword hanging from the saddle-bow.' Minaya said: 'I shall do so with pleasure.'

41

(The Cid continued) 'Here is a boot filled to the brim with gold and silver, to pay for one thousand masses to be said in the church of Santa María at Burgos. The remainder give to my wife and daughters that they may pray for me day and night. If I survive they will be wealthy ladies.'

42

Minaya Álvar Fáñez willingly agreed to do this, and a band of knights were chosen to accompany him. They gave fodder to their horses as night fell, while the Cid took counsel with his followers:

43

'You are bound, Minaya, for fair Castile! You can tell our friends: "God has favoured us and given us the victory." On your return, if you find us here (all well and good); if you do not, follow on to join us when you know our whereabouts. We are obliged to defend ourselves with lance and sword. If we did not do so we could not live in this impoverished land.'

44

Ya es aguisado,   mañanas' fue Minaya
e el Campeador   [*fincó*] con su mesnada.
La tierra es angosta   e sobejana de mala,
todos los días   a Mio Cid aguardavan
moros de las fronteras   e unas yentes estrañas;   [*840*
sanó el rrey Fáriz,   con él se consejavan.
Entre los de Teca   e los de Ter*r*er la casa
e los de Calatayut,   que es más ondrada,
assí lo an asmado   e metudo en carta,
· vendido les á Alcocer   por tres mill marcos de plata.   [*845*

45

Mio Cid Rruy Díaz   Alcocer á ven[*d*]ido,
¡qué bien pagó   a sus vassallos mismos!
A cavalleros e a peones   fechos los ha rricos,
18v en todos los sos   non fallariedes un mesquino;
qui a buen señor sirve   siempre bive en delicio.   [*850*

46

Quando Mio Cid   el castiello quiso quitar,
moros e moras   tomáronse a quexar:
'¡Vaste, Mio Cid!   ¡Nuestras oraciones váyante delante!
Nós pagados finc*a*mos,   señor, de la tu part.'
Quando quitó a Alcocer   Mio Cid el de Bivar,   [*855*
moros e moras   compeçaron de llorar.
Alçó su seña,   el Campeador se va,
passó Salón ayuso,   aguijó cabadelant,
al exir de Salón   mucho ovo buenas aves.
Plogo a los de Terrer   e a los de Calatayut más;   [*860*
pesó a los de Alcocer   ca pro les fazié grant.
Aguijó Mio Cid,   ivas' cabadelant,
í fincó en un poyo   que es sobre Mont Rreal;
alto es el poyo,   maravilloso e grant;
non teme guerra,   sabet, a nulla part.   [*865*
Metió en paria   a Doroca enantes,
desí a Molina,   que es del otra part,
la tercera Teruel,   que estava delant,
en su mano tenié   a Celfa la de Canal.

47

¡Mio Cid Rruy Díaz   de Dios aya su gracia!   [*870*
Ido es a Castiella   Álbar Fáñez Minaya,

44

Now that everything was settled Minaya departed next morning. The Cid and his followers were left behind in that poor and barren land. The frontier Moors, alien folk, kept daily watch on the Cid, and they took counsel with Fáriz, who had recovered from his wound. The inhabitants of Ateca and Terrer, and those of Calatayud, a larger town than either of them, calculated and wrote down the bargain that the Cid had struck in selling Alcocer to them for the sum of three thousand silver marks.

45

The Cid Ruy Díaz had sold Alcocer, and how well he had rewarded his own vassals! He had enriched them all, knights and foot soldiers—you could not have found one poor man among them. Those who serve a good master are always well off!

46

When the Cid decided to leave the fortress all the Moors were sorry to see him go. 'You are going, Cid,' they said. 'May our prayers go before you! We are well satisfied with the way you have treated us.' When at last he took his departure from Alcocer, the Moors wept. The Campeador raised his standard and set off; following the course of the Jalón, he spurred straight ahead, and when he left the river he noted good omens. The inhabitants of Terrer and even more so those of Calatayud were pleased to see him go, but the people of Alcocer were sorry, for he had treated them well. The Cid went straight on and finally halted at a hill above Monreal. This hill is very high, and impregnable to attack from any side. The Cid first laid Daroca under tribute and then Molina, which is on the other side, and thirdly Teruel farther on. He already had possession of Cella de Canal.

47

May God grant His help to the Cid Ruy Díaz! Álvar Fáñez Minaya reached Castile and presented the thirty horses to the

treínta cavallos   al rrey los enpresentava.
19r Violos el rrey,   fermoso sonrrisava:
'¿Quín' los dio éstos,   sí vos vala Dios, Minaya?'
'Mio Cid Rruy Díaz,   que en buen ora cinxo espada.   [875
Venció dos rreyes de moros   en aquesta batalla;
sobejana es, señor,   la su gana[n]cia.
A vós, rrey ondrado,   enbía esta presentaja;
bésavos los pies   e las manos amas
quel' ay[a]des merced,   sí el Criador vos vala.'   [880
Dixo el rrey: 'Mucho es mañana
omne airado   que de señor non ha gracia
por acogello   a cabo de tres semanas.
Mas después que de moros fue,   prendo esta presentaja;
aún me plaze de Mio Cid   que fizo tal ganancia.   [885
Sobr'esto todo   a vós quito, Minaya,
honores e tierras   avellas condonadas,
id e venit,   d'aquí vos do mi gracia;
mas del Cid Campeador   yo non vos digo nada.
Sobre aquesto todo   dezirvos quiero, Minaya,   [890

48
    de todo mio rreino   los que lo quisieren far,
buenos e valientes   pora Mio Cid huyar,
suéltoles los cuerpos   e quítoles las heredades.'
Besóle las manos   Minaya Álbar Fáñez:
'Grado e gracias, rrey,   como a señor natural,   [895
esto feches agora,   ál feredes adelant.'

49
    'Id por Castiella   e déxenvos andar, Minaya,
si[n] nulla dubda   id a Mio Cid buscar ganancia.'
19v Quiero vos dezir   del que en buen ora nasco e cinxo espada.
Aquel poyo,   en él priso posada,   [900
mientra que sea el pueblo de moros   e la yente cristiana
El Poyo de Mio Cid   assil' dirán por carta.
Estando allí,   mucha tierra preava,
el río de Martín   todo lo metió en paria.
A Saragoça   sus nuevas llegavan,   [905
non plaze a los moros,   firmemientre les pesava,
allí sovo Mio Cid   conplidas *quinze* semanas.
Quando vio el caboso   que se tardava Minaya,
con todas sus yentes   fizo una trasnochada;
dexó El Poyo,   todo lo desenparava,   [910

King. When King Alfonso saw them a pleasant smile lit up his face (and he said): 'Tell me, Minaya, who has sent me this present?' 'The Cid Ruy Díaz, who was knighted in a fortunate hour,' answered Minaya. 'He vanquished two Moorish leaders in that battle and won enormous booty. He sends this gift to you, his honoured King, humbly salutes you and sues for your favour in God's name.' The King answered: 'It is rather soon to receive and pardon, after such a short time, a man who has incurred our anger and been disgraced. But as the booty has been taken from the Moors, I accept the gift, and I am even pleased that the Cid has won it. I hereupon pardon you, Minaya, and restore to you your lands and property. You have our permission to come and go freely, but I say nothing about the Cid Campeador. And now I tell you, Álvar Fáñez,

48

that those who wish to go to the assistance of the Cid may do so without fear for their lives or property.' Minaya kissed the King's hands and said: 'I thank you as my king and liege lord! You do this now and you will do more in the future.'

49

(The King answered) 'Travel freely through Castile and return to the Cid without delay to win booty.' We must go back to what the Cid was doing. That hill where he had encamped will be known in the records of both Moors and Christians for all time as El Poyo de Mio Cid—Hill of the Cid. While he was there he ravaged the neighbouring lands extensively and laid (the towns along) the river Martín under tribute. The news of his feats of arms reached Saragossa and angered the Moors greatly. The Cid remained there fully fifteen weeks, but when the great man saw that Minaya was long in coming he marched away by night with all his men. Don Rodrigo abandoned El Poyo for good and left it undefended, and passed beyond Teruel to

allén de Teruel   don Rrodrigo passava,
en el pinar de Tévar   don Rroy Díaz posava,
todas essas tierras   todas las preava,
a Saragoça   metuda la [*á*] en paria.
Quando esto fecho ovo,   a cabo de tres semanas   [915
de Castiella   venido es Minaya,
dozientos con él,   que todos ciñen espadas,
non son en cuenta,   sabet, las peonadas.
Quando vio Mio Cid   asomar a Minaya,
el cavallo corriendo,   valo abraçar sin falla,   [920
besóle la boca   e los ojos de la cara.
Todo ge lo dize,   que nol' encubre nada,
el Campeador   fermoso sonrrisava:
20r   '¡Grado a Dios   e a las sus vertudes sanctas,
mientra vós visquiéredes,   bien me irá a mí, Minaya!'   [925

50

¡Dios, cómo fue alegre   todo aquel fonsado
que Minaya Álbar Fáñez   assí era llegado,
diziéndoles saludes   de primos e de ermanos
e de sus compañas,   aquellas que avién dexadas!

51

¡Dios, cómo es alegre   la barba vellida   [930
que Álbar Fáñez   pagó las mill missas
e quel' dixo saludes   de su mugier e de sus fijas!
¡Dios, cómo fue el Cid pagado   e fizo grand alegría!
'¡Ya Álbar Fáñez,   bivades muchos días!'

52

Non lo tardó   el que en buen ora nasco,   [935
tierras d'Alcañ[i]z   negras las va parando
e aderredor   todo lo va preando;
al tercer día   dón ixo, í es tornado.

53

Ya va el mandado   por las tierras todas,
pesando va a los de Monçón   e a los de Huesca;   [940
porque dan parias   plaze a los de Saragoça,
de Mio Cid Rruy Díaz   que non temién ninguna fonta.

encamp in the pine wood of Tévar. He ravaged all that territory and laid Saragossa under tribute. Three weeks after the Cid had ended these exploits Minaya arrived from Castile, accompanied by two hundred armed knights and innumerable foot soldiers. When the Cid caught sight of Minaya, setting his horse to a gallop he rode to meet him and embraced him, kissing his mouth and eyes. Minaya told him the whole story and kept nothing back from him. A happy smile spread over the face of the Campeador, and he said: 'I thank God and all his holy powers! As long as you live, Minaya, my fortune will never wane.'

50
The whole army was delighted at Minaya's arrival, for he brought them greetings from brothers and cousins and from the companions they had left behind.

51
The Cid was in great spirits. He was pleased that Álvar Fáñez had paid for the thousand masses and had brought him greetings from his wife and daughters. The Cid could not contain his joy, and he cried, 'Long life to you, Álvar Fáñez!'

52
The Campeador made no delay but laid waste the lands of Alcañiz and its neighbourhood, and on the third day returned whence he had come.

53
News of this raid spread through the country round about, filling the inhabitants of Monzón and Huesca with dismay. The people of Saragossa were pleased, for, as they paid tribute, they knew that Ruy Díaz would not dishonour his word.

54

Con estas ganancias   a la posada tornándose van,
todos son alegres,   ganancias traen grandes,
plogo a Mio Cid   e mucho a Álbar Fáñez.   [945
Sonrrisós' el caboso,   que non lo pudo endurar:
'Ya cavalleros,   dezir vos he la verdad:
qui en un logar mora siempre,   lo so puede menguar;
20v   cras a la mañana   pensemos de cavalgar,
dexat estas posadas   e iremos adelant.'   [950
Estonces se mudó el Cid   al puerto de Aluca[n]t,
dent corre Mio Cid   a Huesa e a Mont Alván;
en aquessa corrida   *diez* días ovieron a morar.
Fueron los mandados   a todas partes
que el salido de Castiella   assí los trae tan mal.   [955
Los mandados son idos   a todas partes.

55

Llegaron las nuevas   al conde de Barcilona
que Mio Cid Rruy Díaz   quel' corrié la tierra toda;
ovo grand pesar   e tóvos'lo a grant fonta.

56

El conde es muy follón   e dixo una vanidat: [960
'Grandes tuertos me tiene   Mio Cid el de Bivar.
Dentro en mi cort   tuerto me tovo grand,
firióm' el sobrino   e non' lo enmendó más;
agora córrem' las tierras   que en mi enpara están.
Non lo desafié,   nil' torné enemistad,   [965
mas quando él me lo busca,   ir ge lo he yo demandar.'
Grandes son los poderes   e apriessa llegando se van,
entre moros e cristianos   gentes se le allegan grandes,
adeliñan tras Mio Cid   el bueno de Bivar;
tres días e dos noches   pensaron de andar,   [970
alcançaron a Mio Cid   en Tévar e el pinar;
assí viene esforçado el conde   que a manos se le cuidó tomar.
Mio Cid don Rrodrigo   ganancia trae grand,
21r   dice de una sierra   e llegava a un val.
Del conde don Rremont   venídol' es mensaje,   [975
Mio Cid, quando lo oyó,   enbió pora allá:
'Digades al conde   non lo tenga a mal,
de lo so non lievo nada,   déxem' ir en paz.'

54

When the troops returned to the encampment all were delighted with the great booty, and the Cid and Álvar Fáñez were well satisfied. The great man could not help smiling. 'My good knights,' he said, 'I shall tell you the plain truth. Whoever remains in one spot stands to lose. We must prepare to mount tomorrow morning, leave the camp and go farther afield.' The Cid moved on then to the pass of Gallocanta, and from there he made an expedition as far as Huesa and Montalbán which lasted ten days. The news of the damage the exile from Castile was doing spread far and wide.

55

These widespread rumours that the Cid Ruy Díaz was harrying the whole countryside reached the ears of the Count of Barcelona, who was highly incensed and considered this action as a personal injury.

56

The Count was a hasty and foolish man and spoke without due reflection: 'The Cid, Rodrigo of Vivar, has done me great wrongs. In my own palace he gave me great offence by striking my nephew and never giving satisfaction for it. Now he is ravaging the lands under my protection. I never challenged him nor showed enmity towards him in return, but since he seeks me out, I shall demand redress.' Great numbers of Moors and Christians flocked in haste to join his forces, and they went in search of the Cid, the mighty Ruy Díaz of Vivar. They journeyed three days and two nights and came up with the Cid in the pine wood of Tévar, so confident in their strength that the Count was certain of laying hands on him. The Cid, Don Rodrigo, carrying large quantities of booty, descended from the mountains to a valley. There he received the message of Count Ramón. When the Cid heard it he sent word, saying: 'Tell the Count not to take offence. I am carrying off nothing of his, so let him leave me to go in peace.' The Count replied: 'Not so!

Rrespuso el conde: '¡Esto non será verdad!
Lo de antes e de agora   tódom' lo pechará;   [980
¡sabrá el salido   a quién vino desondrar!'
Tornós' el mandadero   quanto pudo más;
essora lo connosce   Mio Cid el de Bivar
que a menos de batalla   nos' pueden dén quitar.

57

'Ya cavalleros,   apart fazed la ganancia,   [985
apriessa vos guarnid   e metedos en las armas;
el conde don Rremont   dar nos ha grant batalla,
de moros e de cristianos   gentes trae sobejanas,
a menos de batalla   non nos dexarié por nada.
Pues adelant irán tras nós,   aquí sea la batalla;   [990
apretad los cavallos   e bistades las armas.
Ellos vienen cuesta yuso   e todos trahen calças
e las siellas coceras   e las cinchas amojadas;
nós cavalgaremos siellas gallegas   e huesas sobre calças,
ciento cavalleros   devemos vencer aquellas mesnadas.   [995
Antes que ellos lleguen a[l] llano,   presentémosles las lanças,
por uno que firgades,   tres siellas irán vazias;
¡verá Rremont Verenguel   tras quién vino en alcança
oy en este pinar de Tévar   por tollerme la ganancia!'

58

21v   Todos son adobados   quando Mio Cid esto ovo fablado, [1000
las armas avién presas   e sedién sobre los cavallos,
vieron la cuesta yuso   la fuerça de los francos;
al fondón de la cuesta,   cerca es de[l] llano,
mandólos ferir Mio Cid,   el que en buen ora nasco.
Esto fazen los sos   de voluntad e de grado,   [1005
los pendones e las lanças   tan bien las van enpleando,
a los unos firiendo   e a los otros derrocando.
Vencido á esta batalla   el que en buen [ora] nasco;
al conde don Rremont   a presón le an tomado.

59

Í gañó a Colada,   que más vale de mill marcos de plata. [1010
[Í benció] esta batalla   por ó ondró su barba.
Prísolo al conde,   pora su tienda lo levava,
a sos creenderos   guardarlo mandava.
De fuera de la tienda   un salto dava,
de todas partes   los sos se ajuntaron;   [1015

He shall pay for past and present injuries here and now. The exile from Castile will learn what sort of a man he has wronged.' The messenger returned with all speed, and the Cid realised that there was nothing for it but to fight.

57

'Knights' (he said), 'put aside the booty, and make ready quickly to take up arms. Count Ramón is about to engage us in a great battle. He has brought with him a vast host of Moors and Christians and is determined to fight. As they are advancing towards us, let us engage them here. Tighten your saddle-girths and put on your armour. The enemy are coming downhill, all wearing hose (without boots). They have racing saddles and loose girths, but we shall ride with Galician saddles and wear boots over our hose. Though we number only one hundred knights we have got to defeat this large army. Before they reach the plain we shall attack with our lances. For each man you strike, three saddles will go empty. Ramón Berenguer will see the kind of man he has come to find today in the pine wood of Tévar to deprive me of my booty.'

58

All were ready by the time the Cid had finished speaking, with their armour on and mounted on their horses. They watched the forces of the Franks ride down the hill, and when these reached the bottom, close now to the plain, the Cid, fortunate in battle, ordered the attack. His men were delighted to obey and they used their pennoned lances to good effect, striking some and overturning others. The Cid won the battle and took Count Ramón prisoner.

59

There he won for himself Colada, a sword worth more than a thousand silver marks. This was a victorious battle which brought honour to the Cid. He brought the Count as a prisoner to his tent and commanded his faithful vassals to stand guard over him. He then left his tent, in great good humour at the amount of the booty, while his men crowded in from all sides.

plogo a Mio Cid   ca grandes son las ganancias.
A Mio Cid don Rrodrigo   grant cozínal' adobavan;
el conde don Rremont   non ge lo precia nada,
adúzenle los comeres,   delant ge los paravan,
él non lo quiere comer,   a todos los sosañava: [1020
'Non combré un bocado   por quanto ha en toda España,
antes perderé el cuerpo   e dexaré el alma,
pues que tales malcalçados   me vencieron de batalla.'

60
Mio Cid Rruy Díaz   odredes lo que dixo:
22r   'Comed, conde, d'este pan   e beved d'este vino;   [1025
si lo que digo fiziéredes,   saldredes de cativo,
si non, en todos vuestros días   non veredes cristianismo.'

61
Dixo el conde don Rremont: . . . .
'Comede, don Rrodrigo,   e pensedes de fol[gar],   [1028b
que yo dexar me [é] morir,   que non quiero comer.'
Fasta tercer día   nol' pueden acordar;   [1030
ellos partiendo   estas ganancias grandes,
nol' pueden fazer comer   un muesso de pan.

62
Dixo Mio Cid: 'Comed, conde, algo,
ca si non comedes   non veredes [cristianos];   [1033b
e si vós comiéredes   dón yo sea pagado,
a vós   e [a] dos fijos d'algo   [1035
quitar vos he los cuerpos   e dar vos é de [mano].'   [1035b
Quando esto oyó el conde,   yas' iva alegrando:
'Si lo fiziéredes, Cid,   lo que avedes fablado,
tanto quanto yo biva   seré dent maravillado.'
'Pues comed, conde,   e quando fuéredes yantado,
a vós e a otros dos   dar vos he de mano;   [1040
mas quanto avedes perdido   e yo gané en canpo,
sabet, non vos daré   a vós un dinero malo,   [1042
ca huebos me lo he   e pora estos mios vassallos   [1044
que comigo   andan lazrados.   [1045
Prendiendo de vós e de otros   ir nos hemos pagando;
abremos esta vida   mientra ploguiere al Padre sancto,
como que ira á de rrey   e de tierra es echado.'
Alegre es el conde   e pidió agua a las manos
e tiénengelo delant   e diérongelo privado;   [1050

A great feast was prepared for Don Rodrigo, but Count Ramón showed no relish for it. They brought the dishes and placed them in front of him, but he refused to eat and scorned all they offered. 'I shall not eat a mouthful,' he said, 'for all the wealth of Spain. I had rather die outright since such badly shod fellows have defeated me in battle.'

60

To that the Cid replied in these words: 'Eat this bread, Count, and drink this wine. If you do as I say you will go free, but if not, you will never see Christendom again for the rest of your life.'

61

Count Ramón said: 'You eat, Don Rodrigo, and take your ease, for I would rather starve to death than eat anything.' For three days they tried in vain to persuade him. While they were dividing up the great booty they could not get him to eat even a morsel of bread.

62

Then the Cid said: 'Do eat something, Count, for if you do not you will never return to the land of the Christians, but if you eat to my satisfaction I shall set you and two other gentlemen at liberty and let you go free.' When the Count heard this he began to recover his spirits. 'If you do as you say, Cid, I shall never get over my amazement as long as I live.' 'Well, eat, then, Count, and when you have finished your meal I shall let you and two others go. Of what you have lost, however, and I have gained in the field, I shall not return you a penny, as I need it for these vassals of mine who are sharing my hardships. By taking from you and other people we satisfy our wants. This is the life we shall lead while it pleases God, as one who suffers the King's wrath in exile.' The Count was delighted and asked for water to wash his hands, which was quickly brought and handed

22v con los cavalleros que el Cid le avié dados
comiendo va el conde, ¡Dios, qué de buen grado!
Sobr'él sedié el que en buen ora nasco:
'Si bien non comedes, conde, dón yo sea pagado,
aquí feremos la morada, no nos partiremos amos.'   [1055
Aquí dixo el conde: 'De voluntad e de grado.'
Con estos dos cavalleros apriessa va yantando;
pagado es Mio Cid, que lo está aguardando,
porque el conde don Rremont tan bien bolvié la[s] manos.
'Si vos ploguiere, Mio Cid, de ir somos guisados,   [1060
mandad nos dar las bestias e cavalgaremos privado;
del día que fue conde non yanté tan de buen grado,
el sabor que de[n]d é non será olbidado.'
Danle tres palafrés muy bien ensellados
e buenas vestiduras de pelliçones e de mantos.   [1065
El conde don Rremont entre los dos es entrado;
fata cabo del albergada escurriólos el castellano:
'Ya vos ides, conde, a guisa de muy franco,
en grado vos lo tengo lo que me avedes dexado.
Si vos viniere emiente que quisiéredes vengallo,   [1070
si me viniéredes buscar, fallarme podredes;
e si non, mandedes buscar: [1072
o me dexaredes | de lo vuestro, o de lo mío levaredes
                        algo.' [1072b-73

'Folguedes ya, Mio Cid, sodes en vuestro salvo;
pagado vos he por todo aqueste año,   [1075
de venir vos buscar sól non será pensado.'

63
    Aguijava el conde e pensava de andar,
23r tornando va la cabeça e catandos' atrás;
miedo iva aviendo que Mio Cid se rrepintrá;
lo que non ferié el caboso por quanto en el mundo ha, [1080
una deslea[l]tança, ca non la fizo alguandre.
Ido es el conde, tornós' el de Bivar,
juntós' con sus mesnadas, conpeçós' de *pagar*
de la ganancia que an fecha maravillosa e grand.

to him. Together with the knights whom the Cid had set free to go with him, the Count started eating with great zest. Beside him sat the Cid, who said: 'If you do not eat to my satisfaction we shall stay here for ever and part no more.' 'Agreed,' said the Count, and with the two knights he speedily set about his meal, making great play with his hands to the delight of the Cid, who sat watching him. 'Now, if you please, Cid, we are ready to leave. Have our horses brought and we shall ride off at once. I have not eaten so heartily since I became a count, and I shall never forget how good it tasted.' They were given three well saddled palfreys, good fur-lined coats and cloaks. Count Ramón rode between the two knights, and their Castilian host escorted them to the limit of the camp. 'You are off now,' said the Cid, 'like the free Frank you are, and I am grateful to you for what you have left me. If you should take it into your head to get your own back and come to seek me out, you will be able to find me. If not, send out a search party. In that case you will let me have some more of your goods or you will take away some of mine.' 'You can be easy about that, Cid; you are quite safe. I have paid you for the whole of this year and I have not the least intention of coming to look for you again.'

63

The Count set spurs to his horse and rode off, turning his head to look back for fear the Cid should change his mind—a thing that famous man would not do for anything in the world, for never in his life had he gone back on his word. The Count departed, and Rodrigo of Vivar turned and rejoined his men, delighted with the wonderful booty they had taken.

64

Aquís' conpieça la gesta   de Mio Cid el de Bivar.   [1085
Tan rricos son los sos   que non saben qué se an.
Poblado ha Mio Cid   el puerto de Alucant,
dexado á Saragoça   e las tierras ducá
e dexado á Huesa   e las tierras de Mont Alván.
Contra la mar salada   conpeçó de guerrear,   [1090
a orient exe el sol   e tornós' a essa part.
Mio Cid gañó a Xérica   e a Onda e [a] Almenar,
tierras de Borriana   todas conquistas las ha.

65

Ayudól' el Criador,   el Señor que es en cielo.
Él con todo esto   priso a Murviedro;   [1095
ya v[e]yé Mio Cid   que Dios le iva valiendo.
Dentro en Valencia   non es poco el miedo.

66

Pesa a los de Valencia,   sabet, non les plaze,
prisieron so consejo   quel' viniessen cercar;
trasnocharon de noch,   al alva de la man   [1100
acerca de Murviedro   tornan tiendas a fincar.
Violo Mio Cid,   tomós' a maravillar;
'¡Grado a ti,   Padre spiritual!   [1102b
En sus tierras somos   e fémosles todo mal,
bevemos so vino   e comemos el so pan;
si nos cercar vienen,   con derecho lo fazen.   [1105
A menos de lid   aquesto nos' partirá;
vayan los mandados   por los que nos deven ayudar,
los unos a Xérica   e los otros a Alucad,
desí a Onda   e los otros a Almenar,
los de Borriana   luego vengan acá;   [1110
conpeçaremos   aquesta lid campal,
yo fío por Dios   que en nuestro pro eñadrán.'
Al tercer día   todos juntados son,
el que en buen ora nasco   compeçó de fablar:
'¡Oíd, mesnadas,   sí el Criador vos salve!   [1115
Después que nos partiemos   de la linpia cristiandad,
non fue a nuestro grado   ni nós non pudiemos más,
grado a Dios,   lo nuestro fue adelant.
Los de Valencia   cercados nos han,

64

Here begins the story of the great deeds of the Cid of Vivar. His men were rich beyond all reckoning. After the Cid had left Saragossa and its district he passed through Huesa and the lands of Montalbán, and occupied the pass of Olocau. Then he moved on towards the sea to start fighting there, for the sun rises in the east and he turned in that direction. The Cid took Jérica, Onda and Almenara, and he conquered the whole of the country round Burriana.

65

He did all this with God's help, and when he captured Murviedro he was sure the Creator was on his side. Within the walls of Valencia great fear spread.

66

The people of Valencia had grown anxious and distressed. They resolved to go and lay siege to the Cid, so after marching all night they encamped in the morning near Murviedro. When the Cid saw this he wondered and said: 'I give Thee thanks, O Heavenly Father! We have settled in their land and are doing them all kinds of harm, drinking their wine and eating their bread, and they have every right to come and besiege us. This cannot be decided without a fight, so let messengers go to summon those whose duty it is to help us. Let some go to Jérica, others to Olocau, from there on to Onda and the rest to Almenara; let the men in Burriana too come here immediately. We shall engage them in the open field and, as I put my trust in God, I am certain it will turn to our advantage.' By the third day they had all assembled, and the Cid addressed them thus: 'Hear me, vassals, as you hope for salvation. Since we left the fair Christian lands—not of our own free will, for we had no choice—I thank God, our affairs have prospered. Now the

si en estas tierras   quisiéremos durar,   [1120
firmemientre son éstos   a escarmentar.

67

Passe la noche   e venga la mañana,
aparejados me sed   a cavallos e armas,
iremos ver   aquella su almofalla;
como omnes exidos   de tierra estraña,   [1125
allí pareçrá   el que merece la soldada.'

68

Oíd qué dixo   Minaya Álbar Fáñez:
'Campeador, fagamos   lo que a vós plaze.
A mí dedes *ciento* cavalleros,   que non vos pido más,
vós con los otros   firádeslos delant,   [1130
24r bien los ferredes,   que dubda non í avrá;
yo con los ciento   entraré del otra part,
como fío por Dios,   el campo nuestro será.'
Como ge lo á dicho,   al Campeador mucho plaze.
Mañana era   e piénsanse de armar,   [1135
quis cada uno d'ellos   bien sabe lo que ha de far.
Con los alvores   Mio Cid ferirlos va:
'¡En el nombre del Criador   e del apóstol Sancti Yagüe,
feridlos, cavalleros,   d'amor e de grado e de grand voluntad,
ca yo só Rruy Díaz,   Mio Cid el de Bivar!'   [1140
Tanta cuerda de tienda   í veriedes quebrar,
arrancarse las estacas   e acostarse a todas partes los tendales.
[Los] moros son muchos,   ya quieren rreconbrar.
Del otra part   entróles Álbar Fáñez,
maguer les pesa,   oviéronse a dar e a arrancar,   [1145
de pies de cavallo   los ques' pudieron escapar.   [1151
Grand es el gozo   que va por és logar;   [1146
dos rreyes de moros   mataron en és alcanz,
fata Valencia   duró el segudar.
Grandes son las ganancias   que Mio Cid fechas ha, [1149
rrobavan el campo   e piénsanse de tornar.   [1152
Prisieron Cebolla   e quanto que es í adelant,   [1150
entravan a Murviedro   con estas ganancias que traen
                                        grandes.   [1153
Las nuevas de Mio Cid,   sabet, sonando van,
24v miedo an en Valencia   que non saben qué se far. [1155
Sonando van sus nuevas   allent parte del mar.

Valencians are besieging us, and if we wish to remain in this part of the country these men must be given a severe lesson.

67

Let the night go by and when morning comes be armed and on your horses ready to attack their rabble. As men in exile from a distant land you will show in this battle which of you is worthy of his pay.'

68

Then Minaya Álvar Fáñez said: 'Campeador, let us do as you wish. Give me one hundred knights—I want no more. With the rest you will attack the front ranks of the Valencians, striking hard and fearlessly. I shall attack them with my hundred knights in the flank. As I trust in God, the field will be ours.' The Campeador was greatly pleased with what Minaya proposed, and when morning came they began to arm. Each man knew what his task was to be in the battle. With the dawn the Cid advanced to the attack (shouting his battle cry): 'In the name of the Creator and the Apostle St James, strike them hard, knights, with all your might; for I am the Cid, Ruy Díaz of Vivar!' You should have seen how many cords were broken and stakes pulled up and how many tent poles lay fallen on the ground! The Moors, relying on their numbers, tried to rally, but Álvar Fáñez attacked them in the flank. Reluctantly they had to admit defeat and take to flight; those who could escaped by galloping off at full speed. Great joy spread through the place. Two Moorish leaders were killed in this rout, and the pursuit continued as far as Valencia. The Cid captured immense booty, and when they returned after stripping the battlefield they took Cebolla and all the land beyond it, and entered Murviedro laden with the spoils. The Cid's fame was increasing. The Valencians were frightened and at a loss what to do, and the Cid's fame spread far and wide, even to lands beyond the sea.

69

Alegre era el Cid   e todas sus compañas
que Dios le ayudara   e fiziera esta arrancada.
Davan sus corredores   e fazién las trasnochadas,
llegan a Gujera   e llegan a Xátiva,   [1160
aún más ayusso   a Deyna la casa;
cabo del mar tierra de moros   firme la quebranta,
ganaron Peña Cadiella,   las exidas e las entradas.

70

Quando el Cid Campeador   ovo Peña Cadiella,
ma[l] les pesa en Xátiva   e dentro en Gujera,   [1165
non es con rrecabdo   el dolor de Valencia.

71

En tierra de moros   prendiendo e ganando
e durmiendo los días   e las noches tranochando,
en ganar aquellas villas   Mio Cid duró *tres* años.

72

A los de Valencia   escarmentados los ha,   [1170
non osan fueras exir   nin con él se ajuntar;
tajávales las huertas   e fazíales grand mal,
en cada uno d'estos años   Mio Cid les tollió el pan.
Mal se aquexan los de Valencia   que non sabent qués' far,
de ninguna part que sea   non les vinié pan;   [1175
nin da cossejo padre a fijo,   nin fijo a padre,
nin amigo a amigo   nos' pueden consolar.
Mala cueta es, señores,   aver mingua de pan,
fijos e mugieres   verlo[s] murir de fanbre.
25r Delante veyén so duelo,   non se pueden uviar,   [1180
por el rrey de Marruecos   ovieron a enbiar;
con el de los Montes Claros   avié guerra tan grand,
non les dixo cossejo   nin los vino uviar.
Sópolo Mio Cid,   de coraçón le plaz,
salió de Murviedro   una noch en trasnochada,   [1185
amaneció a Mio Cid   en tierras de Mon Rreal.
Por Aragón e por Navarra   pregón mandó echar,
a tierras de Castiella   enbió sus mensajes:
quien quiere perder cueta   e venir a rritad,
viniesse a Mio Cid   que á sabor de cavalgar,   [1190
cercar quiere a Valencia   por a cristianos la dár:

69

The Cid and his companions rejoiced that God had helped them to win this victory. They then sent out scouts and, marching by night, reached Cullera and Játiva and even went farther south, as far as the town of Denia. They laid waste the Moorish territory along the coast, capturing Benicadell and all the roads leading in and out.

70

When the Cid took Benicadell the people in Játiva and Cullera were greatly perturbed, and as for the Valencians, their distress knew no bounds.

71

The Cid spent three years taking those towns and conquering Moorish territory, sleeping by day and marching by night.

72

He had taught the Valencians a severe lesson, and they dared not come out of the town to join him in battle. He cut down their plantations, inflicting great damage on them. Year after year the Cid deprived them of their food. The Valencians lamented loudly, for they were at their wits' end, being cut off from food on all sides. Fathers could not help their sons nor sons their fathers, nor could friends comfort one another. It is indeed a cruel fate for men to be without food and to watch their wives and children dying of hunger. Disaster stared them in the face and there was nothing they could do to help themselves. They sent for aid to the King of Morocco, but he was involved in war with the ruler of the Atlas mountains and could neither relieve them nor come to their assistance. Pleased with this news, the Cid set out one night from Murviedro; he marched all night and dawn found him in the region of Monreal. He sent messengers through Navarre and Aragon and to the land of Castile to proclaim that anyone who was eager to exchange poverty for riches should come to the Cid, who had a mind to ride out to besiege Valencia and restore it to the Christians.

73

'Quien quiere ir comigo   cercar a Valencia,
todos vengan de grado,   ninguno non ha premia;
tres días le speraré   en Canal de Celfa.'

74

Esto dixo Mio Cid,   el que en buen ora nasco.   [1195
Tornavas' a Murviedro   ca él ganada se la á.
Andidieron los pregones,   sabet, a todas partes,
al sabor de la ganancia   non lo quiere[n] detardar,
grandes yentes se le acojen   de la buena cristiandad.
Creciendo va en rriqueza   Mio Cid el de Bivar,   [1200
quando vio Mio Cid las gentes juntadas,   conpeçós' de pagar.
Mio Cid don Rrodrigo   non lo quiso detardar,
adeliñó pora Valencia   e sobr'ellas' va echar,
bien la cerca Mio Cid   que non í avía art,
viédales exir   e viédales entrar.   [1205
25v Sonando va[n] sus nuevas   todas a todas partes,
más le vienen a Mio Cid,   sabet, que nos' le van.
Metióla en plazo,   si les viniessen uviar;
nueve meses complidos,   sabet, sobr'ella yaz[e],
quando vino el dezeno   oviérongela a dar.   [1210
Grandes son los gozos   que van por és logar
quando Mio Cid gañó a Valencia   e entró en la cibdad.
Los que fueron de pie   cavalleros se fazen;
el oro e la plata   ¿quién vos lo podrié contar?
Todos eran rricos,   quantos que allí ha.   [1215
Mio Cid don Rrodrigo   la quinta mandó tomar,
en el aver monedado   treínta mill marcos le caen,
e los otros averes   ¿quién los podrié contar?
Alegre era el Campeador   con todos los que ha
quando su seña cabdal   sedié en somo del alcáçar.   [1220

75

Ya folgava Mio Cid   con todas sus conpañas.
[A] aquel rrey de Sevilla   el mandado llegava
que presa es Valencia,   que non ge la enparan;
vino los ver   con treínta mill de armas.
Aprés de la huerta   ovieron la batalla,   [1225
arrancólos Mio Cid,   el de la luenga barba.
Fata dentro en Xátiva   duró el arrancada,
en el passar de Xúcar   í veriedes barata,
moros en arruenço   amidos bever agua.

73

'Whoever wishes to go with me to besiege Valencia, let him come freely and of his own accord, for there is no compulsion. I shall wait three days for him at Cella.'

74

Those were the words of the Cid, the loyal Campeador, who then returned to Murviedro, which he had taken earlier. The proclamation was carried everywhere, and all who scented plunder came in haste. Crowds of good Christians flocked to join him, and the Cid's riches were steadily mounting. When Don Rodrigo saw these crowds assembled he was filled with joy. Without delay he marched against Valencia and began the siege. He encircled the city completely, allowing no one to go in or come out. The Cid's fame had spread through the lands. Great numbers came and few left. He set a certain time limit for them to surrender if no relief came. For nine whole months he besieged them, and when the tenth month came they were forced to surrender. There was great rejoicing in the whole region when the Cid took Valencia and entered the city. Those who had fought on foot were given horses, and as there were untold quantities of gold and silver, all who took part became rich. The Cid commanded his fifth share of the booty to be set apart, and in this there fell to him thirty thousand marks, while the value of the rest in kind was beyond reckoning. The Campeador and his men rejoiced to see his standard flying from the highest point of the citadel.

75

The Cid and his men could now rest from their labours. When the ruler of Seville heard that Valencia was lost, he came with thirty thousand men to attack the Cid and joined battle with him near the Huerta. The Cid of the flowing beard routed them and carried the pursuit right into Játiva. There you should have seen the confusion the Moors were in as they crossed the river Júcar, struggling with the current and swallowing water

Aquel rrey de Marruecos   con tres colpes escapa.   [1230
Tornado es Mio Cid   con toda esta ganancia;
buena fue la de Valencia   quando ganaron la casa,
26r   más mucho fue provechosa,   sabet, esta arrancada,
a todos los menores   cayeron *ciento* marcos de plata.
Las nuevas del cavallero   ya vedes dó llegavan.   [1235

76
Grand alegría es   entre todos essos cristianos
con Mio Cid Rruy Díaz,   el que en buen ora nasco.
Yal' crece la barba   e vále allongando,
dixo Mio Cid   de la su boca atanto:
'Por amor del rrey Alfonso   que de tierra me á echado',   [1240
nin entrarié en ella tigera,   ni un pelo non avrié tajado
e que fablassen d'esto   moros e cristianos.
Mio Cid don Rrodrigo   en Valencia está folgando,
con él Minaya Álbar Fáñez   que nos' le parte de so braço.
Los que exieron de tierra   de rritad son abondados,   [1245
a todos les dio en Valencia casas,   e heredades | de
                                      que son pagados.   [1246-47
El amor de Mio Cid   ya lo ivan provando,   [1247b
los que fueron con él   e los de después todos son pagados;
véelo Mio Cid   que con los averes que avién tomados
que sis' pudiessen ir   fer lo ien de grado.   [1250
Esto mandó Mio Cid,   Minaya lo ovo consejado,
que ningún omne de los sos ques' le non spidiés,   o nol'
                                      besás la ma[no],
sil' pudiessen prender   o fuesse alcançado,
tomássenle el aver   e pusiéssenle en un palo.
Afevos todo aquesto   puesto en buen rrecabdo,   [1255
con Minaya Álbar Fáñez   él se va consejar:
26v   'Si vós quisiéredes, Minaya,   quiero saber rrecabdo
de los que son aquí   e comigo ganaron algo;
meter los he en escripto   e todos sean contados,
que si algunos' furtare   o menos le fallaren,   [1260
el aver me avrá a tornar | [a] aquestos mios vassallos   [1260b-61
que curian a Valencia   e andan arrobdando.'   [1261b
Allí dixo Minaya: 'Consejo es aguisado.'

77
Mandólos venir a la cort   e a todos los juntar,
quando los falló,   por cuenta fízolos nonbrar;
tres mill e seiscientos   avié Mio Cid el de Bivar,   [1265

much against their will. The King of Morocco escaped with three wounds, while the Campeador returned with the booty. The capture of Valencia had been a great prize, but the gains from this rout were far more substantial, for every common soldier received one hundred silver marks. The Cid's fortunes were improving rapidly.

76

There was much rejoicing among all those Christians who were with him. His beard was growing long and full, for the Cid had said: 'For the love I bear King Alfonso, who has banished me, no shears shall touch it and not a hair shall be cut. Let this be common talk among the Moors and Christians alike.' The Cid Don Rodrigo then took his ease at Valencia, and with him was Minaya Álvar Fáñez, who never left his side. Those who had followed him into exile received houses and possessions in Valencia, and they were contented with this proof of his favour. Those who had set out with him and those who had joined him later were so well satisfied that the Cid saw that they were ready to go off with their gains if they had the chance. On Minaya's advice he gave instructions that every man who had won anything in battle should take leave of him as his leader in the correct manner by kissing his hand; and that if one of them failed to do so he should be pursued, and if they caught him they should take back from him what he had and hang him on the gallows. All that was carefully attended to, and the Cid went to discuss affairs with Minaya Álvar Fáñez: 'If you agree, Minaya, I should like to have a written record of the men here at present who have won riches for themselves while they were fighting under me, so that if any man goes off secretly or is found missing he will be obliged to return his share of the spoils. This I shall distribute among those of my vassals who are on patrol duty outside Valencia.' 'A very wise plan,' said Minaya.

77

All the men were told to assemble in the hall of the palace, and when the Cid came in he had their names called out and noted. They were three thousand six hundred all told, and the

D

alégras'le el coraçón   e tornós' a sonrrisar:
'¡Grado a Dios, Minaya,   e a Sancta María madre!
Con más pocos ixiemos   de la casa de Bivar;
agora avemos rriquiza,   más avremos adelant.
Si a vós ploguiere, Minaya,   e non vos caya en pesar,   [1270
enbiarvos quiero a Castiella,   dó avemos heredades,
al rrey Alfonso   mio señor natural;
d'estas mis ganancias   que avemos fechas acá
darle quiero *ciento* cavallos   e vós ídgelos levar.
Desí por mí besalde la mano   e firme ge lo rrogad   [1275
por mi mugier e mis fijas, ...
si fuere su merced, | quen' las dexe sacar;   [1276b-77
enbiaré por ellas   e vós sabed el mensage:
la mugier de Mio Cid   e sus fijas las infantes
de guisa irán por ellas   que a grand ondra vernán   [1280
a estas tierras estrañas   que nos pudiemos ganar.'
Essora dixo Minaya: 'De buena voluntad.'
27r Pues esto an fablado,   piénsanse de adobar;
ciento omnes le dio   Mio Cid a Álbar Fáñez
por servirle en la carrer[a] . . . . . .   [1284b
e mandó mill marcos de plata   a San Pero levar   [1285
e que los diesse   a don Sancho [e]l abat.

78

En estas nuevas   todos se alegrando,
de parte de orient   vino un coronado;
el obispo don Jerónimo   so nombre es llamado,
bien entendido es de letras   e mucho acordado,   [1290
de pie e de cavallo   mucho era arreziado.
Las provezas de Mio Cid   andávalas demandando,
sospirando el obispo   ques' viesse con moros en el campo,
que sis' fartás lidiando   e firiendo con sus manos
a los días del sieglo   non le llorassen cristianos.   [1295
Quando lo oyó Mio Cid,   de aquesto fue pagado:
'¡Oíd, Minaya Álbar Fáñez,   por Aquel que está en alto!
Quando Dios prestar nos quiere,   nós bien ge lo gradescamos,
en tierras de Valencia   fer quiero obispado
e dárgelo   a este buen cristiano;   [1300
vós, quando ides a Castiella,   levaredes buenos mandados.'

79

Plogo a Álbar Fáñez   de lo que dixo don Rrodrigo;
a este don Jerónimo   yal' otorgan por obispo,

Cid smiled for joy, saying: 'God and His Holy Mother be praised, Minaya, for we left Vivar with far fewer. We are rich now and in the future we shall be richer still. If you are willing to go, Minaya, I should like to send you to Castile, where our lands and possessions are, to King Alfonso, my liege lord. I wish to send him one hundred horses out of the booty I have taken. You go and take them to him; kiss his hand for me and entreat him to allow me as a favour to bring away my wife and my daughters. I shall send for them and this is the message you must give: "Such a fine escort will be sent for the Cid's wife and his little daughters that they will come in great honour to these distant lands which we have made our own." ' 'I shall do so willingly,' said Minaya. After this conversation preparations were made for the journey. The Cid assigned a hundred men to attend Álvar Fáñez on his way, and he asked him to take one thousand silver marks to the monastery of San Pedro and to give them to the Abbot Don Sancho.

78

The news (of Minaya's mission) caused general rejoicing, and (in the meantime) there came from France a cleric called Don Jerome. He was going round enquiring about the Cid's exploits and longing to come to grips with the Moors himself. He said that, if he could have his fill of fighting, Christians need never mourn his death. The Cid was pleased to hear this news, and he said: 'Listen, Minaya, let us give thanks to God in Heaven above for the help he bestows on us. I shall establish a bishopric in Valencia and give it to this good Christian. You will have good tidings to take to them in Castile when you go there.'

79

Álvar Fáñez approved of what Don Rodrigo said, and Don Jerome was appointed Bishop of Valencia, which would be a

diéronle en Valencia   ó bien puede estar rrico.
¡Dios, qué alegre era   todo cristianismo .   [1305
que en tierras de Valencia   señor avié obispo!
Alegre fue Minaya   e spidiós' e vinos'.

80

    Tierras de Valencia   rremanidas en paz,
27v adeliñó pora Castiella   Minaya Álbar Fáñez;
dexarévos las posadas,   non las quiero contar.   [1310
Demandó por Alfonso,   dó lo podrié fallar.
Fuera el rrey a San Fagunt   aún poco ha,
tornós' a Carrión,   í lo podrié fallar.
Alegre fue de aquesto   Minaya Álbar Fáñez,
con esta presenteja   adeliñó pora allá.   [1315

81

    De missa era exido   essora el rrey Alfonso,
afé Minaya Álbar Fáñez   dó llega tan apuesto,
fincó sos inojos   ante tod' el pueblo,
a los pies del rrey Alfonso   cayó con grand duelo,
besávale las manos   e fabló tan apuesto: [1320

82

    '¡Merced, señor Alfonso,   por amor del Criador!
Besávavos las manos   Mio Cid lidiador,
los pies e las manos,   como a tan buen señor,
quel' ayades merced,   ¡sí vos vala el Criador!
Echástesle de tierra,   non ha la vuestra amor,   [1325
maguer en tierra agena   él bien faze lo so:
ganada [á] a Xérica   e a Onda por nombre,
priso a Almenar   e a Murviedro que es miyor,
assí fizo Cebolla   e adelant Castejón
e Peña Cadiella   que es una peña fuert;   [1330
con aquestas todas   de Valencia es señor,
obispo fizo de su mano   el buen Campeador
28r e fizo cinco lides campales   e todas las arrancó.
Grandes son las ganancias   quel' dio el Criador,
fevos aquí las señas,   verdad vos digo yo,   [1335
cient cavallos   gruessos e corredores,
de siellas e de frenos   todos guarnidos son,
bésavos las manos   que los prendades vós;
rrazonas' por vuestro vassallo   e a vós tiene por señor.'
Alçó la mano diestra,   el rrey se sanctigó: [1340
'De tan fieras ganancias   como á fechas el Campeador

wealthy see for him. All Christendom rejoiced to know that
there was once again a bishop in Valencia. Minaya took leave in
good spirits and set off.

80

Peace reigned in Valencia while Álvar Fáñez journeyed
towards Castile. I shall spare you the stages of his journey, as I
have no wish to recount them. When Minaya inquired where
he could find Don Alfonso, he was told that the King had gone
to Sahagún a little while before but had returned to Carrión,
where he was now to be found. Minaya was delighted to hear
this, and made his way there with the present he was bringing
from the Cid.

81

King Alfonso had just come from hearing mass, so Minaya
was arriving at the right moment. He went down on his knees
before all the people, and in an attitude of grief he fell at the
King's feet. He then kissed his hands and made this well timed
speech:

82

'A favour, my lord Alfonso, in God's name! The warrior
Cid makes his most profound obeisance to his excellent lord;
he begs you to grant it, as you hope for God's protection. You
banished him and he is still in disgrace, but he continues doing
mighty deeds in a strange land. He has won Jérica and Onda,
Almenara and, better still, Murviedro; he has also captured
Cebolla, Castellón and the strong fortress of Benicadell. He is
master of all these and lord of Valencia as well; by his own power
he has appointed a bishop there, and he has fought and won
five pitched battles. God gave him rich gains, and here is proof
that I am speaking nothing but the truth. He begs you to accept
as a gift one hundred stout chargers, all saddled and harnessed.
He considers himself your vassal and acknowledges you as his
lord.' The King raised his right hand and crossed himself. 'By
St Isidore' (he exclaimed), 'I am truly pleased at the immense

¡sí me vala Sant Esidro!   plazme de coraçón
e plázem' de las nuevas   que faze el Campeador;
rrecibo estos cavallos   quem' enbía de don.'
Maguer plogo al rrey,   mucho pesó a Garcí Ordóñez: [1345
'Semeja que en tierra de moros   non á bivo omne
quando assí faze a su guisa   el Cid Campeador.'
Dixo el rrey al conde: 'Dexad essa rrazón,
que en todas guisas   mijor me sirve que vós.'
Fablava Minaya í   a guisa de varón: [1350
'Merced vos pide el Cid,   si vos cayesse en sabor,
por su mugier doña Ximena   e sus fijas amas a dos:
saldrién del monesterio   dó elle las dexó
e irién pora Valencia   al buen Campeador.'
Essora dixo el rrey: 'Plazme de coraçón;   [1355
yo les mandaré dar conducho   mientra que por mi tierra fueren,
28v   de fonta e de mal   curiallas e de desonor;
quando en cabo de mi tierra   aquestas dueñas fueren,
catad cómo las sirvades   vós e el Campeador.
¡Oídme, escuelas   e toda la mi cort!   [1360
Non quiero que nada   pierda el Campeador:
a todas las escuelas   que a él dizen señor,
por que los deseredé,   todo ge lo suelto yo;
sírvanle[s] sus herdades   dó fuere el Campeador,
atrégoles los cuerpos   de mal e de ocasión,   [1365
por tal fago aquesto   que sirvan a so señor.'
Minaya Álbar Fáñez   las manos le besó.
Sonrrisós' el rrey,   tan vellido fabló:
'Los que quisieren ir   se[r]vir al Campeador
de mí sean quitos   e vayan a la gracia del Criador.   [1370
Más ganaremos en esto   que en otra desonor.'
Aquí entraron en fabla   los iffantes de Carrión:
'Mucho crecen las nuevas   de Mio Cid el Campeador,
bien casariemos con sus fijas   pora huebos de pro;
non la osariemos   acometer nós esta rrazón,   [1375
Mio Cid es de Bivar   e nós de los condes de Carrión.'
Non lo dizen a nadi   e fincó esta rrazón.
Minaya Álbar Fáñez   al buen rrey se espidió.
'¡Ya vos ides, Minaya,   id a la gracia del Criador!
Levedes un portero,   tengo que vos avrá pro;   [1380
si leváredes las dueñas,   sírvanlas a su sabor,
29r   fata dentro en Medina   denles quanto huebos les fuer,
desí adelant   piense d'ellas el Campeador.'
Espidiós' Minaya   e vasse de la cort.

riches the Campeador has won. I am glad also to hear of the Cid's exploits, and I accept these horses which he has sent me as a gift.' The King was pleased, but on the other hand García Ordóñez was highly annoyed. 'Apparently there are no men at all in Moorish territory,' he said, 'seeing that the Cid can do as he likes there.' To which the King replied: 'No more of that. At least he serves me better than you do.' At this point Minaya spoke up boldly: 'The Cid begs you of your grace to grant him a favour: to give permission for his wife Doña Jimena and his two daughters to come away from the monastery where he left them and to join the good Campeador in Valencia.' The King replied: 'I willingly give my consent. I shall order them to be given provisions for the journey through my territory and to be protected from insult and injury. When the ladies leave my realm, then you and the Campeador must take charge of them. Listen to what I have to say, vassals and all assembled here. I do not wish to deprive the Campeador of any of his rights. I reinstate all those whose property I confiscated because they were faithful to him as his vassals. They may enjoy their revenues wherever they find themselves in his service. I assure them that no harm or hurt will come to them, and I do this so that they may fitly serve their lord.' Minaya kissed the King's hand (in token of thanks), and the King, smiling, pronounced these gracious words: 'I release from my service all those who may wish to go and serve the Campeador, and may God's blessing go with them. We shall gain more by this than by any dishonour.' Then the Infantes of Carrión began to talk together, saying: 'The reputation of the Cid Campeador stands very high. If we married his daughters we should be making a good match; but we dare not suggest such a thing, as the Cid comes from the village of Vivar and we are of the noble house of Carrión.' They told no one of their project, and there the matter rested. Minaya Álvar Fáñez took leave of the good King, who said: 'You are going now, Álvar Fáñez. May God's blessing go with you! Take a royal courier with you; I think you will find him useful. See that the ladies you are accompanying are given all they require until they reach Medinaceli, and from there on let the Campeador provide for their needs.' Minaya said farewell and left the court.

83

Los iffantes de Carrión . . . .   [1385
dando ivan conpaña   a Minaya Álbar Fáñez: [1385b
'En todo sodes pro,   en esto assí lo fagades:
saludadnos a Mio Cid,   el de Bivar,
somos en so pro   quanto lo podemos far;
el Cid que bien nos quiera   nada non perderá.'
Rrespuso Minaya: 'Esto non me á por qué pesar.' [1390
Ido es Minaya,   tórnanse los iffantes.
Adeliñó pora San Pero   ó las dueñas están,
tan grand fue el gozo   quándol' vieron assomar.
Decido es Minaya,   a San Pero va rrogar,
quando acabó la oración,   a las dueñas se tornó: [1395
'Omíllom', doña Ximena,   Dios vos curie de mal,
assí faga   a vuestras fijas amas.
Salúdavos Mio Cid   allá onde elle está;
sano lo dexé   e con tan grand rrictad.
El rrey por su merced   sueltas me vos ha   [1400
por levaros a Valencia   que avemos por heredad.
Si vos viesse el Cid   sanas e sin mal,
todo serié alegre,   que non avrié ningún pesar.'
Dixo doña Ximena: '¡El Criador lo mande!'
Dio tres cavalleros   Minaya Álbar Fáñez,   [1405
enviólos a Mio Cid   a Valencia dó está:
'Dezid al Canpeador,   que Dios le curie de mal,
29v   que su mugier e sus fijas   el rrey sueltas me las ha,
mientra que fuéremos   por sus tierras   conducho nos mandó dar.
De aquestos *quinze* días,   si Dios nos curiare de mal,   [1410
seremos [í] yo e su mugier   e sus fijas que él á
y todas las dueñas con ellas,   quantas buenas ellas han.'
Idos son los cavalleros   e d'ello pensarán,
rremaneció en San Pero   Minaya Álbar Fáñez.
Veriedes cavalleros   venir de todas partes,   [1415
irse quiere[n] a Valencia   a Mio Cid el de Bivar;
que les toviesse pro   rrogavan a Álbar Fáñez,
diziendo esto Mianaya: 'Esto feré de veluntad.'
A Minaya *sessaenta* [e] *cinco* cavalleros   acrecídol' han
e él se tenié *ciento*   que aduxiera d'allá;   [1420
por ir con estas dueñas   buena conpaña se faze.
Los quinientos marcos   dio Minaya al abat,
de los otros quinientos   dezir vos he qué faze:
Minaya a doña Ximina   e a sus fijas que ha
e a las otras dueñas   que las sirven delant,   [1425

83

The Infantes of Carrión saw Minaya on his way. 'You are helpful in all matters,' they said, 'so grant us a favour now. Pay our respects to the Cid of Vivar; tell him that we are well disposed to him and that it would be worth his while to be friends with us.' Minaya replied: 'That will be no trouble.' So Minaya departed and the Infantes turned back. Minaya made for San Pedro, where the ladies were staying, and there was great rejoicing when they saw him approaching. On his arrival Minaya dismounted and went into the church to say a prayer, after which he came back to the ladies and addressed Doña Jimena, saying: 'My respectful greetings to you, Doña Jimena. May God keep you and your noble daughters from harm! The Cid sends you his greetings from Valencia; I left him well and enjoying vast wealth. The King has graciously consented to release you so that I may take you to Valencia, which is now in our possession. If the Cid could see you there safe and sound with his mind free from anxiety he would be completely happy.' 'Please God it may be so!' said Doña Jimena. Minaya Álvar Fáñez chose three knights and sent them to the Cid in Valencia with this message: 'Tell the Campeador, whom God protect, that the King has handed over his wife and daughters to me and that he has made all provision for our journey through his territory. In fifteen days, God willing, we shall be with him, I and his wife and his two daughters and all the good ladies who are in attendance on them.' The knights set off on their mission, prepared to carry out all his instructions, while Minaya remained at San Pedro. Knights could be seen crowding in from all sides, eager to go to Valencia to join the Cid. They begged Minaya for his support, and he promised it willingly. So sixty-five knights were now added to the hundred he had brought with him, and together they would make a fine escort for the ladies. Minaya gave the Abbot his five hundred marks, and this is what he did with the other five hundred. Our good Minaya bought the finest clothes he could find in Burgos for Doña Jimena, her daughters and their

el bueno de Minaya   pensólas de adobar
de los mejores guarnimientos   que en Burgos pudo fallar,
palafrés e mulas,   que non parescan mal.
Quando estas dueñas   adobadas las ha,
el bueno de Minaya   pensar quiere de cavalgar,   [1430
afevos Rrachel e Vidas   a los pies le caen:

3or '¡Merced, Minaya,   cavallero de prestar!
Desfechos nos ha el Cid,   sabet, si no nos val;
soltariemos la ganancia,   que nos diesse el cabdal.'
'Yo lo veré con el Cid,   si Dios me lieva allá;   [1435
por lo que avedes fecho   buen cosiment í avrá.'
Dixo Rrachel e Vidas: '¡El Criador lo mande!
Si non, dexaremos Burgos,   ir lo hemos buscar.'
Ido es pora San Pero   Minaya Álbar Fáñez,
muchas yentes se le acogen,   pensó de cavalgar,   [1440
grand duelo es   al partir del abat:
'¡Sí vos vala el Criador,   Minaya Álbar Fáñez!
Por mí al Campeador   las manos le besad,
aqueste monesterio   no lo quiera olbidar,
todos los días del sieglo   en levarlo adelant   [1445
el Cid   siempre valdrá más.'
Rrespuso Minaya: 'Fer lo he de veluntad.'
Yas' espiden   e piensan de cavalgar,
el portero con ellos   que los ha de aguardar,
por la tierra del rrey   mucho conducho les dan.   [1450
De San Pero fasta Medina   en *cinco* días van,
felos en Medina   las dueñas e Álbar Fáñez.
Dirévos de los cavalleros   que levaron el mensaje,
al ora que lo sopo   Mio Cid el de Bivar,
plógol' de coraçón   e tornós' a alegrar,   [1455
de la su boca   conpeçó de fablar:
'Qui buen mandadero enbía   tal deve sperar.

3ov Tú, Muño Gustioz,   e Pero Vermúez delant,
e Martín Antolínez,   un burgalés leal,
el obispo don Jerónimo,   coronado de prestar,   [1460
cavalguedes con ciento   guisados pora huebos de lidiar;
por Sancta María   vós vayades passar,
vayades a Molina   que yaze más adelant,
tiénela Ave[n]galvón,   mio amigo es de paz,
con otros ciento cavalleros   bien vos consigrá;   [1465
id pora Medina   quanto lo pudiéredes far,
mi mugier e mis fijas   con Minaya Álbar Fáñez,
as[s]í como a mí dixieron,   í los podredes fallar;

ladies in waiting. He bought also palfreys and mules so that they should make a good appearance. When the ladies were arrayed in their finery and Minaya was ready to start, Rachel and Vidas appeared and fell at his feet, saying: 'A favour, worthy and noble Minaya! The Cid has ruined us if he does not keep his word. We would forgo the interest provided he paid us the capital.' 'I shall speak to the Cid about it when, God willing, I get back to Valencia. You will be well rewarded for what you did for him.' 'God grant it!' said Rachel and Vidas. 'If not, we shall set out from Burgos to go and find him.' Minaya Álvar Fáñez returned to San Pedro, where men flocked to his banner. When they were ready to depart, the Abbot was very sorry to see them go. 'God will bless you, Minaya,' he said, 'if you kiss the Cid's hands for me and ask him not to forget this monastery; if he keeps it in mind he will go from strength to strength in his career.' 'I shall certainly give him your message,' replied Minaya. At length they took their leave and rode away, the King's courier accompanying them to see to all their needs. They were abundantly supplied with provisions on their journey through the King's territory. They reached Medinaceli in five days after leaving San Pedro, and there we take our leave of the ladies and Álvar Fáñez and return to the knights who had gone with the message to the Cid. The Cid was very happy when he received the message, and he said: 'He who sends a good messenger may expect a good result! Muño Gustioz, do you and Pedro Bermúdez go on ahead, while Martín Antolínez and you, worthy bishop, Don Jerome, take with you one hundred knights fully armed as for battle. Go by Santa María de Albarracín and farther on to Molina, whose governor is the Moor Abengalbón. I am on terms of peace and friendship with him, and he will be sure to join you with another hundred knights. After that, ride on to Medinaceli as fast as you can, and there you will find my wife and daughters with Minaya Álvar Fáñez, as the

con grand ondra   aduzídmelas delant.
E yo fincaré en Valencia,   que mucho costádom' ha,   [1470
grand locura serié   si la desenparás;
yo fincaré en Valencia   ca la tengo por heredad.'
Esto era dicho,   piensan de cavalgar
e quanto que pueden   non fincan de andar.
Trocieron a Sancta María   e vinieron albergar a Frontael [1475
e el otro día vinieron   a Molina posar.
El moro Ave[n]galvón,   quando sopo el mensaje,
saliólos rrecebir   con grant gozo que faze:
'¡Venides, los vassallos   de mio amigo natural!
A mí non me pesa,   sabet, mucho me plaze.'   [1480
Fabló Muño Gustioz,   non speró a nadi:
'Mio Cid vos saludava   e mandólo rrecabdar
co[n] ciento cavalleros   que privádol' acorrades;
su mugier e sus fijas   en Medina están;
que vayades por ellas,   adugádesgelas acá   [1485
e fata en Valencia   d'ellas non vos partades.'
Dixo Ave[n]galvón: 'Fer lo he de veluntad.'
Essa noch   conducho les dio grand,
a la mañana   piensan de cavalgar;
ciéntol' pidieron,   mas él con dozientos' va.   [1490
Passan las montañas   que son fieras e grandes,
passaron   Mata de Toranz
de tal guisa   que ningún miedo non han,   [1492b
por el val de Arbuxedo   piensan a deprunar.
E en Medina   todo el rrecabdo está,
envió dos cavalleros   Minaya Álbar Fáñez   [1495
. . . .   que sopiesse la verdad;   [1495b
esto non detard[an]   ca de coraçón lo han,
el uno fincó con ellos   e el otro tornó a Álbar Fáñez:
'Virtos del Campeador   a nós vienen buscar;
afevos aquí   Pero Vermúez
e Muño Gustioz,   que vos quieren sin art,   [1499b
e Martín Antolínez,   el burgalés natural,   [1500
e el obispo don Jerónimo,   coranado leal,
e el alcayaz Ave[n]galvón   con sus fuerças que trahe
por sabor de Mio Cid   de grand óndral' dar,
todos vienen en uno,   agora llegarán.'
Essora dixo Minaya: 'Vay[a]mos cavalgar.'   [1505
Esso fue apriessa fecho,   que nos' quieren detardar,
bien salieron dén ciento   que non parecen mal,
en buenos cavallos   a cuberturas de cendales

31r

message says. Escort them to us here with all due honour, for I
shall remain in Valencia, which cost me so much to win. It
would be madness to leave unprotected what is now my own
territory.' When the Cid had finished speaking they rode off,
covering the ground as quickly as they could. They passed
through Santa María de Albarracín, put up at Bronchales, and
on the following day got to Molina, where they stopped.
When the Moor, Abengalbón, heard of their arrival he came out
to give them a joyous welcome, saying: 'Here you are, vassals
of my good friend, the Cid. I am very happy to see you.' Muño
Gustioz spoke up at once: 'The Cid sends his greetings and begs
you to arrange to join us without delay with one hundred
horsemen to meet his wife and daughters in Medinaceli, escort
them here and not leave them until they reach Valencia.' 'I shall
be glad to do so,' said Abengalbón. That night he gave them a
great feast, and the next morning they set off. They had asked
for one hundred horsemen but he brought two hundred with
him. They passed through the wild forest land and crossed
Campo Taranz without fear because of their escort. Then they
began to drop down into the valley of Arbujuelo. In Medinaceli
the greatest precautions were being taken, and when Minaya
saw this body of armed men arriving he sent two knights to
find out who they were. They went out eagerly and did their
work quickly, one of them remaining with the newcomers
while the other returned to Álvar Fáñez. 'They are a company
of the Cid's followers coming to join us' (he said). 'Your good
friends Pedro Bermúdez and Muño Gustioz are there with
Martín Antolínez of Burgos, the worthy bishop Don Jerome
and the Moorish leader Abengalbón, who brings an armed force
with him to do honour to the Cid. They are all coming together
and will be here immediately.' 'Mount your horses,' said
Minaya, and it was no sooner said than done. One hundred
of his men rode out from Medinaceli, and they were a magnifi-
cent sight on their fine horses covered with rich trappings and

  e petrales a cascaveles; e escudos a los cuellos,
  e en las manos lanças que pendones traen,   [1510
  que sopiessen los otros de qué seso era Álbar Fáñez
31v o ćuémo saliera de Castiella con estas dueñas que trahe.
  Los que ivan mesurando e llegando delant
  luego toman armas e tómanse a deportar,
  por cerca de Salón tan grandes gozos van.   [1515
  Dón llegan los otros, a Minaya Álvar Fáñez se van homillar;
  quando llegó Ave[n]galvón, dont a ojo [lo] ha,
  sonrrisándose de la boca ívalo abraçar,
  en el ombro lo saluda ca tal es su usaje:
  '¡Tan buen día convusco, Minaya Álbar Fáñez!   [1520
  Traedes estas dueñas por ó valdremos más,
  mugier del Cid lidiador e sus fijas naturales.
  Ondrar vos hemos todos ca tal es la su auze,
  maguer que mal le queramos, non ge lo podremos fer,
  en paz o en guerra de lo nuestro abrá,   [1525
  múchol' tengo por torpe qui non conosce la verdad.'
  Sorrisós' de la boca Minaya Álbar Fáñez:

84
  '¡Y[a] Ave[n]galvón, amígol' sodes sin falla!
  Si Dios me llegare al Cid e lo vea con el alma,
  d'esto que avedes fecho vós non perderedes nada. [1530
  Vayamos posar, ca la cena es adobada.'
  Dixo Avengalvón: 'Plazme d'esta presentaja,
  antes d'este te[r]cer día vos la daré doblada.'
  Entraron en Medina, sirvíalos Minaya,
  todos fueron alegres del cervicio que tomaron; [1535
  el portero del rrey quitarlo mandava,
32r ondrado es Mio Cid en Valencia dó estava
  de tan grand conducho como en Medínal' sacaron;
  el rrey lo pagó todo e quito se va Minaya.
  Passada es la noche, venida es la mañana,   [1540
  oída es la missa e luego cavalgavan;
  salieron de Medina e Salón passavan,
  Arbuxuelo arriba privado aguijavan,
  el campo de Torancio luégol' atravessavan,
  vinieron a Molina, la que Ave[n]galvón mandava. [1545
  El obispo don Jerónimo, buen cristiano sin falla,
  las noches e los días las dueñas aguarda*va*,
  e buen cavallo en diestro que va ante sus armas;
  entre él e Álbar Fáñez ivan a una compaña,

with bells on their breast-straps. The riders had their shields
slung from their necks, and they carried lances with pennons
attached. This was done to show the others how well Álvar
Fáñez managed things and in what style he had set out from
Castile with the ladies he was escorting. The advance party
of the new arrivals began to amuse themselves by giving a display
of arms, and there was some good sport on the banks of the Jalón.
The others went on to Minaya and greeted him respectfully.
When Abengalbón arrived and saw Minaya he came forward
to embrace him, kissing him on the shoulder as was his custom.
'Good day to you, Minaya Álvar Fáñez,' he said. 'By bringing
these ladies here you are giving us a welcome opportunity to do
honour to the wife and daughters of the Cid Campeador. Such
is his destiny that, even if we wished, we could do him no
harm. He will always get the better of us in peace or in war, and
whoever does not acknowledge this I consider a fool.' Minaya
smiled and said:

84

'You are a loyal friend to the Cid, Abengalbón. If God spares
me to return and see him, you will not be the loser for what you
have done here. And now let us rest, for the supper is ready.'
'I am grateful for the hospitality you are showing me,' said
Abengalbón, 'and before three days have passed I shall do as
much again for you.' They entered the town of Medinaceli,
where Minaya gave them such a feast that they were all in high
spirits. As the royal courier gave orders in the King's name that
everything should be paid for by him, Minaya was put to no
expense, and the Cid, though far away in Valencia, was honoured
by the lavish entertainment in Medinaceli. The whole party spent
the night there, and when morning dawned they attended mass
and rode off immediately after. They left Medinaceli, crossed the
river Jalón and made their way swiftly up the Arbujuelo.
Passing across Campo Taranz, they soon came to Molina, where
Abengalbón was governor. The bishop, Don Jerome, like a
good and faithful Christian, kept day-and-night watch over the
ladies. His fine war horse was led along on his right hand, and
behind it came the pack-horse carrying his armour. He and
Álvar Fáñez rode side by side, and together they entered the

entrados son a Molina,   buena e rrica casa,   [1550
el moro Ave[n]galvón   bien los sirvié sin falla,
de quanto que quisieron   non ovieron falla,
aun las ferraduras   quitárgelas mandava;
a Minaya e a las dueñas   ¡Dios, cómo las ondrava!
Otro día mañana   luego cavalgavan,   [1555
fata en Valencia   sirvíalos sin falla,
lo so despendié el moro,   que d'el[l]os non tomava nada.
Con estas alegrías   e nuevas tan ondradas
aprés son de Valencia   a tres leguas contadas.

85
A Mio Cid,   el que en buen ora nasco,   [1560
dentro a Valencia   liévanle el mandado.
Alegre fue Mio Cid   que nunqua más nin tanto
32v ca de lo que más amava   yal' viene el mandado.
Dozi[en]tos cavalleros   mandó exir privado
que rreciban a Mianaya   e a las dueñas fijas d'algo;   [1565
él sedié en Valencia   curiando e guardando
ca bien sabe que Álbar Fáñez   trahe todo rrecabdo.

86
Afevos todos aquéstos   rreciben a Minaya
e a las dueñas e a las niñas   e a las otras conpañas.
Mandó Mio Cid   a los que ha en su casa   [1570
que guardassen el alcáçar   e las otras torres altas
e todas las puertas   e las exidas e las entradas
e aduxiéssenle a Bavieca,   poco avié quel' ganara,
aún non sabié Mio Cid,   el que en buen ora cinxo espada,
si serié corredor   o si abrié buena parada;   [1575
a la puerta de Valencia,   dó fuesse en so salvo,
delante su mugier e sus fijas   querié tener las armas.
Rrecebidas las dueñas   a una grant ondrança,
el obispo don Jerónimo   adelant se entrava,
í dexava el cavallo,   pora la capiella adeliñava;   [1580
con quantos que él puede,   que con oras se acordaran,
sobrepel[l]iças vestidas   e con cruzes de plata,
rrecibir salién [a] las dueñas   e al bueno de Minaya.
El que en buen ora nasco   non lo detardava,   [1584
vistiós' el sobregonel,   luenga trahe la barba;   [1587
ensiéllanle a Bavieca,   cuberturas le echavan,   [1585
Mio Cid salió sobr'él   e armas de fuste tomava.   [1586
Por nombre el cavallo   Bavieca cavalga,   [1589

prosperous town of Molina. There the Moorish governor
Abengalbón entertained them lavishly and saw to it that they
had all they wanted, even paying for the shoeing of their horses.
He could not do enough to honour Minaya and the ladies.
Early next morning they set off again; Abengalbón continued
faithfully in attendance on them until they reached Valencia,
spending his own money and not taking a penny of theirs.
After this triumphal progress in their honour the ladies arrived,
amid great rejoicing, within three leagues of Valencia.

85

Messages announcing their arrival were brought to the Cid
in the city. The Cid had never been so happy as he was on
hearing the news that those he held dearest had arrived. He
ordered two hundred knights to set out at once to welcome
Minaya and the noble ladies, while he remained in Valencia
to guard and protect it, knowing that Minaya Álvar Fáñez
had things well in hand.

86

The knights bade Minaya welcome with the ladies, the Cid's
daughters and all their attendants. Meanwhile the Cid commanded those of his household to guard the fortress, with its
tall towers and gates, and all the ways in and out. He also
ordered his horse, Babieca, to be brought—he had won him only
a short while before (when he routed the King of Seville in
battle), and he was not sure yet if he would be a good runner and
if he would allow himself to be pulled up sharply. So at the gates
of Valencia, where he would be in complete safety, he decided
to make a display of arms in the presence of his wife and
daughters. When the ladies had been received with every honour,
Bishop Jerome went on ahead and, dismounting from his horse,
made his way to the chapel, where he joined all the clerics
already there for the canonical hours. Wearing their surplices
and carrying silver crosses, they went out to meet the ladies and
the worthy Minaya. The Cid quickly donned his rich tunic—
his long, flowing beard was a fine sight—and when Babieca
was saddled and caparisoned he rode out on him, carrying
wooden jousting weapons. Babieca ran one length with such

33r fizo una corrida, ésta fue tan estraña,   [1588
quando ovo corrido, todos se maravillavan,   [1590
d'és día se preció Bavieca en quant grant fue España.
En cabo del cosso Mio Cid desca[*va*]lgava,
adeliñó a su mugier e a sus fijas amas;
quando lo vio doña Ximena, a pies se le echava:
'¡Merced, Campeador, en buen ora cinxiestes espada! [1595
Sacada me avedes de muchas vergüenças malas;
afeme aquí, señor, yo e vuestras fijas amas;
con Dios e convusco buenas son e criadas.'
A la madre e a las fijas bien las abraçava,
del gozo que avién de los sos ojos lloravan.   [1600
Todas las sus mesnadas en grant deleite estavan,
armas teniendo e tablados quebrantando.
Oíd lo que dixo el que en buen ora nasco:
'Vós, querida mugier e ondrada
e amas mis fijas, | mi coraçón e mi alma,   [1604b-05
entrad comigo en Valencia la casa,
en esta heredad que vos yo he ganada.'
Madre e fijas las manos le besavan,
a tan grand ondra ellas a Valencia entravan.

87
    Adeliñó Mio Cid con ellas al alcáçar,   [1610
allá las subié en el más alto logar.
Ojos vellidos catan a todas partes,
33v miran Valencia cómo yaze la cibdad
e del otra parte a ojo han el mar,
miran la huerta, espessa es e grand;   [1615
alçan las manos por a Dios rrogar
d'esta ganancia cómo es buena e grand.
Mio Cid e sus compañas tan a grand sabor están.
El ivierno es exido, que el março quiere entrar.
Dezirvos quiero nuevas de allent partes del mar,   [1620
de aquel rrey Yúcef que en Marruecos está.

88
    Pesól' al rrey de Marruecos de Mio Cid don Rrodrigo:
'Que en mis heredades fuertemie[*n*]tre es metido
e él non ge lo gradece sinon a Jesu Cristo.'
Aquel rrey de Marruecos ajuntava sus virtos,   [1625

extraordinary vigour that all the onlookers were amazed, and from that day onward he won fame throughout the whole of Spain. At the end of the run the Cid dismounted and approached his wife and daughters. When Doña Jimena saw him she knelt at his feet and said: 'I thank you, my brave Campeador, for having rescued me from many indignities. Here I am, my lord, I and your two daughters who are, thank God, good girls and a credit to their father.' The Cid embraced mother and daughters while they wept for joy. All his vassals were full of jubilation, making displays of skill in arms and breaking down wooden turrets. The Cid then spoke as follows: 'Come, Doña Jimena, my beloved and honoured wife, and you my two daughters, so dear to my heart, come into the town of Valencia with me and take possession of the inheritance that I have won for you.' Mother and daughters thanked him, kissing his hands, and made their entry into Valencia with great ceremony.

87

The Cid then led them up to the fortress and took them up to the highest point, from which their fair eyes could take in the whole scene. They saw how the city of Valencia lay before them, with the sea on one side and on the other the wide, luxuriant plantations of the Huerta. They raised their hands in a prayer of thanks to God for the great fortune which he had won for them. The Cid and his companions were well satisfied. Winter was over and March was coming in, and now I must give you news from beyond the sea of King Yusuf of Morocco.

88

The Cid had roused his anger, and he said: 'He has forcibly invaded my territory and he attributes all his success to Jesus Christ.' So the Moorish king assembled his armed forces,

con *cinquaenta* vezes mill de armas   todos fueron conplidos,
entraron sobre mar,   en las barcas son metidos,
van buscar a Valencia   a Mio Cid don Rrodrigo;
arribado an las naves,   fuera eran exidos.

89
Llegaron a Valencia,   la que Mio Cid á conquista,   [1630
fincaron las tiendas   e posan las yentes descreídas.
Estas nuevas   a Mio Cid eran venidas:

90
'¡Grado al Criador   e a[l] padre espirital!
Todo el bien que yo he,   todo lo tengo delant;
con afán gané a Valencia   e éla por heredad,   [1635
a menos de muert   no la puedo dexar;
grado al Criador   e a Sancta María madre,
34r   mis fijas e mi mugier   que las tengo acá.
Venídom' es delicio   de tierras d'allent mar,
entraré en las armas,   non lo podré dexar,   [1640
mis fijas e mi mugier   ver me an lidiar,
en estas tierras agenas   verán las moradas cómo se fazen,
afarto verán por los ojos   cómo se gana el pan.'
Su mugier e sus fijas   subiólas al alcáçar,
alçavan los ojos,   tiendas vieron fincadas: [1645
'¿Qu'es esto, Cid?   ¡sí el Criador vos salve!'
'¡Ya mugier ondrada,   non ayades pesar!
Rriqueza es que nos acrece   maravillosa e grand,
a poco que viniestes,   presend vos quieren dar,
por casar son vuestras fijas,   adúzenvos axuvar.'   [1650
'A vós grado, Cid,   e al padre spiritual.'
'Mugier, sed en este palacio,   e si quisiéredes, en el alcáçar,
non ayades pavor   porque me veades lidiar;
con la merced de Dios   e de Sancta María madre,
crécem' el coraçón   porque estades delant;   [1655
con Dios aquesta lid   yo la he de arrancar.'

91
Fincadas son las tiendas   e parecen los alvores,
a una grand priessa   tañién los atamores;
alegravas' Mio Cid   e dixo: '¡Tan buen día es oy!'
Miedo á su mugier   e quiérel' quebrar el coraçón,   [1660
assí fazié a las dueñas   e a sus fijas amas a dos,
del día que nasquieran   non vieran tal tremor.

fifty thousand strong, and they embarked in ships and set sail for Valencia in search of the Cid. When the ships arrived they disembarked.

89

When they reached Valencia, which the Cid had conquered, the infidel hordes pitched their tents and encamped there. When this news reached the Cid, he exclaimed:

90

'Thanks be to our Father in Heaven! I have all I cherish most here with me in Valencia, which I won by hard fighting; it belongs to me now, and only death can make me give it up. Thanks to God and His Holy Mother, I have my wife and daughters here with me. A piece of good fortune has come from beyond the sea. I shall take up arms to meet this attack, and my wife and daughters shall see me fight and behold with their eyes how we earn our bread and make our homes in these strange lands.' He took his wife and daughters up to the tower of the fortress, and when they looked and saw the tents pitched Doña Jimena exclaimed: 'In Heaven's name, Cid, what is this? 'Noble wife' (said he), 'do not be alarmed. This is great and wonderful wealth that is coming to us. You have no sooner arrived than they wish to give you a present. Your daughters are of marriageable age and they come with a dowry for them.' 'We owe all this to you and to our Heavenly Father,' said Doña Jimena. 'Stay in this part of the castle, wife, and do not be afraid when you see me fight; with the help of God and His Holy Mother I feel stronger of heart because you are here. By God's grace I shall be victorious in this battle.'

91

Day dawned over the Moorish camp, and soon the Moors began to beat their drums. This made the Cid happy, and he cried out, 'What a good day this is going to be!' His wife was terrified, and so were his daughters and their ladies; they had never been so frightened in their lives. The Campeador stroked

Prisos' a la barba   el buen Cid Campeador:

34v 'Non ayades miedo,   ca todo es vuestra pro;
antes d'estos *quinze* días,   si ploguiere a[l] Criador,   [1665
. . . .   aquellos atamores
a vós los pondrán delant   e veredes quáles son,   [1666b
desí an a ser   del obispo don Jerónimo,
colgar los han en Sancta María   madre del Criador.'
Vocación es que fizo   el Cid Campeador.
Alegre[s] son las dueñas,   perdiendo van el pavor.   [1670
Los moros de Marruecos   cavalgan a vigor,
por las huertas adentro   ent[r]an sines pavor.

92

Violo el atalaya   e tanxo el esquila,
prestas son las mesnadas   de las yentes cristianas,
adóbanse de coraçón   e dan salto de la villa;   [1675
dós' fallan con los moros   cometiénlos tan aína,
sácanlos de las huertas   mucho a fea guisa,
quinientos mataron d'ellos   conplidos en és día.

93

Bien fata las tiendas   dura aqueste alcaz,
mucho avién fecho,   piessan de cavalgar;   [1680
Álbar Salvadórez   preso fincó allá.
Tornados son a Mio Cid   los que comién so pan,
él se lo vio con los ojos,   cuéntangelo delant,
alegre es Mio Cid   por quanto fecho han:
'¡Oídme, cavalleros,   non rrastará por ál!   [1685
Oy es día bueno   e mejor será cras:
por la mañana prieta   todos armados seades,
dezir nos ha la missa   e pensad de cavalgar,
el obispo do Jerónimo   soltura nos dará,
ir los hemos ferir . . . .   [1690

35r en el nombre del Criador   e del apóstol Sancti Yagüe; [1690b
más vale que nós los vezcamos   que ellos cojan el [p]an.'
Essora dixieron todos: 'D'amor e de voluntad.'
Fablava Minaya,   non lo quiso detardar:
'Pues esso queredes, Cid,   a mí mandedes ál,
dadme *ciento* [e] *treínta* cavalleros   pora huebos de lidiar,   [1695
quando vós los fuéredes ferir,   entraré yo del otra part;
o de amas o del una   Dios nos valdrá.'
Essora dixo el Cid: 'De buena voluntad.'

his beard and said: 'Do not be afraid, for it will all turn to your advantage. Before a fortnight is up (we shall capture) those war drums, please God, and I shall set them before you for you to see what they are like. After that they must go to the Bishop, Don Jerome, who will hang them up in the church of our Lady, Mother of God.' This was a vow that the Cid made. The ladies, less frightened now, became more cheerful. The Moroccans rode steadily forward and penetrated fearlessly into the Huerta.

92
The look-out saw them and rang the alarm bell. The Cid's men were on the alert, and donning their full equipment sallied quickly from the town. When they met the Moors they attacked at once and drove them ruthlessly from the Huerta, killing a good five hundred of them before the end of the day.

93
They pressed the Moors hard and pursued them right back to their tents. Then they began to return to their own lines, but Álvar Salvadórez was taken prisoner and remained behind. When the Cid's faithful followers returned they recounted to him their exploits, seen by him from a distance, and the Cid was delighted at their success. (Then he said to them) 'Hear me, knights, today has been a good day and tomorrow is bound to be better. See that you are all armed and ready for battle before daybreak. Bishop Jerome will say mass for us and give us absolution; then we must ride out to the attack in the name of God and of the Apostle St James. We must defeat them rather than let them deprive us of our food.' To this they all replied: 'We shall, with a right good will.' Thereupon Minaya hastened to say: 'Since these are your wishes, Cid, grant me this as well. Give me one hundred and thirty knights fully armed for battle; when you attack the Moors from the front I shall come in from the flank, and with God's help we shall be successful in one or both of these engagements.' 'I grant it willingly,' said the Cid.

94

És día es salido e la noch es entrada,
nos' detardan de adobasse essas yentes cristianas.   [1700
A los mediados gallos, antes de la mañana,
el obispo don Jerónimo la missa les cantava;
la missa dicha, grant sultura les dava:
'El que aquí muriere lidiando de cara
préndol' yo los pecados e Dios le abrá el alma.   [1705
A vós, Cid don Rrodrigo, en buen ora cinxiestes espada,
yo vos canté la missa por aquesta mañana;
pídovos un don e séam' presentado,
las feridas primeras que las aya yo otorgadas.'
Dixo el Campeador: 'Desaquí vos sean mandadas.'   [1710

95

Salidos son todos armados por las torres de Va[le]ncia,
Mio Cid a los sos vassallos tan bien los acordando;
dexan a las puertas omnes de grant rrecabdo.
Dio salto Mio Cid en Bavieca el so cavallo,
de todas guarnizones muy bien es adobado.   [1715
35v   La seña sacan fuera, de Valencia dieron salto,
quatro mill menos *treínta* con Mio Cid van a cabo,
a los cinquaenta mill van los ferir de grado;
Álvar Álvarez e Álvar Salvadórez
e Minaya Álvar Fáñez | entráronles del otro cabo.   [1719b-20
Plogo al Criador e ovieron de arrancarlos.
Mio Cid enpleó la lança, al espada metió mano,
atantos mata de moros que non fueron contados,
por el cobdo ayuso la sangre destellando.
Al rrey Yúcef tres colpes le ovo dados,   [1725
saliós'le de so'l espada ca múchol' andido el cavallo,
metiós'le en Gujera, un castiello palaciano,
Mio Cid el de Bivar fasta allí llegó en alcaz
con otros quel' consiguen de sus buenos vassallos.
Desd' allí se tornó el que en buen ora nasco,   [1730
mucho era alegre de lo que an caçado.
Allí preció a Bavieca de la cabeça fasta a cabo.
Toda esta ganancia en su mano á rrastado.
Los *cinquaenta* mill por cuenta fuero[n] notados,
non escaparon más de ciento e quatro.   [1735
Mesnadas de Mio Cid rrobado an el canpo,
entre oro e plata fallaron tres mill marcos,
las otras ganancias non avía rrecabdo.

94

When the day was over and night had come on, the Christian forces started arming at once, and at three o'clock in the morning, before sunrise, Bishop Jerome said mass and afterwards gave them full absolution in these words: 'I absolve from sin all those who die with their faces to the enemy; God will receive their souls. I have said mass for you this morning, Don Rodrigo, and now I confidently beg you to grant me a favour. Let me have the honour of striking the first blows.' 'I grant it to you here and now,' answered the Campeador.

95

All the men, fully armed, went out by the towers of Valencia, the Cid meanwhile giving them advice and instructions. At the gates of the town they left capable and reliable men. The Cid sallied forth, mounted on Babieca and wearing his full armour. They left Valencia with their standard carried in front, four thousand all but thirty forming the Cid's company, going eagerly to the attack of fifty thousand Moors. Álvar Álvarez and Álvar Salvadórez and Minaya Álvar Fáñez came at them from the flank and with God's help the Moors were routed. The Cid first used his lance and then wielded his sword, killing countless Moors while the blood dripped down to his elbow. He struck three blows at King Yusuf, but the king escaped the Cid's sword and galloped off on his swift horse, not stopping till he was inside the fine fortress of Cullera. The Cid, with some of his men, pursued him right up to the fortress and then turned back, highly satisfied with the chase, in which Babieca too had shown his mettle. All that booty fell to the Cid, and of the fifty thousand Moors they counted not more than one hundred and four as having escaped. The Cid's vassals plundered the field and found three thousand gold and silver marks and enormous quantities

Alegre era Mio Cid   e todos sos vassallos
que Dios les ovo merced   que vencieron el campo.   [1740
Quando al rrey de Marruecos   assí lo an arrancado,
36r   dexó [a] Álbar Fáñez   por saber todo rrecabdo;
con *ciento* cavalleros   a Valencia es entrado,
fronzida trahe la cara,   que era desarmado,
assí entró sobre Bavieca,   el espada en la mano.   [1745
Rrecibiénlo las dueñas   que lo están esperando;
Mio Cid fincó ant'ellas,   tovo la rrienda al cavallo:
'A vós me omillo, dueñas,   grant prez vos he gañado,
vós teniendo Valencia   e yo vencí el campo;
esto Dios se lo quiso   con todos los sos santos   [1750
quando en vuestra venida   tal ganancia nos an dada.
¿Vedes el espada sangrienta   e sudiento el cavallo?
—con tal cum esto   se vencen moros del campo.
Rrogand al Criador   que vos biva algunt año,
entraredes en prez   e besarán vuestras manos.'   [1755
Esto dixo Mio Cid,   diciendo del cavallo.
Quándol' vieron de pie,   que era descavalgado,
las dueñas e las fijas   e la mugier que vale algo
delant el Campeador   los inojos fincaron:
'Somos en vuestra merced   e ¡bivades muchos años!'   [1760
En buelta con él   entraron al palacio
e ivan posar con él   en unos preciosos escaños.
'Ya mugier daña Ximena,   ¿nom' lo aviedes rrogado?
Estas dueñas que aduxiestes,   que vos sirven tanto,
quiero las casar   con de aquestos mios vassallos;   [1765
a cada una d'ellas   doles *dozientos* marcos de plata,
que lo sepan en Castiella   a quién sirvieron tanto.
36v   Lo de vuestras fijas   venir se á más por espacio.'
Levantáronse todas   e besáronle las manos,
grant fue el alegría   que fue por el palacio;   [1770
como lo dixo el Cid   assí lo han acabado.
Minaya Álbar Fáñez   fuera era en el campo
con todas estas yentes   escriviendo e contando,
entre tiendas e armas   e vestidos preciados
tanto fallan d'esto   que es cosa sobejana.   [1775
Quiero vos dezir   lo que es más granado,
non pudieron ellos saber la cuenta   de todos los cavallos
que andan arrad[í]os   e non ha qui tomallos,
los moros de las tierras   ganado se an í algo;
maguer de todo esto,   *al* Campeador contado   [1780
de los buenos e otorgados   cayéronle mill e *quinientos* cavallos;

of other spoils. The Cid and his vassals were overjoyed that by
God's favour they had won the day. Now that they had utterly
routed the King of Morocco, the Cid left Álvar Fáñez to make a
complete reckoning of the booty while he himself went into
Valencia with a hundred knights. His crumpled linen coif could
be seen, for he had thrown back his mailed hood, and, sword in
hand, he entered the town, mounted on Babieca. The Cid drew
rein and stopped before the ladies, who were waiting to receive
him, saying: 'My humble greetings to you, ladies, for whose
sake I have won great renown. While you were holding
Valencia I fought and won in the field. It was the will of God and
of all saints to give us this great victory as soon as you arrived.
Do you see my bloodstained sword and my horse dripping
sweat? That is how Moors are vanquished in battle. Praying
God to spare my life a few years longer, you will come to great
honour and many vassals will do you obeisance.' The Cid made
this speech as he dismounted, and when they saw him standing
before them the ladies, his daughters and his noble wife knelt
down and said: 'May you live long to guard and protect us!'
They entered the palace, and there they all sat down on some
richly ornamented couches. 'Doña Jimena,' said the Cid, 'have
you not asked this favour of me? I want these ladies whom you
have brought with you, and who have served you so well, to
marry some of my vassals. I shall give each of them two hundred
silver marks, so that people in Castile may know to whom these
ladies have given such faithful service. The question of your
daughters' marriages will come up later on.' All the ladies rose
and kissed his hand to thank him, and there was great rejoicing
throughout the whole palace. The Cid carried out faithfully the
promise he had made. Minaya Álvar Fáñez was still out on the
field of battle with all his assistants, counting and taking note
in writing of the booty. Much valuable material was found in
tents, arms and costly garments, but most valuable of all were the
innumerable horses that were wandering loose about the battlefield. The Moors who lived in the district took a certain number
of them, and in spite of that fifteen hundred thoroughbred horses
fell to the Campeador's own share; and if so many fell to him

quando a Mio Cid   cayeron tantos
los otros bien pueden   fincar pagados.   [1782b
¡Tanta tienda preciada   e tanto tendal obrado
que á ganado Mio Cid   con todos sus vassallos!
La tienda del rrey de Marruecos,   que de las otras es cabo, [1785
dos tendales la sufren,   con oro son labrados,
mandó Mio Cid Rruy Díaz   . . . .
que fita soviesse la tienda | e non la tolliesse
                              dent cristiano: [1787b-88
'Tal tienda como ésta,   que de Marruecos es passada,
enbiarla quiero   a Alfonso el castellano,'   [1790
que croviesse sos nuevas   de Mio Cid que avié algo.
Con aquestas rriquezas tantas   a Valencia son entrados.
El obispo don Jerónimo,   caboso coronado,
quando es farto de lidiar   con amas las sus manos,
37r non tiene en cuenta   los moros que ha matados;   [1795
lo que cayé a él   mucho era sobejano,
Mio Cid don Rrodrigo,   el que en buen ora nasco,
de toda la su quinta   el diezmo l'á mandado.

96

Alegres son por Valencia   las yentes cristianas,
tantos avién de averes,   de cavallos e de armas;   [1800
alegre es doña Ximena   e sus fijas amas
e todas la[s] otras dueñas   que[s'] tienen por casadas.
El bueno de Mio Cid   non lo tardó por nada:
'¿Dó sodes, caboso?   Venid acá, Minaya;
de lo que a vós cayó   vós non gradecedes nada;   [1805
d'esta mi quinta,   dígovos sin falla,
prended lo que quisiéredes,   lo otro rremanga;
e cras a la mañana   ir vos hedes sin falla
con cavallos d'esta quinta   que yo he ganada,
con siellas e con frenos   e con señas espadas;   [1810
por amor de mi mugier   e de mis fijas amas,
porque assí las enbió   dond ellas son pagadas,
estos dozientos cavallos   irán en presentajas
que non diga mal el rrey Alfonso   del que Valencia manda.'
Mandó a Pero Vermúez   que fuesse con Minaya.   [1815
Otro día mañana   privado cavalgavan
e dozientos omnes   lievan en su conpaña
con saludes del Cid   que las manos le besava:
d'esta lid   que ha arrancada

the others must have been more than satisfied. Among the many richly decorated tents and carved tent poles that became the spoil of the Cid and his followers was the King of Morocco's tent, the finest of them all, which was supported on two tent poles wrought in gold. The Cid ordered that the tent should remain standing and that no one should take it away. 'A tent like this,' he said, 'which has come from Morocco, I should like to send to King Alfonso of Castile, so that he may believe the rumours he hears of the Cid's great wealth.' With these rich spoils they entered Valencia. The valiant cleric, Bishop Jerome, had had all the fighting he could wish for, and he had lost all count of the Moors he had slain. His share of the booty was considerable, for the Cid assigned to him the tenth of his fifth part.

96

All the Christians in Valencia were very pleased with the money, the horses and the arms they had won. Doña Jimena and her daughters were happy too, as were all the ladies, who saw themselves as good as married already. The Cid lost no time, but called to Álvar Fáñez: 'Come here, my gallant Minaya. You have more than earned your share of the booty, so take what you want out of mine, leaving the rest behind. Tomorrow morning you must set out, taking with you horses from this fifth share of mine, fully equipped with saddle and sword. In this way these two hundred horses will go as a present to King Alfonso, who has allowed my beloved wife and daughters to join me so happily here, so that he may not speak ill of the man who rules Valencia.' He ordered Pedro Bermúdez to accompany Minaya, and next morning they set out with all speed, taking two hundred men with them to carry to the King greetings from the Cid, who kissed his hand (as a loyal vassal). The Cid was

dozientos cavallos   le enbiava en presentaja,   [*1819b*
'E servir lo he sienpre,'   mientra que ovisse el alma.   [*1820*

97

37v   Salidos son de Valencia   e piensan de andar,
tales ganancias traen   que son a aguardar.
Andan los días e las noches . . . . . .
e passada han la sierra | que las otras tierras parte. [*1823b-24*
Por el rrey don Alfonso   tómanse a preguntar.   [*1825*

98

        Passando van las sierras   e los montes e las aguas,
llegan a Valladolid   dó el rrey Alfonso estava;
enviávanle mandado   Per Vermúez e Minaya
que mandasse rrecebir   a esta conpaña;
Mio Cid el de Valencia   enbía su presentaja.   [*1830*

99

        Alegre fue el rrey,   non viestes atanto,
mandó cavalgar apriessa   todos sos fijos d'algo,
í en los primeros   el rrey fuera dio salto
a ver estos mensajes   del que en buen ora nasco.
Los ifantes de Carrión,   sabet, ís' acertaron,   [*1835*
[e] el conde don García,   so enemigo malo.
A los unos plaze   e a los otros va pesando.
A ojo lo[s] avién   los del que en buen ora nasco,
cuédanse que es almofalla   ca non vienen con mandado,
el rrey don Alfonso   seíse sanctiguando.   [*1840*
Minaya e Per Vermúez   adelante son llegados,
firiéronse a tierra,   decendieron de los cavallos,
ante'l rrey Alfonso,   los inojos fincados,
besan la tierra   e los pies amos:
'¡Merced, rrey Alfonso,   sodes tan ondrado!   [*1845*
Por Mio Cid el Campeador   todo esto vos besamos,
38r   a vós llama por señor   e tienes' por vuestro vassallo,
mucho precia la ondra el Cid   quel' avedes dado.
Pocos días ha, rrey,   que una lid á arrancado;
a aquel rrey de Marruecos,   Yúcef por nombrado,   [*1850*
con cinquaenta mill   arrancólos del campo.
Las ganancias que fizo   mucho son sobejanas,
rricos son venidos   todos los sos vassallos
e embíavos dozientos cavallos   e bésavos las manos.'
Dixo el rrey don Alfonso: 'Rrecíbolos de grado;   [*1855*

sending as a gift to King Alfonso the two hundred horses from
the spoils he had won in this battle, with a message saying that
he would always serve him as long as he lived.

97

They left Valencia and began their journey, taking special
care to guard the valuable booty. They travelled night and day
without stopping and crossed the mountain range that separates
the two regions. They inquired where King Alfonso was to be
found.

98

They went on, crossing mountains, woods and rivers, until
they reached Valladolid, where the King was staying at that
time. Pedro Bermúdez and Minaya sent him a message asking
if he would be pleased to receive this deputation from the Cid of
Valencia, who was sending him a present.

99

The King showed how delighted he was by ordering all his
nobles to mount their horses immediately, and he himself rode in
the first rank to meet these envoys from the Cid. The Infantes of
Carrión were there and Count García Ordóñez, the Cid's mortal
enemy. Some of the nobles were pleased and others just the
reverse. When they caught sight of the Cid's men they thought
it was a hostile force, since they did not send a message
ahead; even King Alfonso crossed himself. Minaya and Pedro
Bermúdez came first, and when they drew up they alighted from
their horses and knelt down before King Alfonso, kissing the
ground and his feet as well. (Then they said) 'We beg a favour,
honoured King Alfonso; we pay you this homage on behalf of
the Cid Campeador, who acknowledges you as his liege lord
and considers himself your vassal. He appreciates greatly the
favour you have done him. A few days ago he won a pitched
battle over the king Yúsuf of Morocco. He routed the Moorish
army of fifty thousand and captured such quantities of booty
that all his vassals are now rich men. To you he sends two
hundred horses and begs you humbly to accept them.' 'I accept
them willingly,' said the King, 'and I thank the Cid for sending

gradéscolo a Mio Cid   que tal don me ha enbiado,
aún vea [el] ora   que de mí sea pagado.'
Esto plogo a muchos   e besáronle las manos.
Pesó al conde don García   e mal era irado,
con *diez* de sus parientes   aparte davan salto: [1860
'¡Maravilla es del Cid   que su ondra crece tanto!
En la ondra que él ha   nós seremos abiltados;
por tan biltadamientre   vencer rreyes del campo,
como si los fallasse muertos   aduzirse los cavallos,
por esto que él faze   nós abremos enbargo.'   [1865

100

Fabló el rrey don Alfonso   e dixo esta rrazón:
'Grado al Criador   e al señor Sant Esidro el de León
estos dozientos cavallos   quem' enbía Mio Cid.
Mio rreino adelant   mejor me podrá servir.
A vós, Minaya Álbar Fáñez,   e a Pero Vermúez aquí   [1870
38v   mándovos los cuerpos   ondradamientre servir e vestir
e guarnirvos de todas armas,   como vós dixiéredes aquí,
que bien parescades   ante Rruy Díaz Mio Cid;
dovos *tres* cavallos   e prendedlos aquí.
Assí como semeja   e la veluntad me lo diz,   [1875
todas estas nuevas   a bien abrán de venir.'

101

Besáronle las manos   e entraron a posar;
bien los mandó servir   de quanto huebos han.
De los iffantes de Carrión   yo vos quiero contar,
fablando en su consejo,   aviendo su poridad: [1880
'Las nuevas del Cid   mucho van adelant,
demandemos sus fijas   pora con ellas casar,
creçremos en nuestra ondra   e iremos adelant.'
Vinién al rrey Alfonso   con esta poridad:
'¡Merced vos pidimos   como a rrey e señor natural!   [1885

102

Con vuestro consejo   lo queremos fer nós
que nos demandedes   fijas del Campeador;
casar queremos con ellas   a su ondra e a nuestra pro.'
Una grant ora el rrey   pensó e comidió:
'Yo eché de tierra   al buen Campeador,   [1890
e faziendo yo a él mal   e él a mí grand pro,
del casamiento non sé   sis' abrá sabor,

me such a fine gift. I hope the time will come when I can repay him.' Many of those present were pleased at hearing this, and they kissed the King's hands, but it angered Count García (Ordóñez), who went aside with ten of his relatives and said: 'The Cid is doing wonders and covering himself with glory, but the higher his reputation rises the lower ours will fall. He will make us look small if he goes on defeating kings in battle so basely and taking away their horses as if they were all dead.'

100

King Alfonso then made the following speech: 'Thanks be to God and to St Isidore of León for these two hundred horses which the Cid has sent me. As time goes on he will do me, as his king, even greater service. Minaya Álvar Fáñez and Pedro Bermúdez, I want you both to dress yourselves in the finest clothes and be equipped with arms as you will now bespeak, so as to make a worthy appearance before the Cid Ruy Díaz. I give you three horses, so take them here and now. I feel certain that this whole affair will turn out well.'

101

They kissed the King's hands and withdrew to their lodging, and the King gave command that they should be supplied with all they needed. Now I must tell you about the Infantes of Carrión, who were consulting together privately and saying: 'The Cid has had great success in his affairs, so let us ask for his daughters in marriage, for we shall increase our prestige and better our prospects by making this match.' Accordingly they approached the King with this private proposal, saying: 'We beg a favour of you as our king and lord.

102

We want your help in what we are planning to do. We want you to ask for us the hands of the Cid's daughters in marriage. By marrying them we shall bring honour to them and advantage to ourselves.' The King pondered over the matter for a long time, and then he said: 'I sent the good Campeador into exile and, considering that he has been doing great things on my behalf while I treated him badly, I doubt whether he will care for this

E

mas pues bós lo queredes   entremos en la rrazón.'
A Minaya Álbar Fáñez   e a Pero Vermúez
el rrey don Alfonso   essora los llamó,   [1895
39r   a una quadra   ele los apartó:
'Oídme, Minaya   e vós, Per Vermúez,
sírvem' Mio Cid   el Campeador,
él lo merece | e de mí abrá perdón,   [1898b-99
viniéssem' a vistas,   si oviesse dent sabor.   [1899b
Otros mandados ha   en esta mi cort: [1900
Diego e Ferrando,   los iffantes de Carrión,
sabor han de casar   con sus fijas amas a dos.
Sed buenos mensageros   e rruégovoslo yo
que ge lo digades   al buen Campeador:
abrá í ondra   e creçrá en onor   [1905
por consagrar   con los iffantes de Carrión.'
Fabló Minaya   e plogo a Per Vermúez:
'Rrogar ge lo emos   lo que dezides vós;
después faga el Cid   lo que oviere sabor.'
'Dezid a Rruy Díaz,   el que en buen ora nasco,   [1910
quel' iré a vistas   dó fuere aguisado,
dó él dixiere   í sea el mojón.
Andarle quiero   a Mio Cid en toda pro.'
Espidiénse al rrey,   con esto tornados son,
van pora Valencia   ellos e todos los sos.   [1915
Quando lo sopo   el buen Campeador,
apriessa cavalga,   a rrecebirlos salió,
sonrrisós' Mio Cid   e bien los abraçó:
'¡Venides, Minaya   e vós, Pero Vermúez!
En pocas tierras   á tales dos varones.   [1920
¿Cómo son las saludes   de Alfonso mio señor?
39v   ¿Si es pagado   o rrecibió el don?'
Dixo Minaya: 'D'alma e de coraçón
es pagado   e davos su amor.'
Dixo Mio Cid: '¡Grado al Criador!'   [1925
Esto diziendo,   conpieçan la rrazón,
lo quel' rrogava   Alfonso el de León
de dar sus fijas   a los ifantes de Carrión,
quel' connoscié í ondra   e creç[r]ié en onor,
que ge lo consejava   d'alma e de coraçón.   [1930
Quando lo oyó Mio Cid   el buen Campeador,
una grand ora   pensó e comidió:
'Esto gradesco   a Christus el mio señor.
Echado fu de tierra,   é tollida la onor,

marriage. However, as you wish it, let us open negotiations.'
King Alfonso then summoned Minaya Álvar Fáñez and Pedro
Bermúdez and took them aside with him into a room. 'Listen,
both of you' (he said). 'The Cid Campeador is doing me good
service, and he shall have the pardon he so richly deserves.
Tell him that I wish him to meet me in a full assembly, if he will,
and I have other messages for him from members of my court,
for Diego and Fernando, the Infantes of Carrión, desire to
marry his daughters. Deliver my message faithfully to him,
I beg of you, and tell the Cid that a marriage with the Infantes
of Carrión will bring him honour and increase his prestige.'
Minaya spoke and Pedro Bermúdez nodded agreement: 'We
shall put the matter to him as you suggest, but afterwards the
Cid must decide as he pleases.' (The King went on) 'Tell Ruy
Díaz that I shall call an assembly and meet him in whatever place
he chooses, for I leave the choice of the meeting-place to him.
I wish to show the Cid every possible consideration.' They
took leave of the King and, with all their company, returned to
Valencia. When the good Campeador heard that they had
arrived he rode out in all haste to meet them and, smiling as he
embraced them (he said), 'Welcome back, Minaya and Pedro
Bermúdez. Two such men as you would be hard to find any-
where. What news do you bring from my lord Alfonso the
King? Tell me if he is pleased and if he accepted my gift.'
Minaya replied: 'He is heartily pleased and is ready to receive
you into his favour again.' 'God be praised!' said the Cid, and
they began at once to tell him what Alfonso of León had proposed, namely that he should give his daughters in marriage
to the Infantes of Carrión and by so doing gain honour and
estate. They told him also that the King urged him very strongly
to do it. When the Cid heard this he pondered for a long time
(and then he said), 'I give thanks to our Lord Jesus Christ for this
favour. I was sent into exile and deprived of my property. It

con grand afán gané   lo que he yo.   [1935
A Dios lo gradesco   que del rrey he su gracia
e pídenme mis fijas   pora los ifantes de Carrión.
Ellos son mucho urgullosos   e an part en la cort,
d'este casamiento   non avría sabor,
mas pues lo conseja   el que más vale que nós,   [1940
fablemos en ello,   en la poridad seamos nós.
Afé Dios del cielo   que nos acuerde en lo mijor.'
'Con todo esto   a vós dixo Alfonso
que vos vernié a vistas   dó oviéssedes sabor;
querer vos ie ver   e darvos su amor,   [1945
acordar vos iedes después   a todo lo mejor.'

40r   Essora dixo el Cid: 'Plazme de coraçón.'
'Estas vistas   ó las ayades vós,'
dixo Minaya,   'vós sed sabidor.'
'Non era maravilla   si quisiesse el rrey Alfonso;   [1950
fasta dó lo fallássemos   buscarlo ir[i]emos nós,
por darle grand ondra   como a rrey de tierra.
Mas lo que él quisiere   esso queramos nós.
Sobre Tajo,   que es una agua cabdal,
ayamos vistas   quando lo quiere mio señor.'   [1955
Escrivién cartas,   bien las selló,
con dos cavalleros   luego las enbió:
'Lo que el rrey quisiere   esso ferá el Campeador.'

103

Al rrey ondrado   delant le echaron las cartas;
quando las vio,   de coraçón se paga: [1960
'Saludadme a Mio Cid,   el que en buen ora cinxo espada,
sean las vistas   d'estas *tres* semanas;
s[i] yo bivo só,   allí iré sin falla.'
Non lo detardan,   a Mio Cid se tornavan.
D'ella part e d'ella   pora la[s] vistas se adobavan;   [1965
¿quién vio por Castiella   tanta mula preciada
e tanto palafré   que bien anda,
cavallos gruessos   e corredores sin falla,
tanto buen pendón   meter en buenas astas,
escudos boclados   con oro e con plata,   [1970
mantos e pielles   e buenos cendales d'A[n]dria?

40v   Conduchos largos   el rrey enbiar mandava
a las aguas de Tajo   ó las vistas son aparejadas.
Con el rrey   atantas buenas conpañas;
los iffantes de Carrió[n]   mucho alegres andan,   [1975

has taken hard work for me to gain what I possess. Now, thanks be to God, I have won back the King's favour and I am being asked to give my daughters in marriage to the Infantes of Carrión. They are very proud young men and they belong to the King's household. (Left to myself) I should not wish for this marriage but, as the King, our overlord, urges it so strongly, let us discuss it quietly among ourselves, and may God guide us to do what is best.' (Minaya continued) 'In addition to this, King Alfonso said he would come to meet you in open assembly at a place to be chosen by you. He would like to see you and give you his pardon, and afterwards you could come to some agreement as to what is best.' 'I consent to that with all my heart,' said the Cid. 'It is for you to decide where the assembly is to be held,' said Minaya (and the Cid replied), 'It would not have been surprising if King Alfonso had summoned me to his presence, and I should have gone to honour him as my king and lord; but let us agree to whatever he decides. Let the assembly be held on the banks of the great river Tagus, but let the King fix the date.' Letters were written and the Cid's seal was attached to them; they said that the Cid would comply with the King's wishes, and they were sent off by two knights.

103

The letters were duly presented to the King, and when he had read them he was greatly pleased. 'Take my greetings to the Cid' (he said), 'and tell him that the assembly will take place in three weeks' time. If God spares my life I shall be there without fail.' The messengers went straight back to the Cid, and everywhere great preparations for the assembly were set on foot. Never had Castile seen so many costly mules, such high-stepping palfreys and strong, swift chargers, or so many pennons fixed on lances, and shields with gold and silver bosses, or so many mantles and fur cloaks and beautiful silks from Andros. The King ordered plentiful supplies of provisions to be sent to the banks of the Tagus where the assembly was being prepared, for he was himself bringing a large train of nobles. The Infantes of Carrión were in high feather; and, as they thought that with the

lo uno adebdan   e lo otro pagavan,
como ellos tenién,   crecer les ía la gana[n]cia,
quantos quisiessen   averes d'oro o de plata.
El rrey don Alfonso   apriessa cavalgava,
cuendes e podestades   e muy grandes mesnadas.   [1980
Los ifantes de Carrión   lievan grandes conpañas.
Con el rrey van leoneses   e mesnadas galizianas,
non son en cuenta,   sabet, las castellanas.
Sueltan las rriendas,   a las vistas se van adeliñadas.

104

Dentro en Valencia   Mio Cid el Campeador   [1985
non lo detarda,   pora las vistas se adobó.
Tanta gruessa mula   e tanto palafré de sazón,
tanta buena arma   e tanto buen cavallo corredor,
tanta buena capa   e mantos e pelliçones,
chicos e grandes   vestidos son de colores.   [1990
Minaya Álbar Fáñez   e aquel Pero Vermúez,
Martín Muñoz . . . .
e Martín Antolínez,   el burgalés de pro,   [1992b
el obispo don Jerónimo,   coranado mejor,
Álvar Álvarez   e Álvar Sa[l]vadórez,
Muño Gustioz,   el cavallero de pro,   [1995
Galind Garcíaz,   el que fue de Aragón,
éstos se adoban   por ir con el Campeador

41r   e todos los otros   que í son.
[A] Álbar Salvadórez   e Galind Garcíaz el de Aragón
a aquestos dos   mandó el Campeador   [2000
que curien a Valencia | d'alma e de coraçón   [2000b-01
e todos los [otros]   que en poder d'éssos fossen;   [2001b
las puertas del alcáçar . . . .
que non se abriessen   de día nin de noch;   [2002b
dentro es su mugier   e sus fijas amas a dos,
en que tiene su alma   e su coraçón,
e otras dueñas   que las sirven a su sabor;   [2005
rrecabdado ha,   como tan buen várón,
que del alcáçar   una salir non puede
fata ques' torne   el que en buen ora nasco.
Salién de Valencia,   aguijan e espolonavan,
tantos cavallos en diestro,   gruessos e corredores,   [2010
Mio Cid se los gañara,   que non ge los dieran en don;
yas' va pora las vistas   que con el rrey paró.
De un día es llegado antes   el rrey don Alfonso;

increase of wealth they expected they would have as much gold
and silver as they could wish for, they paid cash for some things
and obtained others on credit. Without delay King Alfonso
rode off with his retinue of counts and barons and a vast company
of vassals. The Infantes of Carrión had their own fine escort;
in the King's suite there were Leonese and Galicians, but the
Castilians outnumbered them all. With slackened reins the whole
company made its way towards the place of assembly.

104

In Valencia the Cid pressed on with his preparations. Many
were the sturdy mules, fine palfreys and swift chargers. Great
was the display of splendid armour, rich capes and fur tunics;
all men, high and low, were dressed in gay colours. Among the
great company of those who were preparing to go with the Cid
to the assembly were Minaya Álvar Fáñez, Pedro Bermúdez,
Martín Muñoz, worthy Martín Antolínez of Burgos, the revered
cleric Bishop Jerome, Álvar Álvarez, Álvar Salvadórez, Muño
Gustioz, a distinguished knight, and Galindo Garcíaz from
Aragon. Álvar Salvadórez and Galindo Garcíaz, however,
were ordered by the Campeador to keep close guard over
Valencia, and all who remained there were placed under their
authority. (The Cid's orders were that) the gates of the fortress
which housed his dearly beloved wife and daughters, and their
ladies in waiting, should be kept closed night and day. In this
way he ensured that none of them could leave the fortress until
he returned. The Cid's party left Valencia and rode off quickly,
taking with them a great many strong, swift chargers which the
Cid had won for himself in battle and had not received as a
gift. In this fashion the Campeador set out for the assembly
arranged with the King. King Alfonso, who had arrived on the

quando vieron que vinié el buen Campeador
rrecebirlo salen con tan grand onor.   [2015
Dón lo ovo a ojo el que en buen ora nasco,
a todos los sos estar los mandó
sinon a estos cavalleros que querié de coraçó[n];
con unos *quinze* a tierras’ firió,
como lo comidía el que en buen ora nació,   [2020
los inojos e las manos en tierra los fincó,
las yerbas del campo a dientes las tomó,
41v llorando de los ojos tanto avié el gozo mayor;
assí sabe dar omildança a Alfonso so señor.
De aquesta guisa a los pies le cayó;   [2025
tan grand pesar ovo el rrey don Alfonso:
‘Levantados en pie, ya Cid Campeador,
besad las manos ca los pies no[n];
si esto non feches, non avredes mi amor.’
Inojos fitos sedié el Campeador: [2030
‘Merced vos pido a vós, mio natural señor,
assí estando, dédesme vuestra amor,
que lo oyan quantos aquí son.’   [2032b
Dixo el rrey: ‘Esto feré d’alma e de coraçón;
aquí vos perdono e dovos mi amor
[e] en todo mio rreino parte desde oy.’   [2035
Fabló Mio Cid e dixo:
‘¡Merced! Yo lo rrecibo, Alfonso mio señor;   [2036b
gradéscolo a Dios del cielo e después a vós
e a estas mesnadas que están aderredor.’
Inojos fitos las manos le besó,
levós’ en pie e en la bóca l’ saludó.   [2040
Todos los demás d’esto avién sabor;
pesó a Álbar Díaz e a Garcí Ordóñez.
Fabló Mio Cid e dixo esta rrazón:
‘Esto gradesco al Criador   [2043b
quando he la gracia de don Alfonso mio señor;
valer me á Dios de día e de noch.   [2045
Fuéssedes mi huésped, si vos ploguiesse, señor.’
Dixo el rrey: ‘Non es aguisado oy,
42r vós agora llegastes e nós viniemos anoch;
mio huésped seredes, Cid Campeador,
e cras feremos lo que ploguiere a vós.’   [2050
Besóle la mano, Mio Cid lo otorgó.
Essora se le omillan los iffantes de Carrión:
‘¡Omillámosnos, Cid, en buen ora nasquiestes vós!

previous day, went out when he saw the Cid approaching, with
all due ceremony, to meet him. As soon as the Cid caught sight
of the King he ordered all his men to halt, while he, with some
fifteen of his chosen knights, dismounted, and then he carried
out what he had planned to do. He knelt down on his hands and
knees on the ground and with his teeth he pulled up a mouthful
of grass. With tears of joy streaming from his eyes he showed
in this way his complete submission to his liege lord. Alfonso,
however, was distressed at this display of humility, and he said:
'Stand up, Cid Campeador, and kiss my hands but not my feet.
You will have no pardon from me unless you do so.' But the
Cid remained on his knees and said: 'I beg a favour of you, my
liege lord, that as I kneel here you grant me your pardon in the
hearing of all this assembled company.' The King replied: 'I
shall do so with all my heart. Here and now I pardon you and
restore you to my favour and welcome your return to my
kingdom.' The Cid answered: 'I receive your pardon with
gratitude, my lord Alfonso. For it I thank God, then you and
these my vassals who stand here with me.' Still on his knees,
the Cid kissed the King's hands, and then, rising to his feet, he
kissed him on the mouth. The whole assembly rejoiced at this,
except Álvar Díaz and García Ordóñez, who were annoyed.
The Cid spoke again and said: 'I give thanks to our heavenly
Father that I am restored to my Lord Alfonso's favour; God's
grace will be with me always. Now, my lord, if you will give
your consent, I should like you to be my guest.' But the King
replied: 'That would not be right or suitable, for you have only
just arrived, and we have been here since last night. You, Cid,
must be my guest, and tomorrow you shall have your way.'
The Cid agreed to this and kissed the King's hand. The Infantes
of Carrión chose this moment to pay their respects. They said:
'Greetings to you, Cid, whom good fortune always attends.

En quanto podemos   andamos en vuestro pro.'
Rrespuso Mio Cid: '¡Assí lo mande el Criador!'   [2055
Mio Cid Rruy Díaz   que en ora buena nasco,
en aquel día   del rrey so huésped fue;
non se puede fartar d'él,   tántol' querié de coraçón,
catándol' sedié la barba,   que tan aínal' creciera.
Maravíllanse de Mio Cid   quantos que í son.   [2060
És día es passado   e entrada es la noch;
otro día mañana   claro salié el sol,
el Campeador   a los sos lo mandó
que adobassen cozina   pora quantos que í son.
De tal guisa los paga   Mio Cid el Campeador,   [2065
todos eran alegres   e acuerdan en una rrazón:
passado avié *tres* años   no comieran mejor.
Al otro día mañana,   assí como salió el sol,
el obispo don Jerónimo   la missa cantó.
Al salir de la missa   todos juntados son,   [2070
non lo tardó el rrey,   la rrazón conpeçó:
'¡Oídme, las escuelas,   cuendes e ifançones!

42v   Cometer quiero un rruego   a Mio Cid el Campeador,
assí lo mande Christus   que sea a so pro.
Vuestras fijas vos pido,   don Elvira e doña Sol,   [2075
que las dedes por mugieres   a los ifantes de Carrión.
Seméjam' el casamiento   ondrado e con grant pro,
ellos vos las piden   e mándovoslo yo.
D'ella e d'ella parte   quantos que aquí son,
los míos e los vuestros   que sean rrogadores;   [2080
¡dándoslas, Mio Cid,   sí vos vala el Criador!'
'Non abría fijas de casar,'   rrespuso el Campeador,
'ca non han grant edad   e de días pequeñas son.
De grandes nuevas son   los ifantes de Carrión,
pertenecen pora mis fijas   e aun pora mejores.   [2085
Yo las engendré amas   e criásteslas vós,
entre yo y ellas   en vuestra merced somos nós;
afellas en vuestra mano   don Elvira e doña Sol,
dadlas a qui quisiéredes vós,   ca yo pagado só.'
'Gracias', dixo el rrey,   'a vós e a tod' esta cort.'   [2090
Luego se levantaron   los iffantes de Carrión,
ban besar las manos   al que en ora buena nació,
camearon las espadas   ant'el rrey don Alfonso.
Fabló el rrey don Alfonso   como tan buen señor:
'Grado e gracias, Cid,   como tan bueno   e primero
                                  al Criador   [2095

We wish to do all we can to prove our friendship to you.'
'God grant it!' was the Cid's answer. That day the Cid was the
guest of the King, who could not do enough to show him his
love and favour. He could not keep his eyes off the Cid's beard,
which had grown so long in such a short time. All those present
at the assembly were much impressed by the Cid's appearance.
The day passed and night followed, and the next morning when
the sun shone out brightly the Cid ordered his men to prepare
a feast for the whole company. The Cid gave them such splendid
fare that they were more than satisfied, and one and all declared
that for fully three years they had not had such a meal. At
sunrise on the following day Bishop Jerome said mass, and
afterwards, when they were all assembled again, the King
addressed them thus: 'Hear me, my vassals, counts and baronets!
I wish to make a proposal to the Cid Campeador, and may God
grant that it turn out to his advantage. I ask the hands of your
daughters, Doña Elvira and Doña Sol, in marriage for the
Infantes of Carrión. I consider this marriage an honourable and
advantageous alliance. They ask you for your daughters and I
support their petition. Let sponsors be chosen from both sides
among my vassals and yours who are present at this assembly.
Give your consent, Cid, as you hope for God's grace.' 'I ought
not to give my daughters in marriage,' replied the Cid, 'for they
are hardly grown up and still too young. Besides, the Infantes
come of a distinguished family and could aspire to far better
marriages. Though they are my daughters, you brought them up
and both they and I are subject to you in this matter. I am content
to place them in your hands to dispose of as you choose.' 'I
thank you,' said the King, 'and all those assembled here.' The
Infantes of Carrión rose and approached the Cid to kiss his hands,
and then in the King's presence they exchanged swords with him
(in token of kinship). The King then spoke, as his liege lord, to
the Cid, saying: 'I give thanks to God and then to you, my good

43r   quem' dades vuestras fijas   pora los ifantes de Carrión.
D'aquí las prendo por mis manos   don Elvira e doña Sol
e dolas por veladas   a los ifantes de Carrión.
Yo las caso a vuestras fijas   con vuestro amor,
al Criador plega   que ayades ende sabor.   [2100
Afellos en vuestras manos   los ifantes de Carrión,
ellos vayan convusco,   ca d'aquén me torno yo.
Trezientos marcos de plata   en ayuda les do yo
que metan en sus bodas   o dó quisiéredes vós;
pues fueren en vuestro poder   en Valencia la mayor,   [2105
los yernos e las fijas   todos vuestros fijos son;
lo que vos ploguiere   d'ellos fet, Campeador.'
Mio Cid ge los rrecibe,   las manos le besó:
'Mucho vos lo gradesco,   como a rrey e a señor.
Vós casades mis fijas   ca non ge las do yo.'   [2110
Las palabras son puestas . . . .
que otro día mañana, | quando salie*s*[s]e el sol,   [2111b-12
ques' tornasse cada uno   dón salidos son.   [2112b
Aquís' metió en nuevas   Mio Cid el Campeador:
tanta gruessa mula   e tanto palafré de sazón,
tantas buenas vestiduras   que d'alfaya son,   [2116
conpeçó Mio Cid a dar   a quien quiere prender so don; [2115
cada uno lo que pide   nadi nol' dize de no.   [2117
Mio Cid de los cavallos   *sessaenta* dio en don.

43v   Todos son pagados de las vistas,   quantos que í son;
partirse quieren   que entrada era la noch.   [2120
El rrey a los ifantes   a las manos les tomó,
metiólos en poder   de Mio Cid el Campeador:
'Evad aquí vuestros fijos,   quando vuestros yernos son;
oy de más sabed   qué fer d'ellos, Campeador.'
'Gradéscolo, rrey,   e prendo vuestro don;   [2125
Dios que está en cielo   dém' dent buen galardón.'
Sobr'el so cavallo Bavieca   Mio Cid salto dava:
'Aquí lo digo   ante mio señor el rrey Alfonso:
qui quiere ir a las bodas   o rrecebir mi don,
d'aquend vaya comigo,   cuedo quel' avrá pro.   [2130

105

Yo vos pido merced   a vós, rrey natural:
pues que casades mis fijas   assí como a vós plaz,
dad manero a qui las dé,   quando vós las tomades;
non ge las daré yo con mi mano,   nin de[n]d non se alabarán.'
Rrespondió el rrey: 'Afé aquí Álbar Fáñez,   [2135

Cid, for your gracious permission to marry your daughters
to the Infantes of Carrión. I take them now and with my own
hands I give them to the Infantes to be their lawful wedded
wives. I marry your daughters with your approval, and may God
grant that this marriage may bring you satisfaction. I deliver
the Infantes into your keeping to go with you, for I am about
to return. I give them three hundred silver marks to help with the
expenses of the wedding or to be used as you think fit. Your
sons-in-law and their brides are all your children now, and will
be under your authority in the great city of Valencia, so make
any arrangements for them that you choose.' The Cid received
the Infantes from the King and kissed his hands, saying: 'I
thank you with all my heart as my king and lord, but it is you,
not I, who are giving my daughters in marriage.' The marriage
promises having been given, it was agreed that at daybreak on
the following morning each party should return home. Then the
Cid attracted great attention by presenting to anyone who liked
to accept them many strong mules, fine palfreys and beautiful
costly garments. Every man (took) what he wanted and no one
refused the offer. The Cid gave away sixty horses all told. All
those who had attended the assembly were well pleased, but now
that night had fallen they were eager to be off. The King took
the Infantes by the hand and delivered them into the Cid's
keeping. (He said) 'Here are your sons, for they are now your
sons-in-law. Henceforward, Campeador, they are your responsi-
bility.' 'I thank you, King Alfonso' (said the Cid), 'and I accept
your gift. God reward me for it with his blessing from on high.'
The Cid sprang on to his horse, Babieca, (calling out) 'I say here,
in King Alfonso's presence, that anyone who wishes to attend
the wedding and receive a gift from me may go with me now.
I am sure they will find it worth their while.

105

I beg a favour of you as my lawful king; you are marrying
my daughters as you think best, and I ask you to appoint a
sponsor into whose care I can entrust them, since you are taking
them from me. I shall not give them away myself so that (the
Infantes) may not have that satisfaction.' The King called Álvar

prendellas con vuestras manos   e daldas a los ifantes,
assí como yo las prendo d'aquent,   como si fosse delant,
sed padrino d'el*l*as   a tod' el velar;
quando vos juntáredes comigo,   quem' digades la verdat.'
Dixo Álbar Fáñez: 'Señor, afé que me plaz.'   [2140

106

Tod' esto es puesto,   sabed, en grant rrecabdo.
'Ya rrey don Alfonso,   señor tan ondrado,
44r   d'estas vistas que oviemos,   de mí tomedes algo.
Tráyovos *veínte* palafrés,   éstos bien adobados,
e *treínta* cavallos corredores,   éstos bien ensellados;   [2145
tomad aquesto   e beso vuestras manos.'
Dixo el rrey don Alfonso: 'Mucho me avedes enbargado;
rrecibo este don   que me avedes mandado;
plega al Criador   con todos los sos sanctos
este plazer | quem' feches   que bien sea galardonado. [2149b-50
Mio Cid Rruy Díaz,   mucho me avedes ondrado,
de vós bien só servido   e tengon' por pagado,
aún bivo seyendo   de mí ayades algo.
A Dios vos acomiendo,   d'estas vistas me parto.
¡Afé Dios del cielo   que lo ponga en buen logar!'   [2155

107

Yas' espidió Mio Cid   de so señor Alfonso,
non quiere quel' escurra,   quitól' dessí luego.
Veriedes cavalleros   que bien andantes son
besar las manos   [e] espedirse del rrey Alfonso:
'Merced vos sea   e fazednos este perdón: [2160
iremos en poder de Mio Cid   a Valencia la mayor,
seremos a las bodas   de los ifantes de Carrión
e de las fijas de Mio Cid,   de don Elvira e doña Sol.'
Esto plogo al rrey   e a todos los soltó,
la conpaña del Cid crece   e la del rrey mengó,   [2165
44v   grandes son las yentes   que van con el Canpeador,
adeliñan pora Valencia,   la que en buen punto ganó.
E a don Fernando e a don Diego   aguardarlos mandó
a Pero Vermúez   e Muño Gustioz,
en casa de Mio Cid   non á dos mejores,   [2170
que sopiessen sos mañas   de los ifantes de Carrión.
E va í A[s]sur Gonçález,   que era bullidor,
que es largo de lengua   mas en lo ál non es tan pro.

Fáñez to him and said: 'You must take the brides by their hands and give them to the Infantes, just as I take them from the Cid as if they were present here. You be the sponsor for them throughout the marriage ceremony. When we meet next you can give me an account of all that happens.' Álvar Fáñez replied: 'My lord, I shall be pleased to do this.'

106

In this way all the details were very carefully arranged. (Before taking his leave the Cid spoke as follows) 'My honoured lord, King Alfonso, you must take something of mine away with you from this assembly. I have brought you twenty palfreys with all their trappings and thirty horses with their saddles. I kiss your hands and beg you to accept this present.' Alfonso replied: 'Your generosity embarrasses me, but I accept your gift and pray God and all his saints to reward you for the pleasure you have given me. Ruy Díaz Cid Campeador, you have brought me great honour and have served me well. I am well satisfied, and as long as I live I shall protect and favour you. I commend you to God as I leave this assembly and I pray that, by God's grace, all will turn out for the best.'

107

Finally the Cid took leave of King Alfonso and then rode off at once, not wishing the King to escort him for the usual short distance. You should have seen the numbers of splendid knights who came to kiss the King's hands and take formal leave of him! (They said) 'Grant us your permission to join the Cid's retinue and go with him to the great city of Valencia to attend the wedding of his daughters, Doña Elvira and Doña Sol, with the Infantes of Carrión.' The King gladly agreed to free them from their obligations to him, and so many wished to accompany the Cid that his party increased in number while the King's grew smaller. They rode away in the direction of Valencia, which the Cid had so successfully captured. The Campeador asked Pedro Bermúdez and Muño Gustioz—two better men he could not have found among those of his household—to attend on Fernando and Diego and learn of their ways. With them also came (their brother) Ansur González, a noisy, boisterous fellow, a great talker but otherwise a man of no great importance. The

Grant ondra les dan   a los ifantes de Carrión.
Afelos en Valencia,   la que Mio Cid gañó,   [2175
quando a ella assomaron   los gozos son mayores.
Dixo Mio Cid a don Pero   e a Muño Gustioz:
'Dadles un rreyal   a los ifantes de Carrión,
[e] vós con ellos sed,   que assí vos lo mando yo.
Quando viniere la mañana,   que apuntare el sol,   [2180
verán a sus esposas,   a don Elvira e a doña Sol.'

108

Todos essa noch   fueron a sus posadas,
Mio Cid el Campeador   al alcáçar entrava,
rrecibiólo doña Ximena   e sus fijas amas:
'¡Venides, Campeador,   en buena ora cinxiestes espada!   [2185
¡Muchos días vos veamos   con los ojos de las caras!'
'¡Grado al Criador,   vengo, mugier ondrada!
Yernos vos adugo   de que avremos ondrança;
¡gradídmelo, mis fijas,   ca bien vos he casadas!'
45r   Besáronle las manos   la mugier e las fijas amas   [2190
e todas las dueñas   que las sirven:

109

'¡Grado al Criador   e a vós, Cid, barba vellida!
Todo lo que vós feches   es de buena guisa;
non serán menguadas   en todos vuestros días.'
'Quando vós nos casáredes   bien seremos rricas.'   [2195

110

'Mugier doña Ximena,   ¡grado al Criador!
A vós digo, mis fijas,   don Elvira e doña Sol:
d'este vu[e]stro casamiento   creçremos en onor,
mas bien sabed verdad   que non lo levanté yo;
pedidas vos ha e rrogadas   el mio señor Alfonso   [2200
atan firmemientre   e de todo coraçón
que yo nulla cosa   nol' sope dezir de no.
Metívos en sus manos,   fijas amas a dos,
bien me lo creades   que él vos casa, ca non yo.'

111

Pensaron de adobar   essora el palacio,   [2205
por el suelo e suso   tan bien encortinado,
tanta pórpola e tanto xamed   e tanto paño preciado.

Infantes were shown every mark of honour and respect, and when they reached the conquered city of Valencia they were given a great welcome. Then the Cid said to Don Pedro and Muño Gustioz: 'I bid you find suitable lodging for the Infantes of Carrión and remain with them there. Tomorrow morning when the sun is up they may see their brides, Doña Elvira and Doña Sol.'

108

That night they all went to their quarters, and the Cid entered the castle, where he was met by Doña Jimena and his two daughters. 'Welcome to you on your return, Campeador, successful as ever in all you undertake! May you be spared to us for many years to come!' (The Cid replied) 'Thanks be to God, my noble wife, I have returned, bringing you sons-in-law who will enhance the honour of our family. Thank me, my daughters, for the good marriages I have arranged for you.' 'Mother and daughters kissed his hands, as did all the ladies who were in attendance on them.

109

(Doña Jimena said) 'Thanks be to God and to you, my honoured husband, for all you do is well done. Your daughters will lack for nothing as long as you live.' (The two girls added) 'Since you have arranged these marriages, we are sure to be very rich.'

110

(The Cid, however, continued as follows) 'I join you, Doña Jimena, in thanks to God. To you, my daughters, I say that we shall gain honour by this marriage, but you must know the truth. I did not raise the matter myself; it was King Alfonso who asked for your hands and pressed me so hard and earnestly that I could by no means refuse. I placed you both in his hands, so it is he who is giving you in marriage and not I.'

111

They now began to get the castle hall ready for the festivities. Rich silks, satins and other precious cloths were hung on the walls and laid on the floor. What a pleasure it would be to have

Sabor abriedes de ser   e de comer en el palacio.
Todos sus cavalleros   apriessa son juntados;
por los iffantes de Carrión   essora enbiaron,   [2210
cavalgan los iffantes,   adelant adeliñavan al palacio
con buenas vestiduras   e fuertemientre adobados,
de pie e a sabor,   ¡Dios, qué quedos entraron!

45v   Rrecibiólos Mio Cid   con todos sus vas[s]allos;
a él e a su mugier   delant se le[s] omillaron   [2215
e ivan posar   en un precioso escaño.
Todos los de Mio Cid   tan bien son acordados,
están parando mientes   al que en buen ora nasco.
El Campeador   en pie es levantado:
'Pues que a fazer lo avemos,   ¿por qué lo imos tardando? [2220
¡Venit acá, Álbar Fáñez,   el que yo quiero e amo!
Afé amas mis fijas,   métolas en vuestra mano,
sabedes que al rrey   assí ge lo he mandado,
no lo quiero fallir por nada   de quanto á í parado,
a los ifantes de Carrión   dadlas con vuestra mano   [2225
e prendan bendiciones   e vayamos rrecabdando.'
Esto[n]z dixo Minaya: 'Esto faré yo de grado.'
Levántanse derechas   e metiógelas en mano;
a los ifantes de Carrión   Minaya va fablando:
'Afevos delant Minaya,   amos sodes ermanos,   [2230
por mano del rrey Alfonso   que a mí lo ovo mandado
dovos estas dueñas,   amas son fijas d'algo,
que las tomássedes por mugieres   a ondra e a rrecabdo.'
Amos las rreciben   d'amor e de grado,
a Mio Cid e a su mugier   van besar la mano.   [2235
Quando ovieron aquesto fecho,   salieron del palacio,
pora Sancta María   apriessa adeliñando;

46r   el obispo don Jerónimo   vistiós' tan privado,
a la puerta de la eclegia   sediéllos sperando;
dioles bendictiones,   la missa á cantado.   [2240
Al salir de la eclesia   cavalgaron tan privado,
a la glera de Valencia   fuera dieron salto;
¡Dios, qué bien tovieron armas   el Cid e sus vassallos!
Tres cavallos cameó   el que en buen ora nasco.
Mio Cid de lo que veyé   mucho era pagado,   [2245
los ifantes de Carrión   bien an cavalgado.
Tórnanse con las dueñas,   a Valencia an entrado,
rricas fueron las bodas   en el alcáçar ondrado,
e al otro día fizo Mio Cid   fincar siete tablados;
antes que entrassen a yantar   todos los quebrantaron. [2250

been one of the party and enjoy the good fare! So all the knights came crowding to the palace. When the Infantes of Carrión were summoned they rode to the castle, magnificently arrayed in all their finery. Having dismounted, they walked into the hall with propriety, and how quietly they entered! Surrounded by his vassals, the Cid received them; they bowed low before him and his wife, Doña Jimena, and went to sit down on a richly carved bench. The Cid's wise and trusty followers were all attention when he rose to speak: 'As this ceremony is to be performed, why should we delay? Come here, my well loved Álvar Fáñez. Here are my two daughters, whom I place in your hands, as I promised the King to do. I wish to carry out everything exactly as it was agreed upon. Give them to the Infantes of Carrión and let them receive the marriage blessing, and in this way the whole thing will be settled.' Minaya replied: 'I shall gladly do so.' The girls stood up and the Cid handed them over to Minaya, who addressed the Infantes in these words: 'I, Minaya, stand before you two brothers. The King has passed his authority on to me, so on his behalf I give you these two noble ladies to be your lawful wives.' The Infantes received their brides with every sign of affection and pleasure, and went up to kiss the hands of the Cid and Doña Jimena. When this ceremony was over, the whole party left the palace and made their way at once to the church of Santa María, where Bishop Jerome, having quickly donned his vestments, was waiting for them at the door. He blessed them and sang the mass. On leaving the church all the men went off at a gallop to the sea-shore, where the Cid and his vassals gave a splendid display of arms, the Cid changing his mount three times. He was well pleased with the whole display and with the skill in riding shown by the Infantes. They then joined the ladies and returned to Valencia. The wedding festivities were celebrated with great magnificence in the castle. On the following day the Cid had seven plank turrets set up, which were all knocked down before the company went in to the

Quinze días conplidos   en las bodas duraron,
cerca de los *quinze* días   yas' van los fijos d'algo.
Mio Cid don Rrodrigo,   el que en buen ora nasco,
entre palafrés e mulas   e corredores cavallos,
en bestias sines ál   *ciento á* mandados;   [2255
mantos e pelliçones   e otros vestidos largos;
non fueron en cuenta   los averes monedados.
Los vassallos de Mio Cid   assí son acordados,
cada uno por sí   sos dones avién dados.
Qui aver quiere prender   bien era abastado;   [2260
46v rricos' tornan a Castiella   los que a las bodas llegaron.
Yas' ivan partiendo   aquestos ospedados,
espidiendos' de Rruy Díaz,   el que en buen ora nasco,
e a todas las dueñas   e a los fijos d'algo;
por pagados se parten   de Mio Cid e de sus vassallos,   [2265
grant bien dizen d'ellos,   ca será aguisado.
Mucho eran alegres   Diego e Fernando,
estos fueron fijos   del conde don Gonçalo.
Venidos son a Castiella   aquestos ospedados,
el Cid e sos yernos   en Valencia son rrastados.   [2270
Í moran los ifantes   bien cerca de dos años,
los amores que les fazen   mucho eran sobejanos.
Alegre era el Cid   e todos sus vassallos.
¡Plega a Sancta María   e al Padre sancto
ques' pague d'és casamiento Mio Cid   o el que lo
                              [ovo *a* algo]! [2275
Las coplas d'este cantar   aquís' van acabando.
¡El Criador vos vala   con todos los sos sanctos!

banquet. The celebrations lasted fifteen whole days, after which the nobles began to leave for home. The Cid gave them palfreys, mules and chargers—a hundred in all—mantles and fur tunics and other fine garments, together with vast sums of money. The Cid's vassals too with one accord gave them rich presents. Everyone who wished to accept them was well supplied with these fine gifts, and all who had come to the wedding returned to Castile rich men. The guests departed, bidding farewell to the Cid, the ladies and the noble knights. All were in high spirits as they parted from the Cid and his vassals, and praised their hosts, as indeed was only right. Diego and Fernando, the sons of Don Gonzalo, were highly delighted with it all. When the guests went back to Castile the Cid and his sons-in-law stayed in Valencia, where the Infantes remained for nearly two years and were the objects of much friendly attention, which gave great pleasure to the Cid and his vassals. Holy Mary and our Heavenly Father grant that this marriage bring satisfaction to the Cid and to the King, who expected so much from it! Here the verses of this song come to an end. God and all His holy saints protect you!

112

En Valencia seí Mio Cid   con todos sus vassallos,
con él amos sus yernos   los ifantes de Carrión.
Yaziés' en un escaño,   durmié el Campeador,   *[2280*
mala sobrevienta,   sabed, que les cuntió:
saliós' de la rred   e desatós' el león.
En grant miedo se vieron   por medio de la cort;
enbraçan los mantos   los del Campeador
e cercan el escaño   e fincan sobre so señor.   *[2285*

47r   Ferrán Gonçález . . . .
non vio allí dós' alçasse,   nin cámara abierta nin torre,   *[2286b*
metiós' so'l escaño,   tanto ovo el pavor.
Diego Gonçález   por la puerta salió,
diziendo de la boca: '¡Non veré Carrión!'
Tras una viga lagar   metiós' con grant pavor,   *[2290*
el manto e el brial   todo suzio lo sacó.
En esto despertó   el que en buen ora nació,
vio cercado el escaño   de sus buenos varones:
'¿Qué's esto, mesnadas,   o qué queredes vós?'
'Ya señor ondrado,   rrebata nos dio el león.'   *[2295*
Mio Cid fincó el cobdo,   en pie se levantó,
el manto trae al cuello   e adeliñó pora'[l] león.
El león, quando lo vio,   assí envergonçó,
ante Mio Cid la cabeça premió   e el rrostro fincó.
Mio Cid don Rrodrigo   al cuello lo tomó   *[2300*
e liévalo adestrando,   en la rred le metió.
A maravilla lo han   quantos que í son
e tornáronse al palacio   pora la cort.
Mio Cid por sos yernos   demandó e no los falló,
maguer los están llamando,   ninguno non rresponde.   *[2305*
Quando los fallaron,   assí vinieron sin color,
non viestes tal juego   como iva por la cort;
mandó lo vedar   Mio Cid el Campeador.
Muchos' tovieron por enbaídos   los ifantes de Carrión,
fiera cosa les pesa   d'esto que les cuntió.   *[2310*

113

Ellos en esto estando,   dón avién grant pesar,
47v   fuerças de Marruecos   Valencia vienen cercar,
cinquaenta mill tiendas   fincadas ha de las cabdales,
aquéste era el rrey Búcar,   sil' ouyestes contar.

112

The Cid was at Valencia with his followers, and with him too were his sons-in-law, the Infantes of Carrión. The Cid was lying asleep on his couch when they had a nasty surprise. The lion struggled loose and escaped from his net. Great fear seized them in the middle of the hall, and the Cid's men wrapped their cloaks about their arms and surrounded the couch to protect their lord. Fernando González (one of the Infantes) looked round for somewhere to hide, but found no open door nor tower; so in his panic he crawled under the couch. Diego González made off through the door, crying: 'I shall never see (my home in) Carrión again!' In his terror he got behind the wine press and made his cloak and tunic all filthy. At that moment the Cid awoke and saw his couch surrounded by his brave followers. 'What is the matter?' he asked. 'What are you doing here, my good men?' 'Honoured lord,' they replied, 'the lion has given us all a fright.' The Cid leaned on his elbow and rose to his feet, and leaving his cloak over his shoulder he walked towards the lion. When the lion saw him, it was so taken aback that it hung its head and nosed the ground. Don Rodrigo took it by the neck, led it along with his right hand and put it in the net. All the onlookers, amazed at his courage, returned through the hall to the apartment. When the Cid asked for his sons-in-law they were nowhere to be found. Everyone was calling to them, but they made no answer. When they were discovered they were pale with fear. You never saw such jesting and mockery as then went round the palace. The Cid forbade it to continue, but the Infantes felt that they had been put to shame and deeply resented all that had happened.

113

While the young men were still grieving over their discomfiture, the forces of King Búcar, of whom you may have heard, arrived from Morocco to lay siege to Valencia, and fifty thousand great tents were pitched.

114

Alegravas' el Cid   e todos sus varones   [*2315*
que les crece la ganancia,   grado al Criador;
mas, sabed, de cuer les pesa   a los ifantes de Carrión
ca veyén tantas tiendas de moros   de que non avié[*n*] sabor.
Amos ermanos   apart salidos son:
'Catamos la ganancia   e la pérdida no,   [*2320*
ya en esta batalla   a entrar abremos nós,
esto es aguisado   por non ver Carrión,
bibdas rremandrán   fijas del Campeador.'
Oyó la poridad   aquel Muño Gustioz,
vino con estas nuevas   a Mio Cid Rruy Díaz el Canpeador:[*2325*
'Evades qué pavor han   vuestros yernos tan osados,
por entrar en batalla   desean Carrión.
Idlos conortar,   sí vos vala el Criador,
que sean en paz   e non ayan í rración.
Nós convusco la vençremos   e valer nos ha el Criador.' [*2330*
Mio Cid don Rrodrigo   sonrrisando salió:
'Dios vos salve, yernos,   ifantes de Carrión.
En braços tenedes mis fijas   tan blancas como el sol.
Yo desseo lides   e vós a Carrión,
en Valencia folgad   a todo vuestro sabor   [*2335*
ca d'aquellos moros   yo só sabidor,
arrancar me los trevo   con la merced del Criador.'

[*Lacuna of about fifty lines: one folio missing*]

115

48r   'aún vea el ora   que vos meresca dos tanto.'   [*2338*
En una conpaña   tornados son amos,
assí lo otorga don Pero   cuemo se alaba Ferrando;   [*2340*
plogo a Mio Cid   e a todos sos vassallos:
'Aún, si Dios quisiere   e el Padre que está en alto,
amos los mios yernos   buenos serán en ca[*m*]po.'
Esto van diziendo   e las yentes se allegando,
en la hueste de los moros   los atamores sonando,   [*2345*
a marav[*i*]lla lo avién   muchos d'essos cristianos
ca nunqua lo vieran,   ca nuevos son llegados.
Más se maravillan   entre Diego e Ferrando,
por la su voluntad   non serién allí llegados.
Oíd lo que fabló   el que en buen ora nasco: [*2350*
'¡Ala, Pero Vermúez,   el mio sobrino caro!
Cúriesme a [*don*] Diego   e cúriesme a don Fernando,

114

The Cid and all his men were delighted at the prospect of the booty which, with God's help, they hoped to win, but the Infantes of Carrión were heavy at heart at the sight of so many Moorish tents, which was not at all to their taste. The two brothers went aside and consulted together. 'When we made this match' (they said) 'we thought of what we should gain and not of what we might lose. Now we shall have to take part in this battle, and it looks as if we shall never see Carrión again, and the Cid's daughters will be left widows.' Muño Gustioz overheard their private conversation and reported it to the Cid, saying: 'Here are your brave sons-in-law longing to return to Carrión instead of going into battle. Go and comfort them, in the name of Heaven! Tell them to stay quietly behind and take no part in the fighting. With God's help we shall be victorious under your leadership.' The Cid came out, smiling, and said: 'God keep you, my sons-in-law, Infantes of Carrión! You have but lately married my fair daughters and so may be excused the fight. I long for battles and you for Carrión. You may take your ease in Valencia, for I am a match for any Moors. I can be certain of defeating them with God on my side.'

[*Lacuna of about fifty lines: one folio missing*]

115

'... I hope I may have the chance of repaying you twice over.' Then the two of them returned together, and Don Pedro confirmed all Fernando's boasting. The Cid and his followers were pleased, and the Campeador said: 'Please God my two sons-in-law will yet prove good men in the field.' In the meantime the troops were assembling and the drums were sounding in the Moorish host. Many Christians were struck with amazement at the sight of these drums, for they had only just arrived and had never seen such things before. Diego and Fernando were even more amazed, and would not have been there of their own accord. Then the Cid spoke, saying: 'Come, now, Pedro Bermúdez, my dear nephew, will you look after Diego and Fernando,

mios yernos amos a dos,   la cosa que mucho amo,
ca los moros, con Dios,   non fincarán en canpo.'

116
'Yo vos digo, Cid,   por toda caridad,   [2355
que oy los ifantes   a mí por amo non abrán;
cúrielos qui quier,   ca d'ellos poco m'incal.
Yo con los míos   ferir quiero delant,
vós con los vuestros   firmemientre a la çaga tengades,
si cueta fuere,   bien me podredes uviar.'   [2360
Aquí llegó   Minaya Álbar Fáñez:
'¡Oíd, ya Cid,   Canpeador leal!   [2361b
Esta batalla   el Criador la ferá
e vós tan dinno   que con él avedes part.
Mandadno' los ferir   de quál part vos semejar,
48v   el debdo que á cada uno   a conplir será.   [2365
Ver lo hemos con Dios   e con la vuestra auze.'
Dixo Mio Cid: 'Ayamos más de vagar.'
Afevos el obispo don Jerónimo   muy bien armado,
paravas' delant al Campeador   siempre con la buen auze:
'Oy vos dix la missa   de Sancta Trinidade;   [2370
por esso salí de mi tierra   e vin vos buscar
por sabor que avía   de algún moro matar;
mi orden e mis manos   querría las ondrar
e a estas feridas   yo quiero ir delant.
Pendón trayo a corças   e armas de señal,   [2375
si ploguiesse a Dios   querríalas ensayar,
mio coraçón   que pudiesse folgar
e vós, Mio Cid,   de mí más vos pagar.
Si este amor non' feches,   yo de vós me quiero quitar.'
Essora dixo Mio Cid: 'Lo que vós queredes plazme.   [2380
Afé los moros a ojo,   idlos ensayar.
Nós d'aquent veremos   cómo lidia el abat.'

117
El obispo don Jerónimo   priso a espolonada
e ívalos ferir   a cabo del albergada.
Por la su ventura   e Dios quel' amava   [2385
a los primeros colpes   dos moros matava de la lanç[a];
el astil á quebrado   e metió mano al espada,
ensayavas' el obispo,   ¡Dios, qué bien lidiava!
Dos mató con lança   e *cinco* con el espada;

my two beloved sons-in-law, for with the help of God the Moors will be driven from the field?'

116

'For pity's sake, Cid, I refuse to be responsible for the Infantes today. Let anyone who likes take that on, as I have little concern for them. I wish to make a frontal attack with my men while you hold the rear with yours; if I am in any difficulty you will be able to come to my aid.' Minaya Álvar Fáñez then came up, saying: 'Listen to me, Cid, valiant warrior. This battle is in God's hands, and you are worthy to take part in it with Him. Order us to attack wherever you think best; each one of us will know how to do his duty. God and your good fortune will see us through.' 'Let us take things calmly,' said the Cid. Then the bishop, Don Jerome, came along, fully armed, stood in front of the Campeador, and said: 'Today I have said Mass of the Holy Trinity for your success. I left my country and came here to join you for the desire I felt to kill a Moor or two. Wishing to honour myself and my order, I demand of you the privilege of striking the first blows. I carry a banner and a shield with emblem of roe deer emblazoned on them. I wish to essay my arms, as it may please God, to bring me joy and give you greater satisfaction. If you do not grant me this favour I shall leave you and go my way.' Then the Cid spoke, saying: 'That is the right spirit. There are the Moors; attack them. We shall look on from here to see how the prelate fights.'

117

The bishop Don Jerome spurred forward to the charge and attacked at the edge of their camp. By good fortune and the grace of God he killed two Moors at the first blows he dealt. When the shaft of his lance broke he laid hand on his sword. The bishop showed his mettle; heavens, how well he fought! Two he killed with his lance, five with his sword! A crowd of Moors

49r los moros son muchos,   derredor le cercavan,   [*2390*
dávanle grandes colpes   mas nol' falsan las armas.
El que en buen ora nasco   los ojos le fincava,
enbraçó el escudo   e abaxó el asta,
aguijó a Bavieca,   el cavallo que bien anda,
ívalos ferir   de coraçón e de alma.   [*2395*
En las azes primeras   el Campeador entrava,
abatió a *siete*   e a *quatro* matava.
Plogo a Dios,   aquésta fue el arrancada.
Mio Cid con los suyos   cae en alcança,
veriedes quebrar tantas cuerdas   e arrancarse las estacas   [*2400*
e acostarse los tendales,   con huebras eran tantas.
Los de Mio Cid a los de Búcar   de las tiendas los sacan.

118

Sácanlos de las tiendas,   cáenlos en alcaz,
tanto braço con loriga   veriedes caer apart,
tantas cabeças con yelmos   que por el campo caen,   [*2405*
cavallos sin dueños   salir a todas partes;
siete migeros conplidos   duró el segudar.
Mio Cid al rrey Búcar   cayól' en alcaz:
'¡Acá torna, Búcar!   Venist d'allent mar,
ver te as con el Cid,   el de la barba grant,
saludar nos hemos amos   e tajaremos amista*d*.'   [*2410*
Rrespuso Búcar al Cid: '¡Cofonda Dios tal amistad!
El espada tienes desnuda en la mano   e véot' aguijar,
assí como semeja,   en mí la quieres ensayar;
49v mas si el cavallo non estropieça   o comigo non caye,   [*2415*
non te juntarás comigo   fata dentro en la mar.'
Aquí rrespuso Mio Cid: '¡Esto non será verdad!'
Buen cavallo tiene Búcar   e grandes saltos faz,
mas Bavieca el de Mio Cid   alcançándolo va.
Alcançólo el Cid a Búcar   a tres braças del mar,   [*2420*
arriba alçó Colada,   un grant colpe dádol' ha,
las carbonclas del yelmo   tollidas ge la[*s*] ha,
cortól' el yelmo   e, librado todo lo ál,
fata la cintura   el espada llegado ha.
Mató a Búcar,   al rrey de allén mar,   [*2425*
e ganó a Tizón   que mill marcos d'oro val.
Venció la batalla   maravillosa e grant,
aquís' ondró Mio Cid   e quantos con él son.

surrounded him and heaved great blows, but they did not succeed in piercing his armour. The Cid stood watching the fight; then he embraced his shield, lowered his lance, put spurs to Babieca, his swift horse, and dashed into the fray, laying about him with heart and soul. The Campeador, bursting through the first ranks, overthrew seven and killed four. It pleased God to give the victory to the Cid and his men, for they put the Moors to flight. You should have seen how many ropes were broken and stakes torn up and how many tent poles, adorned with fine work, lay fallen on the ground! The Cid's men drove Búcar's men out of their tents.

118

When they had driven them out they fell to the pursuit. You might have seen many a mailed arm hacked off, many a head with its helmet fall to the ground, while riderless horses ran hither and thither. The pursuit lasted a full seven miles. The Cid followed up King Búcar, calling out to him: 'Come back, Búcar, you who have come from beyond the sea! You have to reckon with the Cid, the man with the flowing beard. We shall kiss and strike up a friendship.' Búcar replied: 'God confound such friendship! I see you spurring after me, sword in hand. It seems you are anxious to test it on me. But if my horse does not stumble or fall with me, I shall reach the sea before you overtake me.' To which the Cid replied: 'I shall give you the lie.' Búcar had a good horse and he galloped well, but Babieca, the Cid's horse, gradually gained on him. The Cid overtook Búcar six yards from the sea. He raised his sword, Colada, and dealt him a mighty blow which struck the garnets off his helmet; he cut straight through the helmet and slashed through everything else until the sword reached his waist. Thus he killed King Búcar, the king from beyond the sea, and won his sword, Tizón, which was worth a thousand golden marks. This was a wonderful victory, in which the Cid acquitted himself with honour, as did all those who fought on his side.

119

Con estas ganancias   yas' ivan tornando,
sabet, todos de firme   rrobavan el campo.   [2430
A las tiendas eran llegados   dó estava | el que en buen
                                ora nasco.   [2431-32
Mio Cid Rruy Díaz   el Campeador contado
con dos espadas   que él preciava algo
por la matança   vinía tan privado,   [2435
la cara fronzida   e almófar soltado,
cofia sobre los pelos   fronzida d'ella yaquanto.
Algo v[e]yé Mio Cid   de lo que era pagado,
alçó sos ojos,   esteva adelant catando
5or e vio venir a Diego   e a Fernando;   [2440
amos son fijos   del conde don Go[n]çalo.
Alegrós' Mio Cid,   fermoso sonrrisando:
'¡Venides, mios yernos,   mios fijos sodes amos!
Sé que de lidiar   bien sodes pagados,
a Carrión de vós   irán buenos mandados   [2445
cómo al rrey Búcar   avemos arrancado.
Como yo fío por Dios   e en todos los sos sanctos,
d'esta arrancada   nós iremos pagados.'   [2448
De todas partes   sos vassallos van llegando,   [2455
Minaya Álbar Fáñez   essora es llegado,   [2449
el escudo trae al cuello   e todo espad[ad]o,   [2450
de los colpes de las lanças   non avié rrecabdo,
aquellos que ge los dieran   non ge lo avién logrado.
Por el cobdo ayuso   la sangre destellando,
de *veínte* arriba   ha moros matado: [2454
'Grado a Dios   e al padre que está en alto   [2456
e a vós, Cid,   que en buen ora fuestes nado.
Matastes a Búcar   e arrancamos el canpo.
Todos estos bienes de vós son   e de vuestros vassallos,
e vuestros yernos   aquí son ensayados,   [2460
fartos de lidiar   con moros en el campo.'
Dixo Mio Cid: 'Yo d'esto só pagado,
quando agora son buenos,   adelant serán preciados.'
Por bien lo dixo el Cid,   mas ellos lo tovieron a mal.
5ov Todas las ganancias   a Valencia son llegadas,   [2465
alegre es Mio Cid   con todas sus conpañas
que a la rración caye   seiscientos marcos de plata.
Los yernos de Mio Cid   quando este aver tomaron
d'esta arrancada,   que lo tenién en so salvo,
cuidaron que en sus días   nunqua serién minguados,   [2470

119

As they returned with the booty they thoroughly stripped the battlefield, and they reached the tents where the Cid Ruy Díaz was. The far-famed Campeador, carrying two swords which he valued highly, rode swiftly over the scene of slaughter with his mail thrown back, showing his creased face and his coif somewhat rumpled on his hair. There was one thing the Cid saw that gave him great satisfaction. As he raised his eyes and looked ahead, there coming towards him were Diego and Fernando, the sons of Don Gonzalo. The Cid smiled a happy smile and said: 'Here you come, my sons-in-law, nay, rather my sons, both of you. I know you have borne yourselves well in the fighting. Good reports of you will reach Carrión telling how we have defeated King Búcar. As I trust in God and all His saints we shall have reason to be proud of this victory.' His vassals were approaching from all directions. Minaya Álvar Fáñez now came up, his shield, which hung from his neck, bearing the marks of the sword-thrusts and of the countless lance-thrusts he had parried; not one had succeeded in piercing it. Blood was dripping down to his elbow, the blood of more than twenty Moors whom he had dispatched. 'Thanks be to God, our Father in Heaven, and to you, Cid, whose good fortune has never failed! You have killed Búcar, and we have won the fight. All this wealth now belongs to you and your vassals, and your sons-in-law have proved their courage to the hilt fighting with Moors in the battlefield.' The Cid said: 'I am content; if they do well now, they will in time distinguish themselves even more.' This was said in all seriousness, but the Infantes thought it was spoken in mockery. All the booty was taken to Valencia, giving great pleasure to the Cid and his men, for each man's share amounted to six hundred silver marks. Now that the Cid's sons-in-law had in their possession all the wealth they had gained in this victory they believed that they were rich for life. They spent the

fúeron en Valencia   muy bien arreados,
conduchos a sazones,   buenas pieles e buenos mantos.
Mucho son alegres   Mio Cid e sus vassallos.

120
  Grant fue el día   [*por*] la cort del Campeador
después que esta batalla vencieron   e al rrey Búcar mató,   [*2475*
alçó la mano,   a la barba se tomó:
'Grado a Christus,   que del mundo es señor,
quando veo   lo que avía sabor
que lidiaran comigo en campo   mios yernos amos a dos;
mandados buenos irán   d'ellos a Carrión   [*2480*
cómo son ondrados   e aver vos [*an*] grant pro.

121
  Sobejanas son las ganancias   que todos an ganadas,
lo uno es nuestro,   lo otro han en salvo.'
Mandó Mio Cid,   el que en buen ora nasco,
d'esta batalla   que han arrancado   [*2485*
que todos prisiessen   so derecho contado
e la su quinta   non fuesse olbidado.
Assí lo fazen todos,   ca eran acordados,
cayéronle en quinta   al Cid seixcientos cavallos
51r   e otras azémilas   e camellos largos,   [*2490*
tantos son de muchos   que non serién contados.

122
  Todas estas ganancias   fizo el Canpeador:
'¡Grado a Dios   que del mundo es señor!
Antes fu minguado,   agora rrico só,
que he aver e tierra   e oro e onor   [*2495*
e son mios yernos   ifantes de Carrión.
Arranco las lides   como plaze al Criador,
moros e cristianos   de mí han grant pavor;
allá dentro en Marruecos,   ó las mezquitas son,
que abrán de mí salto   quiçab alguna noch;   [*2500*
ellos lo temen,   ca non lo piesso yo.
No los iré buscar,   en Valencia seré yo,
ellos me darán parias,   con ayuda del Criador,
que paguen a mí   o a qui yo ovier sabor.'
Grandes son los gozos en Valencia   con Mio Cid el
                                    Canpeado[*r*]   [*2505*
de todas sus conpañas   e de todos sus vassallos;

money on excellent food, fine clothes, good fur tunics and cloaks. The Cid and his vassals were highly delighted.

120

There was great rejoicing in the Campeador's palace after this victory and the death of King Búcar. The Cid raised his hand and grasped his beard. 'Thanks be to Christ, Lord of this world,' he said, 'I have seen my desire fulfilled! My sons-in-law have both fought in battle by my side; good news of them will go to Carrión, for they have won honour for themselves and will hereafter be a great help to us.'

121

The booty won by all is immense; this is our share, the rest they can keep for themselves.' The Cid gave orders that each man should take his rightful share of the spoils of victory and that his own fifth share should be set aside. His followers, like wise men, obeyed the Cid's command. Six hundred horses were included in the Cid's portion, as well as many pack animals and countless camels.

122

Contemplating his great gains, the Cid said: 'Thanks be to God, the Lord of this world. Once I was poor and now I am rich, for I have wealth, lands and property, and the Infantes of Carrión are my sons-in-law. I win battles as it pleases the Creator, and both Moors and Christians fear me. Over the sea in Morocco, where the mosques are, they are afraid that I shall perhaps attack them one night. I have no intention of doing so, for I shall not go to seek them out, but shall remain in Valencia. They will, please God, render me tribute to be paid to me or to anyone whom I shall appoint to receive it.' All the Cid's followers in Valencia rejoiced over the victory which they had won by

grandes son los gozos   de sus yernos amos a dos:
d'aquesta arrancada   que lidiaron de coraçón
valía de cinco mill marcos   ganaron amos a dos;
muchos' tienen por rricos   los ifantes de Carrión;   [2510
ellos con los otros   vinieron a la cort.
Aquí está con Mio Cid   el obispo do Jerónimo,
el bueno de Álbar Fáñez,   cavallero lidiador,
e otros muchos   que crió el Campeador;
quando entraron   los ifantes de Carrión,   [2515
51v rrecibiólos Minaya   por Mio Cid el Campeador:
'Acá venid, cuñados,   que más valemos por vós.'
Assí como llegaron,   pagós' el Campeador:
'Evades aquí, yernos,   la mi mugier de pro
e amas la[s] mis fijas,   don Elvira e doña Sol;   [2520
bien vos abracen   e sírvanvos de coraçón.
Venciemos moros en campo   e matamos
a aquel rrey Búcar,   provado traidor.
Grado a Sancta María,   madre del nuestro señor Dios,
d'estos nuestros casamientos   vós abredes honor.   [2525
Buenos mandados irán   a tierras de Carrión.'

123

A estas palabras   fabló Ferrán Gonçález:
'Grado al Criador   e a vós, Cid ondrado,
tantos avemos de averes   que no son contados,
por vós avemos ondra   e avemos lidiado;   [2530
pensad de lo otro,   que lo nuestro tenémoslo en salvo.'
Vassallos de Mio Cid   seyénse sonrrisando:
quien lidiara mejor   o quien fuera en alcanço,
mas non fallavan í   a Diego ni a Ferrando.
Por aquestos juegos   que ivan levantando   [2535
e las noches e los días   tan mal los escarmentando,
tan mal se consejaron   estos iffantes amos.
Amos saliero[n] apart,   veramientre son ermanos,
d'esto que ellos fablaron   nós parte non ayamos:
'Vayamos pora Carrión,   aquí mucho detardamos;   [2540
los averes que tenemos   grandes son e sobejanos,
mientra que visquiéremos   despender no lo podremos.

124

Pidamos nuestras mugieres   al Cid Campeador,
52r digamos que las levaremos   a tierras de Carrión
[e] enseñar las hemos   dó las heredades son.   [2545

their bravery in the field. His sons-in-law were delighted, for their gains were valued at five thousand marks and they considered themselves rich men. They came with the others to the hall of the Cid's palace. The Cid was there with Bishop Jerome, worthy Álvar Fáñez, that warrior knight, and many others of the Cid's household. When the Infantes entered they were received by Minaya on behalf of the Cid. 'Here you come, my cousins. Your brave conduct has helped in our success.' When they came up to him the Cid expressed his pleasure in these words: 'My sons-in-law, here are my honoured wife and my two daughters, Doña Elvira and Doña Sol. Let them embrace you and serve you faithfully. We have defeated Moors in battle and have killed King Búcar, that manifest traitor. Thanks to the Holy Virgin, Mother of Our Lord, by marrying into our family you will receive estate. Good news of you will go to the land of Carrión.' Fernando answered, saying:

123

'Thanks to the Creator and to you, illustrious Cid, we now possess vast wealth, and on your behalf we have fought honourably. Our property we have safely in our hands; you must see to the rest.' The Cid's vassals smiled and, as they commented on the part played by each one in the battle, they remarked that Diego and Fernando had not been seen in the thick of the fight and had not joined in the pursuit. Day and night they kept up their jokes, making mock of the Infantes, until these two decided to plan their revenge. They went aside to talk in private, a fine pair of brothers—their plot should be no affair of ours. (This is what they said) 'Let us go to Carrión, for we have delayed too long here. We have now such enormous wealth that it will take us the rest of our lives to spend it.

124

Let us ask the Cid for our wives, saying that we shall bring them to Carrión and show them their estates. We shall take them

Sacar las hemos de Valencia   de poder del Campeador,
después en la carrera   feremos nuestro sabor,
ante que nos rretrayan   lo que cuntió del león;
nós de natura somos   de condes de Carrión.
Averes levaremos grandes   que valen grant valor,   [2550
escarniremos   las fijas del Canpeador.
D'aquestos averes   sienpre seremos rricos omnes,
podremos casar con fijas   de rreyes o de enperadores,
ca de natura somos   de condes de Carrión.
Assí las escarniremos   a las fijas del Campeador,   [2555
antes que nos rretrayan   lo que fue del león.'
Con aqueste consejo   amos tornados son,
fabló Ferrán Gonçález   e fizo callar la cort:
'¡Sí vos vala el Criador,   Cid Campeador!
Que plega a doña Ximena   e primero a vós   [2560
e a Minaya Álbar Fáñez   e a quantos aquí son:
dadnos nuestras mugieres   que avemos a bendiciones,
levar las hemos   a nuestras tierras de Carrión,
meter las hemos   en las villas
que les diemos por arras   e por onores,   [2565
verán vuestras fijas   lo que avemos nós,
los fijos que oviéremos   en qué avrán partición.'
Nos' curiava de ser afontado   el Cid | Campeador: [2569-68
'Dar vos he mis fijas   e algo de lo mío;   [2568b
vós les diestes villas por arras   en tierras de Carrión,   [2570
yo quiero les dar axuvar   *tres* mill marcos de plata;
dar vos é mulas e palafrés   muy gruessos de sazón,
52v   cavallos pora en diestro,   fuertes e corredores,
e muchas vestiduras   de paños de ciclatones;
dar vos he dos espadas,   a Colada e a Tizón,   [2575
bien lo sabedes vós   que las gané a guisa de varón.
Mios fijos sodes amos   quando mis fijas vos do,
allá me levades   las telas del coraçón.
Que lo sepan en Gallizia   e en Castiella e en León
con qué rriqueza enbío   mios yernos amos a dos.   [2580
A mis fijas sirvades,   que vuestras mugieres son,
si bien las servides   yo vos rrendré buen galardón.'
Atorgado lo han esto   los iffantes de Carrión,
aquí rreciben   las fijas del Campeador,
conpieçan a rrecebir   lo que el Cid mandó;   [2585
quando son pagados   a todo so sabor,
ya mandavan cargar   iffantes de Carrión.
Grandes son las nuevas   por Valencia la mayor,

away from Valencia out of the power of the Cid; afterwards, on the road home, we shall do as we like, rather than stay here to have the episode of the lion cast in our teeth. We are of the Counts of Carrión by blood! We shall carry off our great wealth and we shall show our contempt for the daughters of the Cid! With these great possessions we shall be rich for life, we shall be able to marry daughters of kings or emperors, for we are descended from the counts of Carrión. We shall make a mock of the Cid's daughters rather than have any harping on what happened with the lion.' After this conversation the two young men returned to the hall and Fernando, having asked for silence, said: 'As you may hope for God's grace, Cid Campeador, I appeal to you first and then to Doña Jimena, Minaya Álvar Fáñez and all those assembled here, to give us our wives to whom we are joined in holy matrimony. We shall take them to our lands in Carrión and we shall hand over the properties which we settled on them. Your daughters will see those possessions of ours that will pass as a heritage to any children we may have.' The Cid had no suspicion of any intended injury, and he answered: 'I shall hand over my daughters to you and with them a considerable dowry. You have settled on them manors in Carrión, and I shall give them as a dowry the sum of three thousand silver marks. I shall give you sturdy mules and palfreys, strong, swift chargers and a good supply of garments made of cloth of gold. I shall give you two swords, Colada and Tizón, won by my valour, as you well know. You are my sons, for I give you my daughters, though it is like tearing my very heart-strings to do so. Let it be noised abroad in Galicia, Castile and León that I am endowing my sons-in-law richly. Care for my daughters, for they are your wives. If you treat them well you will be well rewarded.' The young men assented and received from the Cid his daughters and all the gifts he bestowed on them. When they had received all that they could wish for, they ordered it to be loaded on the pack animals. There was great activity in Valencia in honour of their departure. All seized their

todos prenden armas   e cavalgan a vigor
porque escurren sus fijas del Campeador   a tierras
                                        de Carrión.   [2590
Ya quieren cavalgar,   en espidimiento son;
amas ermanas   don Elvira e doña Sol
fincaron los inojos   ant'el Cid Campeador:
'¡Merced vos pedimos, padre,   sí vos vala el Criador!
Vós nos engendrastes,   nuestra madre nos parió;   [2595
delant sodes amos,   señora e señor.
Agora nos enviades   a tierras de Carrión,
53r   debdo nos es a cunplir   lo que mandáredes vós.
Assí vos pedimos merced   nós amas a dos
que ayades vuestros mensajes   en tierras de Carrión.'   [2600
Abraçólas Mio Cid   e saludólas amas a dos.

125
Él fizo aquesto,   la madre lo doblava:
'Andad, fijas, d'aquí   el Criador vos vala,
de mí e de vuestro padre   bien avedes nuestra gracia.
Id a Carrión   dó sodes heredadas,   [2605
assí como yo tengo,   bien vos he casadas.'
Al padre e a la madre   las manos les besavan;
amos las bendixieron   e diéronles su gracia.
Mio Cid e los otros   de cavalgar pensavan
a grandes guarnimientos,   a cavallos e armas.   [2610
Ya salién los ifantes   de Valencia la clara
espi[di]endos' de las dueñas   e de todas sus compañas.
Por la huerta de Valencia   teniendo salién armas,
alegre va Mio Cid   con todas sus compañas.
Violo en los avueros   el que en buen ora cinxo espada   [2615
que estos casamientos   non serién sin alguna tacha;
nos' puede rrepentir,   que casadas las ha amas.

126
'¿Ó eres mio sobrino,   tú, Félez Muñoz?
Primo eres de mis fijas amas   d'alma e de coraçón.
Mándot' que vayas con ellas   fata dentro en Carrión,   [2620
verás las heredades   que a mis fijas dadas son,
con aquestas nuevas   vernás al Campeador.'
Dixo Félez Muñoz: 'Plazme d'alma e de coraçón.'
53v   Minaya Álbar Fáñez   ante Mio Cid se paró:
'Tornémosnos, Cid,   a Valencia la mayor,   [2625

arms and rode out in style to see the Cid's daughters off on the journey to Carrión. They were about to ride away and were taking their leave when the two sisters, Doña Elvira and Doña Sol, knelt down before the Campeador and said: 'We ask you a favour in God's name! You begat us and our mother bore us. We kneel before you both, to whom we owe respect. Now you are sending us to the land of Carrión and it is our duty to obey your command. So we both together beg you to send us news of you to Carrión.' The Cid embraced and kissed his daughters.

125

Their mother did the same, saying: 'Go, my daughters, and may God protect you! You have your father's blessing and mine. Go to Carrión and take possession of your estates there. I think we have made a good match for you.' They kissed their father's and mother's hands and received their love and blessing. The Cid and his followers rode out, magnificently dressed and armed, on caparisoned horses. The Infantes left the renowned city of Valencia, taking leave of the ladies and all the company there. With display of arms and horsemanship the Cid and his men went gaily out through the farmlands of Valencia. The Cid perceived from the omens that some dishonour would result from these marriages, but he could not undo what had been done, for he had given them in marriage.

126

(He called Félez Muñoz to him and said) 'Are you there, my nephew, Félez Muñoz? You are cousin to my well beloved daughters. Go with them as far as Carrión to see the estates which have been settled on them. Return to me with news of what you see.' Félez Muñoz replied: 'I shall do as you say most willingly.' Minaya Álvar Fáñez came and stood before the Cid and said: 'Let us return to Valencia now, and later, if it please

que si a Dios ploguiere   e al padre Criador,
ir las hemos ver   a tierras de Carrión.'
'A Dios vos acomendamos,   don Elvira e doña Sol,
atales cosas fed   que en plazer caya a nós.'
Rrespondién los yernos: '¡Assí lo mande Dios!'   [2630
Grandes fueron los duelos   a la departición,
el padre con las fijas   lloran de coraçón,
assí fazían   los cavalleros del Campeador.
'¡Oyas, sobrino,   tú, Félez Muñoz!
Por Molina iredes,   í yazredes una noch,   [2635
saludad a mio amigo   el moro Avengalvón;
rreciba a mios yernos   como él pudier mejor.
Dil' que enbío mis fijas   a tierras de Carrión,
de lo que ovieren huebos   sírvalas a so sabor,
desí escúrralas fasta Medina   por la mi amor;   [2640
de quanto él fiziere   yol' dar[é] por ello buen galardón.'
Cuemo la uña de la carne   ellos partidos son,
yas' tornó pora Valencia   el que en buen ora nasció.
Piénsanse de ir   los ifantes de Carrión,
por Sancta María d'Alvarrazín   fazían la posada.   [2645
Aguijan quanto pueden   ifantes de Carrión:
felos en Molina   con el moro Avengalvón.
El moro, quando lo sopo,   plógol' de coraçón,
saliólos rrecebir   con grandes avorozes,
¡Dios, qué bien los sirvió   a todo so sabor!   [2650
54r Otro día mañana   con ellos cavalgó,
con dozientos cavalleros   escurrirlos mandó;
ivan trocir los montes,   los que dizen de Luzón.
A las fijas del Cid   el moro sus donas dio,
buenos seños cavallos   a los ifantes de Carrión.   [2655
Trocieron Arbuxuelo   e llegaron a Salón,
ó dizen el Ansarera   ellos posados son.
Tod' esto les fizo el moro   por el amor del Cid Campead[or].
Ellos veyén la rriqueza   que el moro sacó,
entr'amos ermanos   consejaron tración: [2660
'Ya pues que a dexar avemos   fijas del Campeador,
si pudiéssemos matar   el moro Avengalvón,
quanta rriquiza tiene   aver la iemos nós.
Tan en salvo lo abremos   como lo de Carrión,
nunqua avrié derecho de nós   el Cid Campeador.'   [2665
Quando esta falsedad   dizién los de Carrión,
un moro latinado   bien ge lo entendió;
non tiene poridad,   díxolo [a] Avengalvón:

God, we shall visit them in Carrión.' (Then, turning to the
young wives, he continued) 'We commend you to God's care,
Doña Elvira and Doña Sol; may your lives be such as to give us
pleasure.' Their husbands replied: 'May God so dispose it!'
There was great sorrow at the moment of parting. Both father
and daughters wept bitterly, and so also did the knights of the
Cid's following. 'Listen to me, my nephew, Félez Muñoz,' said
the Cid. 'You shall go to Molina and spend the night there.
Greet my Moorish friend Abengalbón, and ask him to give my
sons-in-law the best possible welcome. Tell him that I am sending
my daughters to Carrión and I should like him to provide them
with anything they may need and then escort them as far as
Medinaceli. I shall give him rich recompense for all he does for
them.' They parted with such pain as when a finger-nail is torn
from the flesh. The Cid returned to Valencia, and the Infantes
of Carrión set out for Santa María de Albarracín, where they all
spent the night. Next day, travelling in great haste, they
reached Molina, the town governed by Abengalbón. When
the Moor heard of their arrival he was delighted and went out of
the town to give them a joyful welcome, doing everything
possible to please them. Next morning Abengalbón rode out
with them, accompanied by two hundred horsemen at his
command to see them on their way. The whole party first
crossed the heights of Luzón. Abengalbón presented gifts to the
Cid's daughters and gave their husbands a good horse each.
Then they passed along the valley of the Arbujuelo, reached the
river Jalón and halted to rest at a place called Ansarera. The
Moor did all this (service) for the love he bore to the Campeador.
When the Infantes saw the wealth displayed by the Moor they
plotted an act of treachery. 'We have already decided' (they said
to each other) 'to abandon the Cid's daughters; now if we can
kill Abengalbón we shall get hold of all his wealth. We can be
as sure of it as we are of our possessions in Carrión; the Cid is
very unlikely to demand satisfaction from us.' However, a Moor
who understood Spanish heard them concocting this treachery
and reported it without delay to Abengalbón, saying: 'My lord

'Acayaz, cúriate d'éstos,   ca eres mio señor,
tu muert oí cossejar   a los ifantes de Carrión.'   [2670

127

El moro Avengalvón   mucho era buen barragán,
co[n] dozientos que tiene   iva cavalgar,
armas iva teniendo,   parós' ante los ifantes,
de lo que el moro dixo   a los ifantes non plaze:
'¡Dezidme qué vos fiz,   ifantes de Carrión!   [2675
Yo sirviéndovos sin art   e vós, pora mí, muert consejastes.
Si no lo dexás   por Mio Cid el de Bivar,
54v   tal cosa vos faría   que por el mundo sonás
e luego levaría sus fijas   al Campeador leal;
vós nu[n]qua en Carrión   entrariedes jamás.   [2680

128

Aquím' parto de vós   como de malos e de traidores.
Iré con vuestra gracia,   don Elvira e doña Sol,
poco precio las nuevas   de los de Carrión.
Dios lo quiera e lo mande,   que de tod' el mundo es señor,
d'aqueste casamiento   que grade el Canpeador.'   [2685
Esto les ha dicho   e el moro se tornó,
teniendo iva armas   al trocir de Salón,
cuemo de buen seso   a Molina se tornó.
Ya movieron del Ansarera   los ifantes de Carrión,
acójense a andar   de día e de noch,   [2690
a siniestro dexan Atienza,   una peña muy fuert,
la sierra de Miedes   passáronla esto[n]z,
por los Montes Claros   aguijan a espolón,
a siniestro dexan a Griza   que Álamos pobló,
allí son caños   dó a Elpha encerró,   [2695
a diestro dexan a Sant Estevan,   más cae aluén.
Entrados son los ifantes   al rrobredo de Corpes,
los montes son altos,   las rramas pujan con las núes;
¡e las bestias fieras   que andan aderredor!
Fallaron un vergel   con una linpia fuent,   [2700
mandan fincar la tienda   ifantes de Carrión,
con quantos que ellos traen   í yazen essa noch,
con sus mugieres en braços   demuéstranles amor,
¡mal ge lo cunplieron   quando salié el sol!
Mandaron cargar las azémilas   con grandes averes,   [2705
55r   cogida han la tienda   dó albergaron de noch,
adelant eran idos   los de criazón,

governor, beware of these two Infantes of Carrión, for I have
heard them discussing a plan to kill you.'

127

Abengalbón, who was a fine brave fellow, rode out with his
two hundred horsemen displaying feats of arms. He halted in
front of the Infantes and uttered these harsh words: 'Tell me,
what have I done to you, Infantes of Carrión? I have kept faith
with you and in return you have plotted my death. If I did not
forbear for the sake of the Cid, Rodrigo of Vivar, I should exact
such vengeance as would startle the world. Then I should escort
his daughters to the loyal Campeador, and you would never
return to Carrión.

128

Here I take leave of you as evildoers and traitors. With your
permission, Doña Elvira and Doña Sol, I shall depart; I go with
the poorest possible opinion of the Infantes of Carrión. God
grant that the Campeador may not have cause to regret this
marriage.' When he had finished speaking the Moor turned away,
recrossed the river Jalón, displaying his skill in horsemanship and
arms, and prudently returned to Molina. The Infantes moved
on from Ansarera and travelled without stopping day or night.
Leaving the mighty cliff of Atienza on the left, they crossed the
Sierra de Miedes and spurred hastily through the Montes Claros.
They passed to the right of Griza, founded by Álamos, and the
caves where he imprisoned Elpha. They left on the right San
Esteban, which lies further on. Then they entered the oak forest
of Corpes, where the branches of the lofty trees seemed to stretch
up to the clouds, and the wild beasts roamed at large. They found
a grassy clearing with a fresh spring, and there the Infantes
ordered a tent to be set up. On this spot they spent the night with
all their company, and with their wives, to whom they showed
signs of tender love. They proved that love in a strange way when
the sun rose next morning. They gave orders that the pack
animals should be loaded with all their valuables, that the tent
in which they had spent the night should be folded and that all
members of their household should go on ahead. No man or

assí lo mandaron los ifantes de Carrión
que non í fincás ninguno, mugier nin varón,
sinon amas sus mugieres doña Elvira e doña Sol: [2710
deportarse quieren con ellas a todo su sabor.
Todos eran idos, ellos *quatro* solos son,
tanto mal comidieron los ifantes de Carrión:
'Bien lo creades, don Elvira e doña Sol,
aquí seredes escarnidas en estos fieros montes. [2715
Oy nos partiremos e dexadas seredes de nós,
non abredes part en tierras de Carrión.
Irán aquestos mandados al Cid Campeador,
nós vengaremos por aquésta la [*desondra*] del león.'
Allí les tuellen los mantos e los pelliçones, [2720
páranlas en cuerpos e en camisas e en ciclatones.
Espuelas tienen calçadas los malos traidores,
en mano prenden las cinchas fuertes e duradores.
Quando esto vieron las dueñas, fablava doña Sol:
'¡Por Dios vos rrogamos, don Diego e don Ferrando! [2725
Dos espadas tenedes fuertes e tajadores,
al una dizen Colada e al otra Tizón,
cortandos las cabeças, mártires seremos nós,
moros e cristianos departirán d'esta rrazón,
que por lo que nós merecemos no lo prendemos nós. [2730
Atan malos ensienplos non fagades sobre nós;
si nós fuéremos majadas, abiltaredes a vós,
rretraer vos lo an en vistas o en cortes.'
55v Lo que rruegan las dueñas non les ha ningún pro,
essora les conpieçan a dar los ifantes de Carrión, [2735
con las cinchas corredizas májanlas tan sin sabor,
con las espuelas agudas dón ellas an mal sabor
rronpién las camisas e las carnes a ellas amas a dos,
linpia salié la sangre sobre los ciclatones;
ya lo sienten ellas en los sos coraçones. [2740
¡Quál ventura serié ésta, si ploguiesse al Criador,
que assomasse essora el Cid Campeador!
Tanto las majaron que sin cosimente son,
sangrientas en las camisas e todos los ciclatones.
Cansados son de ferir ellos amos a dos, [2745
ensayandos' amos quál dará mejores colpes.
Ya non pueden fablar don Elvira e doña Sol;
por muertas las dexaron en el rrobredo de Corpes.

woman was to remain behind except their wives, Doña Elvira and Doña Sol, with whom they wished to disport themselves. When all the rest had gone on and only those four were left alone, the Infantes set about carrying out their wicked plan. (To their wives they said) 'Do you hear, Doña Elvira and Doña Sol? We are going to show our contempt and scorn for you here in this wild forest. Today we shall separate and you will be abandoned by us. You will then have no claim to any of our lands in Carrión. This is the news that will go to the Cid Campeador; this is our vengeance for the dishonour with the lion.' There and then the young men took off their wives' cloaks and fur tunics and left them in nothing but their shifts and tunics of cloth of gold. These wicked traitors put on their spurs and took hold of their strong, hard straps. When the ladies saw them do this Doña Sol cried: 'We implore you, Don Diego and Don Fernando, in God's name! You have two sharp swords, Colada and Tizón. Cut off our heads and make martyrs of us. Everyone will condemn this action of yours, for we have done nothing to deserve it. Do not ill-treat us like this, for if we are beaten you will be disgraced and men will charge you with this crime in assemblies and courts of justice.' The ladies pleaded in vain. The Infantes began at once to beat them with their buckled straps and to hack their flesh cruelly with their sharp spurs. They tore through their shifts to the flesh and the clear red blood poured out over their golden tunics. They were pierced to the heart with shame. If only it had pleased God to send the Cid Campeador at this moment! The Infantes beat them so hard that they were benumbed with pain, their shifts and tunics all stained with blood. The two young men struck till they were weary, trying to see which of them could deal the hardest blows. Doña Elvira and Doña Sol could not utter a word, and were left for dead in the oak forest of Corpes.

129

Leváronles los mantos   e las pieles armiñas,
mas déxanlas marridas   en briales e en camisas   [2750
e a las aves del monte   e a las bestias de la fiera guisa.
Por muertas la[s] dexaron,   sabed, que non por bivas.
¡Quál ventura serié   si assomás essora el Cid Campeador!

130

Los ifantes de Carrión en el rrobredo de Corpes |
                            por muertas las dexaron   [2754-55
que el una al otra   nol' torna rrecabdo.
Por los montes dó ivan   ellos ívanse alabando:
'De nuestros casamientos   agora somos vengados;
56r   non las deviemos tomar por varraganas | si non
                            fuéssemos rrogados,   [2759-60
pues nuestras parejas   non eran pora en braços.
La desondra del león   assís' irá vengando.'

131

Alabandos' ivan   los ifantes de Carrión,
mas yo vos diré   d'aquel Félez Muñoz:
sobrino era   del Cid Campeador;   [2765
mandáronle ir adelante,   mas de su grado non fue.
En la carrera dó iva   dolió' el coraçón,
de todos los otros   aparte se salió,
en un monte espesso   Félez Muñoz se metió
fasta que viesse venir   sus primas amas a dos   [2770
o qué an fecho   los ifantes de Carrión.
Violos venir   e oyó una rrazón,
ellos nol' v[e]yén   ni dend sabién rración;
sabet bien que si ellos le viessen   non escapara de muert.
Vanse los ifantes,   aguijan a espolón;   [2775
por el rrastro   tornós' Félez Muñoz,
falló sus primas   amortecidas amas a dos.
Llamando: '¡Primas, primas!',   luego descavalgó,
arrendó el cavallo,   a ellas adeliñó:
'¡Ya primas, las mis primas,   don Elvira e doña Sol,   [2780
mal se ensayaron   los ifantes de Carrión!
¡A Dios plega e a Sancta María   que dent prendan ellos
                            mal galardón!'
Valas tornando   a ellas amas a dos,
tanto son de traspuestas   que non pueden dezir nada.
Partiéronsele las telas   de dentro del coraçón,   [2785

129

They stripped them of their cloaks and ermine furs. They left them there, distressed, in their tunics and shifts, a prey to the wild beasts and birds of the forest. They left them for dead, indeed, not (thinking them) still alive. How fortunate it would be if the Cid Campeador were to appear at this moment!

130

After the Infantes of Carrión had left their wives for dead in the oak forest of Corpes, unable to give each other any help, they went off through the woods, highly pleased with themselves. As they went they said boastfully: 'Now we are avenged for our marriages. We should not have taken them even as concubines, unless we had been formally asked; they were not our equals in rank or fit to be our lawful wives. By acting as we have done we have our revenge for the dishonour we suffered in the episode of the lion.'

131

Let us leave them boasting of their evil deeds and return to Félez Muñoz, the Cid's nephew. He had been ordered to go on, but did so unwillingly. As he went he was sore at heart, and left the rest of the company. He penetrated into the dense wood, hoping to meet his cousins or to find out what the Infantes had done. He saw them coming and heard what they said, but they did not see him or note any sign of his presence. If they had seen him, you may be sure he would not have escaped with his life. The Infantes rode on, setting spurs to their horses, while Félez Muñoz followed their tracks back into the forest. He found his cousins lying there unconscious. Calling out 'Cousins, cousins!' he dismounted, tied his horse up and went towards them. 'Cousins, cousins,' he cried, 'Doña Elvira and Doña Sol! The Infantes of Carrión have given poor proof of their courage! Please God and Holy Mary they receive the recompense they deserve!' He turned them over, but they were so overcome they could not answer. He felt as if his heart would break, and in

llamando: '¡Primas, primas,   don Elvira e don Sol!
¡Despertedes, primas,   por amor del Criador!

56v   ¡Mie[n]tra es el día,   ante que entre la noch,
los ganados fieros   non nos coman en aqueste mont!'
Van rrecordando   don Elvira e doña Sol,   [2790
abrieron los ojos   e vieron a Félez Muñoz:
'¡Esforçadvos, primas,   por amor del Criador!
De que non me fallaren   los ifantes de Carrión,
a grant priessa   seré buscado yo;
si Dios non nos vale   aquí morremos nós.'   [2795
Tan a grant duelo   fablava doña Sol:
'Sí vos lo meresca, mio primo,   nuestro padre el Canpeador,
¡dandos del agua,   sí vos vala el Criador!'
Con un sonbrero   que tiene Félez Muñoz,
nuevo era e fresco,   que de Valéncial' sacó,   [2800
cogió del agua en él   e a sus primas dio,
mucho son lazradas   e amas las fartó.
Tanto las rrogó   fata que las assentó,
valas conortando   e metiendo coraçón
fata que esfuerçan,   e amas las tomó   [2805
e privado   en el cavallo las cavalgó,
con el so manto   a amas las cubrió.
El cavallo priso por la rrienda   e luego dent las part[ió],
todos tres señeros   por los rrobredos de Corpes,
entre noch e día   salieron de los montes,   [2810
a las aguas de Duero   ellos arribados son,
a la torre de don Urraca   elle las dexó.
A Sant Estevan   vino Félez Muñoz,
falló a Diego Téllez,   el que de Álbar Fáñez fue.
57r   Quando él lo oyó,   pesól' de coraçón,   [2815
priso bestias   e vestidos de pro,
iva rrecebir   a don Elvira e a doña Sol;
en Sant Estevan   dentro las metió,
quanto él mejor puede   allí las ondró.
Los de Sant Estevan   siempre mesurados son,   [2820
quando sabién esto,   pesóles de coraçón,
a llas fijas del Cid   danles esfuerço;
allí sovieron ellas   fata que sanas son.
Alabandos' seían   los ifantes de Carrión.
De cuer pesó esto   al buen rrey don Alfonso.   [2825
Van aquestos mandados   a Valencia la mayor,
quando ge lo dizen   a Mio Cid el Campeador,
una grand ora   pensó e comidió;

great distress he called to them: 'Cousins, cousins, open your eyes, for God's sake, while it is still daylight, before night comes on and the wild beasts devour us in this forest.' Doña Elvira and Doña Sol began to recover consciousness, and, opening their eyes, they saw Félez Muñoz. 'Wake up, cousins, for the love of God! As soon as the Infantes miss me they will send in haste to search for me, and if God does not come to our aid we shall all die in this place.' Doña Sol then spoke in anguished tones: 'Water, in God's name, for the sake of our father, the Campeador!' Félez Muñoz fetched water in a clean new hat which he had brought from Valencia and gave it to his suffering cousins to quench their thirst. He entreated them till he got them sitting up, and he continued to comfort and encourage them until they made an effort. Then he lifted them up and seated them on his horse straight away. He covered them with his cloak, took his horse by the reins and led them off. The three of them went by themselves through the oak forest of Corpes and came out into the open country at dusk. When they reached the river Douro, Félez Muñoz left his cousins at the Tower of Doña Urraca. He himself went on as far as San Esteban, and there he found Diego Téllez, a vassal of Álvar Fáñez. When Diego Téllez heard what had happened he was greatly distressed. He took mounts and fine clothes and went to welcome Doña Elvira and Doña Sol; he brought them to San Esteban and gave them lodging there with all due honour and respect. The inhabitants of San Esteban were thoughtful, kindly people, and when they heard the whole story they were very sorry for the Cid's daughters and put heart into them. They stayed there until they had quite regained their health and strength. Meanwhile the Infantes of Carrión were boasting openly of what they had done. When good King Alfonso heard of it he was greatly grieved. The news reached the great city of Valencia, and when they told the Cid he meditated for a long time. Then he raised his hand and

alçó la su mano,   a la barba se tomó:
'Grado a Christus,   que del mundo es señor,   [2830
quando tal ondra me an dada   los ifantes de Carrión;
par aquesta barba   que nadi non messó,
non la lograrán   los ifantes de Carrión,
¡que a mis fijas   bien las casaré yo!'
Pesó a Mio Cid   e a toda su cort   [2835
e [a] Álbar Fáñez   d'alma e de coraçón.   [2835b
Cavalgó Minaya   con Pero Vermúez
e Martín Antolínez,   el burgalés de pro,
con *dozientos* cavalleros   quales Mio Cid mandó;
díxoles fuertemientre   que andidiessen de día e de noch,
aduxiessen a sus fijas   a Valencia la mayor.   [2840
57v Non lo detardan   el mandado de su señor,
apriessa cavalgan,   andan los días e las noches,
vinieron a Gormaz,   un castiello tan fuert,
í albergaron   por verdad una noch.
A Sant Estevan   el mandado llegó   [2845
que vinié Minaya   por sus primas amas a dos.
Varones de Sant Estevan   a guisa de muy pros
rreciben a Minaya   e a todos sus varones,
presentan a Minaya   essa noch grant enfurción,
non ge lo quiso tomar,   mas mucho ge lo gradió: [2850
'Gracias, varones de Sant Estevan,   que sodes coñoscedores,
por aquesta ondra que vós diestes   a esto que nos cuntió;
mucho vos lo gradece,   allá dó está, Mio Cid el Canpeador,
assí lo fago yo   que aquí estó.
Afé Dios de los cielos   que vos dé dent buen galardón.' [2855
Todos ge lo gradecen   e sos pagados son,
adeliñan a posar   pora folgar essa noch.
Minaya va ver   sus primas dó son,
en él fincan los ojos   don Elvira e doña Sol:
'Atanto vos lo gradimos   como si viéssemos al Criador [2860
e vós a él lo gradid   quando bivas somos nós.

132

En los días de vagar   toda nuestra rrencura sabremos contar.'
Lloravan de los ojos   las dueñas e Álbar Fáñez
e Pero Vermúez   otro tantó las ha:
'Don Elvira e doña Sol,   cuidado non ayades   [2865
quando vós sodes sanas e bivas   e sin otro mal.
Buen casamiento perdiestes,   mejor podredes ganar.
58r ¡Aún veamos el día   que vos podamos vengar!'

gripped his beard. 'Thanks be to our Lord Jesus Christ' (he said) 'for this honour the Infantes of Carrión have done me. By this beard which no one has ever plucked, they will not succeed in dishonouring me, for I shall make much better marriages for my daughters.' The Cid, Álvar Fáñez and the whole household were greatly distressed. The Cid sent Minaya with Pedro Bermúdez, Martín Antolínez and two hundred knights with strict instructions to ride day and night and bring his daughters back to Valencia. They obeyed their lord's command without delay; they mounted their horses and travelled day and night until they came to the strong fortress of Gormaz, where they did, in truth, spend one night. News reached San Esteban that Minaya was coming to fetch his two cousins. The excellent men of the town welcomed him and his companions and offered Minaya a great feast that night. He was reluctant to accept it but expressed his gratitude, saying: 'Thanks, good men of San Esteban, for the honour you show me, understanding as you do this shame that has come upon us. The Cid Campeador sends you his thanks from where he is in Valencia and I give you mine here. May God in Heaven reward you for your action.' All expressed their gratitude and pleasure at his words, and Minaya's party went to their lodging to rest for the night. Minaya went to see his cousins, and when they saw him arrive they said: 'We are thankful to see you as if it were the Lord Himself. Be grateful to Him that you find us alive here.

132

When we have more leisure, we shall be able to tell you all we have suffered.' The ladies and Álvar Fáñez wept, and Pedro Bermúdez spoke these comforting words: 'Doña Elvira and Doña Sol, do not distress yourselves, seeing that you are safe and alive and have nothing more to trouble you. One good marriage has been dissolved but you will be able to make a better one. We hope a time will come when we may avenge

Í yazen essa noche   e tan grand gozo que fazen.
Otro día mañana   piensan de cavalgar,   [2870
los de Sant Estevan   escurriéndolos van
fata Rrío d'Amor,   dándoles solaz;
d'allent se espidieron d'ellos,   piénsanse de tornar
e Minaya con las dueñas   iva cabadelant.
Trocieron Alcoceva,   a diestro dexan Gormaz,   [2875
ó dizen Bado de Rrey   allá ivan pas[s]ar,
a la casa de Berlanga   posada presa han.
Otro día mañana   métense a andar,
a qual dizen Medina   ivan albergar
e de Medina a Molina   en otro día van.   [2880
Al moro Avengalvón   de coraçón le plaz,
saliólos a rrecebir   de buena voluntad,
por amor de Mio Cid   rrica cena les da.
Dent pora Valencia   adeliñechos van;
al que en buen ora nasco   llegava el mensaje,   [2885
privado cavalga,   a rrecebirlos sale,
armas iva teniendo   e grand gozo que faze,
Mio Cid a sus fijas   ívalas abraçar,
besándolas a amas,   tornós' de sonrrisar:
'¡Venides, mis fijas,   Dios vos curie de mal!   [2890
Yo tomé el casamiento,   mas non osé dezir ál.
Plega al Criador,   que en cielo está,
que vos vea mejor casadas   d'aquí en adelant.
¡De mios yernos de Carrión   Dios me faga vengar!'
Besaron las manos   las fijas al padre.   [2895
58v Teniendo ivan armas,   entráronse a la cibdad,
grand gozo fizo con ellas   doña Ximena su madre.
El que en buen ora nasco   non quiso tardar,
fablós' con los sos   en su poridad,
al rrey Alfonso de Castiella   pensó de enbiar: [2900

133

'¿Ó eres, Muño Gustioz,   mio vassallo de pro?
¡En buen ora te crié   a ti en la mi cort!
Lieves el mandado   a Castiella al rrey Alfonso,
por mí bésale la mano   d'alma e de coraçón,
cuemo yo só su vassallo   e él es mio señor,   [2905
d'esta desondra que me an fecha   los ifantes de Carrión
quel' pese al buen rrey   d'alma e de coraçón.
Él casó mis fijas,   ca non ge las di yo;
quando las han dexadas   a grant desonor,

you!' They rested there that night in joy and thankfulness. The next morning they mounted ready for the road. The men of San Esteban, wishing to give them pleasure, escorted them as far as Río d'Amor, and there they bade them farewell and turned back. Minaya and the ladies went on their way across the gully of the Alcoceba; passing Gormaz on their right, they crossed the Douro at Vadorrey and reached the town of Berlanga, where they lodged for the night. Early next day they started off again, reached Medinaceli that night and spent another day on the journey from Medinaceli to Molina. The Moorish governor, Abengalbón, was delighted and went out to bid them a cordial welcome for the love he bore the Cid, and entertained them later to a rich feast. From Molina they went straight on to Valencia. News of their arrival reached the Cid, who mounted quickly and went out to welcome them. As he rode he showed his joy by displaying his skill in arms. The Cid embraced his daughters, kissing them both and smiling with pleasure. 'Here you are, my daughters! May God protect you from all harm! I accepted this marriage, for I did not dare do otherwise. May it please Heaven to let me see you better married in the future! May God grant me vengeance on my sons-in-law of Carrión!' The young women kissed their father's hands and, escorted by the knights performing feats of skill, they entered the city, where their mother, Doña Jimena, received them with great joy. The Cid wasted no time but took counsel immediately with his vassals in private and decided to send a message to King Alfonso of Castile.

133

(He called Muño Gustioz and said to him) 'Muño Gustioz, my brave vassal, I am fortunate in having you among those of my household. You shall carry this message to King Alfonso in Castile. Kiss his hand with cordial respect from me—for I am his vassal and he is my lord. Entreat him to consider as a deep and serious grievance the dishonour done to me by the Infantes of Carrión. The King was responsible for this marriage of my daughters, for I myself did not give them away. The dis-honourable desertion they have suffered is not merely an insult

si desondra í cabe   alguna contra nós,   [2910
la poca e la grant   toda es de mio señor.
Mios averes se me an levado,   que sobejanos son,
esso me puede pesar   con la otra desonor.
Adúgamelos a vistas,   o a juntas o a cortes
como aya derecho   de ifantes de Carrión,   [2915
ca tan grant es la rrencura   dentro en mi coraçón.'
Muño Gustioz   privado cavalgó,
con él dos cavalleros   quel' sirvan a so sabor
e con él escuderos   que son de criazón.
Salién de Valencia   e andan quanto pueden,   [2920
nos' dan vagar   los días e las noches;
59r al rrey   en San Fagunt lo falló.
Rrey es de Castiella   e rrey es de León
e de las Asturias   bien a San Çalvador,
fasta dentro en Sancti Yaguo   de todo es señor,   [2925
e llos condes gallizanos   a él tienen por señor.
Assí como descavalga   aquel Muño Gustioz,
omillós' a los santos   e rrogó a[l] Criador;
adeliñó pora'l palacio   dó estava la cort,
con él dos cavalleros   quel' aguardan cum a señor.   [2930
Assí como entraron   por medio de la cort,
violos el rrey   e connosció a Muño Gustioz,
levantós' el rrey,   tan bien los rrecibió.
Delant el rrey fincó los inojos   aquel Muño Gustioz,
besávale los pies   aquel Muño Gustioz: [2935
'¡Merced, rrey Alfonso,   de largos rreinos a vós dizen señor!
Los pies e las manos   vos besa el Campeador,
ele es vuestro vassallo   e vós sodes so señor.
Casastes sus fijas   con ifantes de Carrión,
alto fue el casamien[t]o   ca lo quisiestes vós.   [2940
Ya vós sabedes la ondra   que es cuntida a nós,
cuemo nos han abiltados   ifantes de Carrión:
mal majaron sus fijas   del Cid Campeador,
majadas e desnudas   a grande desonor,
desenparadas las dexaron   en el rrobredo de Corpes,   [2945
a las bestias fieras   e a las aves del mont.
Afelas sus fijas   en Valencia dó son.
59v Por esto vos besa las manos   como vassallo a señor
que ge los levedes a vistas,   o a juntas o a cortes;
tienes' por desondrado,   mas la vuestra es mayor,   [2950
e que vos pese, rrey,   como sodes sabidor;
que aya Mio Cid derecho   de ifantes de Carrión.'

to me, it is a far greater one to my lord the King, who is responsible for both. They have taken great sums of money from me, which I also consider as an injury. Let the King summon the Infantes to judicial meetings, assemblies or solemn courts to render me justice for the wrong they have done me, which rankles in my heart.' Muño Gustioz rode quickly off with two knights and squires of the Cid's household to attend on him. They left Valencia and travelled with all speed continuously day and night. In Sahagún, Muño Gustioz found Don Alfonso, King of Castile and León, lord of the Asturias and its capital, Oviedo, ruling all the country as far as Santiago, where the Galician counts acknowledged his sovereignty. As soon as he dismounted Muño Gustioz knelt to the saints and prayed to God (in the church of San Facundo). Then he proceeded to the palace where the King held his court, and with him went two knights who attended him as their lord. As they entered the hall of the palace the King saw them and recognised Muño Gustioz. He rose and gave them a friendly welcome. Muño Gustioz knelt before the King and kissed his feet, saying: 'A favour, King and acknowledged lord of many realms! The Campeador kisses your hands and feet, acknowledging himself your vassal and you as his lord. You gave his daughters in marriage to the Infantes of Carrión and in your opinion it was an honour to marry into such a noble family. Now you know what honour has befallen us and how the Infantes of Carrión have disgraced us by their ill-treatment of the Cid's daughters, whom they abandoned, bruised and stripped, in the oak forest of Corpes, exposed to attack from wild beasts and birds of prey. Now that his daughters are safely back in Valencia, the Cid kisses your hands, doing vassal's homage to his lord, and begs you to summon these young men to judicial meetings or assemblies, or to the high court of the land. He considers himself as dishonoured, but that your dishonour is greater still than his. As a wise and prudent lord, you will surely be grieved at this and will grant the Cid satisfaction for the injury done to him by the Infantes of Carrión.'

El rrey una grant ora   calló e comidió:
'Verdad te digo yo   que me pesa de coraçón
e verdad dizes en esto,   tú, Muño Gustioz,   [2955
ca yo casé sus fijas   con ifantes de Carrión;
fizlo por bien   que fuesse a su pro.
¡Si quier el casamiento   fecho non fuesse oy!
Entre yo e Mio Cid   pésanos de coraçón,
ayudar le [é] a derecho,   ¡sín' salve el Criador!   [2960
Lo que non cuidava fer   de toda esta sazón,
andarán mios porteros   por todo mio rreino,
pora dentro en Toledo   pregonarán mi cort,
que allá me vayan   cuendes e ifançones,
mandaré cómo í vayan   ifantes de Carrión   [2965
e cómo den derecho   a Mio Cid el Campeador,

134

e que non aya rrencura   podiendo yo vedallo.
Dezidle al Campeador,   que en buen ora nasco,
que d'estas *siete* semanas   adobes' con sus vassallos,
véngam' a Toledo,   éstol' do de plazo.   [2970
Por amor de Mio Cid   esta cort yo fago.
Saludádmelos a todos,   entr'ellos aya espacio,
6or   d'esto que les abino   aún bien serán ondrados.'
Espidiós' Muño Gustioz,   a Mio Cid es tornado.
Assí como lo dixo,   suyo era el cuidado,   [2975
non lo detiene por nada   Alfonso el castellano,
enbía sus cartas   pora Léon e a Sancti Yaguo,
a los portogaleses   e a galizianos
e a los de Carrión   e a varones castellanos,
que cort fazié en Toledo   aquel rrey ondrado,   [2980
a cabo de *siete* semanas   que í fuessen juntados;
qui non viniesse a la cort   non se toviesse por su vassallo.
Por todas sus tierras   assí lo ivan pensando
que non falliessen   de lo que el rrey avié mandado.

135

Ya les va pesando   a los ifantes de Carrión   [2985
porque en Toledo   el rrey fazié cort;
miedo han que í verná   Mio Cid el Campeador.
Prenden so consejo   assí parientes como son,
rruegan al rrey   que los quite d'esta cort.
Dixo el rrey: 'No lo feré,   ¡sín' salve Dios!   [2990
Ca í verná   Mio Cid el Campeador;

The King remained silent for a long time, reflecting on the matter. 'I am gravely concerned about this, Muño Gustioz' (he said). 'What you say is true, for I did give the Cid's daughters in marriage to the Infantes of Carrión. I did it for the best, thinking that it would be to their advantage. Now I wish the marriage had never taken place. I am as much grieved about it as the Cid, and I promise to do him justice, as I hope for salvation. I shall do something I have not considered doing for a long time. My royal couriers will travel throughout the kingdom, announcing the assembly of a solemn court of justice at Toledo and requiring all counts and baronets to attend. To it I shall summon the Infantes and demand that they give satisfaction to the Cid.

134

No wrong shall be done to him if I can prevent it. Tell the Campeador to prepare to come to Toledo with his vassals within seven weeks—which is the term I allow him. I am calling this court for the Cid's sake. Greet them all in Valencia on my behalf and tell them to be of good cheer, for from this disgrace which has befallen them honour will accrue.' Muño Gustioz took his leave and returned to the Cid. The King took measures to carry out his promise without delay. Alfonso, King of Castile, sent letters to León and Santiago, to the Portuguese and the Galicians, to the lords of Carrión and to the Castilians, announcing that their honoured king would assemble his court in Toledo, and that they should attend it within seven weeks. Anyone who did not attend should cease to be his vassal. Throughout the whole country everyone considered that they should carry out the King's commands in every particular.

135

The Infantes of Carrión were greatly vexed that the King should summon a solemn court of justice at Toledo, for they were afraid that the Cid would attend it. All the members of the family consulted together and begged the King to exempt them from attending this court. The King answered: 'Most certainly not. The Cid will attend this court and I shall see that

dar le [e]des derecho,   ca rrencura ha de vós.
Qui lo fer non quisiesse   o no ir a mi cort,
quite mio rreino,   ca d'él non he sabor.'
Ya lo vieron que es a fer   los ifantes de Carrión,   [2995
prenden consejo   parientes como son;
el conde don García   en estas nuevas fue,
enemigo de Mio Cid   que mal siémprel' buscó,
60v   aquéste consejó   los ifantes de Carrión.
Llegava el plazo,   querién ir a la cort,   [3000
en los primeros va   el buen rrey don Alfonso,
el conde don Anrrich   e el conde don Rremond,
aquéste fue padre   del buen enperador,
el conde don Fruella   e el conde don Beltrán.
Fueron í de su rreino   otros muchos sabidores,   [3005
de toda Castiella   todos los mejores.
El conde don García   con ifantes de Carrión
e As[s]ur Gonçález   e Gonçalo Assúrez,
e Diego e Ferrando   í son amos a dos,
e con ellos grand bando   que aduxieron a la cort: [3010
e[n]baírle cuidan   a Mio Cid el Campeador.
De todas partes   allí juntados son.
Aún non era llegado   el que en buen ora nació,
porque se tarda   el rrey non ha sabor.
Al quinto día   venido es Mio Cid el Campeador,   [3015
[a] Álbar Fáñez   adelántel' enbió
que besasse las manos   al rrey so señor:
bien lo sopiesse   que í serié essa noch.
Quando lo oyó el rrey,   plógol' de coraçón,
con grandes yentes   el rrey cavalgó   [3020
e iva rrecebir   al que en buen ora nació.
Bien aguisado viene   el Cid con todos los sos,
buenas conpañas   que assí an tal señor.
Quando lo ovo a ojo   el buen rrey don Alfonso,
61r   firiós' a tierra   Mio Cid el Campeador,   [3025
biltarse quiere   e ondrar a so señor.
Quando lo oyó el rrey   por nada non tardó:
'¡Par Sant Esidro   verdad non será oy!
Cavalgad, Cid, si non,   non avría de[n]d sabor,
saludar nos hemos   d'alma e de coraçón.   [3030
De lo que a vós pesa   a mí duele el coraçón,
¡Dios lo mande que por vós   se ondre oy la cort!'
'Amen,' dixo   Mio Cid el Campeador,
besóle la mano   e después le saludó:

justice is done him, for he has a complaint to make of you. Whoever refuses to attend my court let him go into exile, for he will have forfeited my favour.' When the Infantes saw that attendance at court could not be avoided they took counsel with their whole family. Count García (Ordóñez), an enemy of the Cid, always ready to do him an ill turn, gave them his advice also. The term allowed had elapsed, and all prepared to attend the court. Among the first to arrive were King Alfonso, Count Henry and Count Raymond of Burgundy—the last was the father of the good emperor Alfonso—Count Fruela and Count Beltrán. A great many other legal experts were there—all the best in the whole of Castile. Others who attended the court were Count García (Ordóñez) with the Infantes of Carrión, and Ansur González and Gonzalo Ansúrez. Diego and Fernando came with a large band of supporters, whom they had brought to the court with the intention of assaulting the Cid. The members of the court had assembled from all directions, but the Cid had not yet arrived, which rather annoyed the King. He came, however, on the fifth day, having sent Álvar Fáñez ahead to announce respectfully to the King his arrival that very night. When the King received this news he was very pleased, and he rode out with a great company of followers to bid the Cid welcome. The Campeador came well prepared, with a great following of vassals worthy of such a lord. When he caught sight of the King the Cid dismounted and prepared to humble himself to do honour to his lord. On seeing this the King came forward at once and said: 'By St Isidore, I shall not allow that! Mount your horse, Cid, otherwise I shall be displeased. We shall exchange the kiss of greeting. I am much grieved for your trouble. God grant that the court may acquit itself well in your case.' 'Amen,' said the Campeador. He kissed the King's hand and then his mouth.

'Grado a Dios quando vos veo, señor. [3035

Omíllom' a vós e al conde do Rremond

e al conde don A[n]rrich e a quantos que í son,

¡Dios salve a nuestros amigos e a vós más, señor!

Mi mugier doña Ximena, dueña es de pro,

bésavos las manos, e mis fijas amas a dos, [3040

d'esto que nos abino que vos pese, señor.'

Rrespondió el rrey: 'Sí fago, ¡sín' salve Dios!'

136

Pora Toledo el rrey tornada da,

essa noch Mio Cid Tajo non quiso passar:

'¡Merced, ya rrey, sí el Criador vos salve! [3045

Pensad, señor, de entrar a la cibdad

e yo con los míos posaré a San Serván;

las mis compañas esta noche llegarán.

Terné vigilia en aqueste sancto logar,

cras mañana entraré a la cibdad [3050

e iré a la cort enantes de yantar.'

Dixo el rrey: 'Plazme de veluntad.'

61v   El rrey don Alfonso a Toledo es entrado,

Mio Cid Rruy Díaz en San Serván posado.

Mandó fazer candelas e poner en el altar, [3055

sabor á de velar en essa santidad,

al Criador rrogando e fablando en poridad.

Entre Minaya e los buenos que í ha

acordados fueron quando vino la man.

Matines e prima dixieron faza'l alba. [3060

137

Suelta fue la missa antes que saliesse el sol

e su ofrenda han fecha muy buena e conplida.

'Vós, Minaya Álbar Fáñez, el mio braço mejor,

vós iredes comigo e el obispo don Jerónimo

e Pero Vermúez e aqueste Muño Gustioz [3065

e Martín Antolínez, el burgalés de pro,

e Álbar Álbarez e Álbar Salvadórez

e Martín Muñoz, que en buen punto nació,

e mio sobrino Félez Muñoz;

comigo irá Mal Anda, que es bien sabidor, [3070

e Galind Garcíez, el bueno d'Aragón;

con éstos cúnplanse ciento de los buenos que í son.

Velmezes vestidos por sufrir las guarnizones,

'I am thankful to see you here. I give you my humble greetings, Count Raymond, Count Henry and all here present. God save our friends and above all you, our lord and King. My noble wife, Doña Jimena, and my two daughters beg you to sympathise with them in their misfortune.' The King answered: 'I do so, as I hope for salvation.'

136

The King made ready to return to Toledo, but the Cid decided not to cross the Tagus that night. 'I beg a favour in God's name. Do you, my liege lord, return to the city while I remain in San Servando, for I expect the rest of my company to arrive tonight. I shall keep vigil in this consecrated place, and tomorrow morning I shall enter the town and shall meet you at the palace before the mid-day meal.' The King replied: 'I give you free permission to do this.' King Alfonso then went back to Toledo, while the Cid Ruy Díaz retired to San Servando. He requested that candles be placed on the altar, for he desired to keep vigil in that holy place, praying to God and communing in secret. Minaya and the Cid's loyal men were ready when morning came. Towards dawn matins and prime were said.

137

Mass was over before the sun rose, and they all made fitting and generous offerings. The Cid then gave these instructions to his followers: 'You, Minaya Álvar Fáñez, my good right arm, will accompany me and so also will the bishop, Don Jerome, Pedro Bermúdez, Muño Gustioz, Martín Antolínez, worthy citizen of Burgos, Álvar Álvarez, the ever fortunate Martín Muñoz, and my nephew Félez Muñoz. Mal Anda, an expert in law, will also accompany me and Galindo Garcíaz, the worthy Aragonese. One hundred good men here present will make up your numbers. I wish you all to put on your padded tunics which help you to bear the armour, over them your coats of

de suso las lorigas   tan blancas como el sol;
sobre las lorigas   armiños e pelliçones   [3075
e, que non parescan las armas,   bien presos los cordones,
so los mantos las espadas   dulces e tajadores;
d'aquesta guisa   quiero ir a la cort
62r   por demandar mios derechos   e dezir mi rrazón.
Si desobra buscaren   ifantes de Carrión,   [3080
dó tales ciento tovier,   bien seré sin pavor.'
Rrespondieron todos: 'Nós esso queremos, señor.'
Assí como lo á dicho,   todos adobados son.
Nos' detiene por nada   el que en buen ora nació:
calças de buen paño   en sus camas metió,   [3085
sobr'ellas unos çapatos   que a grant huebra son,
vistió camisa de rrançal   tan blanca como el sol,
con oro e con plata   todas las presas son,
al puño bien están,   ca él se lo mandó;
sobr'ella un brial   primo de ciclatón,   [3090
obrado es con oro,   parecen por ó son;
sobr'esto una piel vermeja,   las bandas d'oro son,
siempre la viste   Mio Cid el Campeador;
una cofia sobre los pelos   d'un escarín de pro,
con oro es obrada,   fecha por rrazón,   [3095
que non le contal[l]assen los pelos   al buen Cid Canpeador;
la barba avié luenga   e prísola con el cordón,
por tal lo faze esto   que rrecabdar quiere todo lo suyo;
de suso cubrió un manto,   que es de grant valor.
En él abrién que ver   quantos que í son.   [3100
Con aquestos ciento   que adobar mandó
apriessa cavalga,   de San Serván salió;
assí iva Mio Cid   adobado a lla cort.
A la puerta de fuera   descavalga a sabor,
cuerdamientre entra   Mio Cid con todos los sos: [3105
62v   él va en medio   e los ciento aderredor.
Quando lo vieron entrar   al que en buen ora nació,
levantós' en pie   el buen rrey don Alfonso
e el conde don Anrrich   e el conde don Rremont
e desí adelant,   sabet, todos los otros;   [3110
a grant ondra lo rreciben   al que en buen ora nació.
Nos' quiso levantar   el Crespo de Grañón,
nin todos los del bando   de ifantes de Carrión.
El rrey dixo al Cid: 'Venid acá ser, Campeador,
en aqueste escaño   quem' diestes vós en don;   [3115
maguer que [a] algunos pesa,   mejor sodes que nós.'

mail shining like the sun and, over these, ermine or other fur
tunics with strings pulled tight to hide the coats of mail; under
your cloaks carry your sharp, well tempered swords. That is how
I wish to go to the court to demand justice and plead my case.
If the Infantes of Carrión should commit any breach of the peace,
I shall fear nothing with a hundred like you behind me.' They
answered with one accord: 'We agree to do what you wish.'
As they said this they all made ready. Thereupon the Cid
covered his legs with good cloth hose, and over these he drew
his finely worked shoes. He then put on a linen shirt, snow-white
and fastened neatly at the wrist with gold and silver links according to his own instructions. Over this undergarment he wore an
elegant silk gown beautifully worked in gold brocade. His
fur-lined coat was red, with fringes of gold—the one he always
wore. On his head he wore a cambric coif embroidered in gold,
made on purpose so that no one might pluck his hair. The good
Campeador wore his beard long but caught in with a circlet of
cord to avoid any possibility of insult. He then covered everything with a cloak so rich that it would attract the attention of
all beholders. Dressed like this for his appearance at court, he
mounted quickly and left San Servando with those hundred
knights whom he had ordered to get ready. At the main entrance
to the palace the Cid alighted and entered with sober mien,
surrounded by his hundred followers. On seeing the Cid enter,
good King Alfonso and Counts Henry and Raymond of
Burgundy rose, and after them all other members of the court,
to give him an honourable welcome. Neither Count García
Ordóñez nor any of the Carrión faction took the trouble to rise.
The King took the Cid by the hand, saying: 'Come and sit near
me, Campeador, on this bench which was a gift to me from you.
Although many will begrudge it to you, I give you the place of

Essora dixo muchas mercedes   el que Valencia gañó:
'Sed en vuestro escaño   como rrey e señor,
acá posaré   con todos aquestos míos.'
Lo que dixo el Cid   al rrey plogo de coraçón.   [3120
En un escaño torniño   essora Mio Cid posó,
los ciento quel' aguardan   posan aderredor.
Catando están a Mio Cid   quantos ha en la cort,
a la barba que avié luenga   e presa con el cordón,
en sos aguisamientos   bien semeja varón,   [3125
nol' pueden catar de vergüença   ifantes de Carrión.
Essora se levó en pie   el buen rrey don Alfonso:
'¡Oíd, mesnadas,   sí vos vala el Criador!
Yo, de que fu rrey,   non fiz más de dos cortes,
la una fue en Burgos   e la otra en Carrión;   [3130
esta tercera   a Toledo la vin fer oy
por el amor de Mio Cid,   el que en buen ora nació,
63r   que rreciba derecho   de ifantes de Carrión.
Grande tuerto le han tenido,   sabémoslo todos nós;
alcaldes sean d'esto   el conde don Anrrich e el conde
                             don Rremond   [3135
e estos otros condes   que del vando non sodes.
Todos meted í mientes,   ca sodes coñoscedores,
por escoger el derecho,   ca tuerto non mando yo.
D'ella e d'ella part   en paz seamos oy:
juro par Sant Esidro,   el que bolviere mi cort   [3140
quitar me á el rreino,   perderá mi amor.
Con el que toviere derecho   yo d'essa parte me só.
Agora demande   Mio Cid el Campeador;
sabremos qué rresponden   ifantes de Carrión.'
Mio Cid la mano besó al rrey   e en pie se levantó: [3145
'Mucho vos lo gradesco   como a rrey e a señor
por quanto esta cort   fiziestes por mi amor.
Esto les demando   a ifantes de Carrión:
por mis fijas quem' dexaron   yo non he desonor,
ca vós las casastes, rrey,   sabredes qué fer oy;   [3150
mas quando sacaron mis fijas   de Valencia la mayor,
yo bien los quería   d'alma e de coraçón,
diles dos espadas   a Colada e a Tizón,
éstas yo las gané   a guisa de varón,
ques' ondrassen con ellas   e sirviessen a vós;   [3155
quando dexaron mis fijas   en el rrobredo de Corpes
comigo non quisieron aver nada   e perdieron mi amor;
denme mis espadas   quando mios yernos non son.'

greatest honour.' The conqueror of Valencia thanked the King warmly and said: 'Remain in the seat of honour as king and liege lord; I shall stay where I am with these followers of mine.' These words of the Cid pleased the King greatly. The Campeador then took his seat on a finely turned bench with his hundred men in attendance around him. All the court gazed at the Cid, with his long beard caught in with the cord, displaying his manly worth in all his accoutrements—all except the Infantes of Carrión, who dared not look at him for shame. Then King Alfonso stood up and addressed the assembly: 'Listen, my vassals, as you hope for God's protection. Since I became king I have not held more than two full courts of justice, one in Burgos and the other in Carrión. I have come to Toledo to hold a third today for the Cid's sake, so that he may receive satisfaction from the Infantes of Carrión, for we all know they have done him a great wrong. Let Counts Henry and Raymond act as judges in this case and with them the other counts who do not belong to the Carrión faction. All of you give it your closest attention as experts to choose the right, for I will authorise no wrong. Let peace reign between the two parties. I swear by St Isidore that anyone who disturbs the court shall lose my favour and leave my kingdom. I side with the party which is proved to be in the right. Now let the Cid pronounce his accusation and we shall then hear what answer the Infantes of Carrión will make.' The Cid stood up and did obeisance to the King. 'I am truly grateful', he said, 'to you as my king and lord for summoning this court for my sake. With regard to the Infantes of Carrión, my complaint is this. In deserting my daughters they did no dishonour to me, for you gave them in marriage and you will know what to do on that score today. When they took my dearly beloved daughters away from Valencia I gave them two swords, Colada and Tizón—which I won by my own skill—that they might gain honour with them in your service. When they abandoned my daughters in the oak forest of Corpes they showed that they wished to have no more connexion with me and broke all bonds of friendship and affection. Let them give me back the swords, as they are no longer my sons-in-law.' The judges confirmed the

G

63v Atorgan los alcaldes: 'Tod' esto es rrazón.'
Dixo el conde don García: 'A esto fablemos nós.'   [3160
Essora salién aparte   iffantes de Carrión
con todos sus parientes   e el vando que í son,
apriessa lo ivan trayendo   e acuerdan la rrazón:
'Aún grand amor nos faze   el Cid Campeador
quando desondra de sus fijas   no nos demanda oy,   [3165
bien nos abendremos   con el rrey don Alfonso.
Démosle sus espadas   quando assí finca la boz,
e quando las toviere   partir se á la cort;
ya más non avrá derecho   de nós el Cid Canpeador.'
Con aquesta fabla   tornaron a la cort: [3170
'¡Merced, ya rrey don Alfonso,   sodes nuestro señor!
No lo podemos negar   ca dos espadas nos dio,
quando las demanda   e d'ellas ha sabor
dárgelas queremos   delant estando vós.'
Sacaron las espadas   Colada e Tizón,   [3175
pusiéronlas en mano   del rrey so señor,
saca las espadas   e rrelumbra toda la cort,
las maçanas e los arriazes   todos d'oro son.
Maravíllanse d'ellas   todos los omnes buenos de la cort.
Rrecibió [*el Cid*] las espadas,   las manos le besó,   [3180
tornós' al escaño   dón se levantó,
en las manos las tiene   e amas las cató,
nos' le pueden camear   ca el Cid bien las connosce,
alegrós'le tod' el cuerpo,   sonrrisós' de coraçón,
alçava la mano,   a la barba se tomó: [3185
'¡Par aquesta barba   que nadi non' messó,
64r assís' irán vengando   don Elvira e doña Sol!'
A so sobrino   por nónbrel' llamó,
tendió el braço,   la espada Tizón le dio:
'Prendetla, sobrino,   ca mejora en señor.'   [3190
A Martín Antolínez,   el burgalés de pro,
tendió el braço,   el espada Coládal' dio:
'Martín Antolínez,   mio vassallo de pro,
prended a Colada,   ganéla de buen señor,
del conde d*o* Rremont Verenguel   de Barcilona la mayor. [3195
Por esso vos la do   que la bien curiedes vós;
sé que si vos acaeciere   . . . . . .
con ella ganaredes   grand prez e grand valor.'   [3197b
Besóle la mano,   el espada tomó e rrecibió.
Luego se levantó   Mio Cid el Campeador:
'Grado al Criador   e a vós, rrey señor,   [3200

justice of this plea. Count García (Ordóñez) said: 'We should like to consult about this matter.' Then the Infantes of Carrión went aside to discuss the question with all their relations and their party there. They decided at once to accede to the request, saying: 'The Cid Campeador does us a great favour by not demanding satisfaction today for the insult to his daughters. We shall easily come to an understanding with King Alfonso. Let us give the Cid his swords, as he has ended his pleading, so that when he has received them he will leave the court and make no more demands on us.' They returned to the court to announce this decision: 'We beg permission to speak, King Alfonso, our liege lord. We cannot deny that the Cid gave us two swords. As he demands them and wishes to have them returned we shall give them to him here in your presence.' They brought out the swords, Colada and Tizón, and placed them in the hands of the King, their liege lord. When the swords were drawn they dazzled the whole court with their golden pommels and cross-guards, to the amazement of all beholders. The Cid received them, kissed the King's hands and returned to the bench from which he had risen. Holding up the swords he examined them closely; there was no possibility of their having been changed, for he knew them well. The joy that filled his heart was seen in his smile and every movement of his body. He raised his hand and grasped his beard, saying: 'By this beard that none has ever plucked, they will help me to take vengeance for Doña Elvira and Doña Sol.' The Cid then called his nephew (Pedro Bermúdez) to him and, handing him the sword Tizón, he said: 'Take it, nephew, you will prove a better master.' To Martín Antolínez he handed the sword Colada, saying: 'Martín Antolínez, my staunch vassal, take Colada, which I won from a good master, Ramón Berenguer of the great city of Barcelona. I give it to you that you may guard it with great care. I know that, if an occasion arises for you to use it, this sword will bring you great honour and esteem.' Martín Antolínez kissed the Cid's hand and accepted the sword. Then the Campeador rose and spoke again: 'Thanks be to God, the Creator, and to you, my liege lord and

ya pagado só de mis espadas,   de Colada e de Tizón.
Otra rrencura he   de ifantes de Carrión:
quando sacaron de Valencia   mis fijas amas a dos
en oro e en plata   tres mill marcos les di [γ]o,
yo faziendo esto,   ellos acabaron lo so;   [3205
denme mis averes   quando mios yernos non son.'
¡Aquí veriedes quexarse   ifantes de Carrión!
Dize el conde don Rremond: 'Dezid de sí o de no.'
Essora rresponden   ifantes de Carrión:
'Por éssol' diemos sus espadas   al Cid Campeador   [3210
que ál no nos demandasse,   que aquí fincó la boz.'
'Si ploguiere al rrey,   assí dezimos nós:
a lo que demanda el Cid   quel' rrecudades vós.'

64v   Dixo el buen rrey: 'Assí lo otorgo yo.'
Levantós' en pie   el Cid Campeador: [3215
'D'estos averes   que vos di yo
si me los dades,   o dedes [d'ello rraçón].'   [3216b
Essora salién aparte   ifantes de Carrión,
non acuerdan en consejo   ca los haveres grandes son,
espesos los han   ifantes de Carrión.
Tornan con el consejo   e fablavan a so *señor*:   [3220
'Mucho nos afinca   el que Valencia gañó
quando de nuestros averes   assil' prende sabor,
pagar le hemos de heredades   en tierras de Carrión.'
Dixieron los alcaldes   quando manifestados son:
'Si esso ploguiere al Cid,   non ge lo vedamos nós,   [3225
mas en nuestro juvizio   assí lo mandamos nós
que aquí lo enterguedes   dentro en la cort.'
A estas palabras   fabló el rrey don Alfonso:
'Nós bien la sabemos   aquesta rrazón
que derecho demanda   el Cid Campeador.   [3230
D'estos *tres* mill marcos   los *dozientos* tengo yo,
entr'amos me los dieron   los ifantes de Carrión;
tornárgelos quiero,   ca *tan des*fechos son,
enterguen a Mio Cid,   el que en buen ora nació;
quando ellos los an a pechar,   non ge los quiero yo.'   [3235
Fabló Ferrán Go[n]çález: 'Averes monedados non tenemos nós.'
Luego rrespondió   el conde don Rremond:
'El oro e la plata   espendiésteslo vós,
por juvizio lo damos   ant'el rrey don Alfonso:
páguenle en apreciadura   e préndalo el Campeador.'   [3240
Ya vieron que es a fer   los ifantes de Carrión:

65r   veriedes aduzir   tanto cavallo corredor,

king, I have now received satisfaction for my swords, Colada and Tizón. I have a further complaint to make against the Infantes of Carrión. When they took my daughters away from Valencia, I gave them three thousand marks in gold and silver. In spite of this generosity on my part, they carried out what they had planned to do. Let them give me back my money as they have ceased to be my sons-in-law.' When the Infantes began to show distress, Count Raymond of Burgundy said: 'Say yes or no.' The young men answered: 'We gave the Cid his swords so that he should ask for nothing more, and his claim ended there.' Count Raymond answered: 'We decide this, subject to the King's pleasure, that you satisfy the demand of the Cid.' The King said: 'I confirm your decision.' Then the Cid Campeador rose again to his feet and said: 'Either return me the money I gave you or justify your action.' The Infantes of Carrión went aside to talk it over, but could find no solution to the problem, for it involved a considerable amount of money which they had already spent. The young men returned and said to the King: 'The conqueror of Valencia' (they said) 'is pressing us hard in his demand for our money. We shall pay him in property and land in Carrión.' When they had recognised their debt in these words the judges spoke as follows: 'We shall authorise this if it satisfies the Cid, but the sentence we pronounce is that they pay him here in the court.' At this point King Alfonso spoke, saying: 'We realise that the Cid has right on his side in this matter. Of these three thousand marks I hold two hundred which the Infantes gave to me on the conclusion of the match. As they are so impoverished, I shall return this sum to them. Let them pass it on to the Cid, for, if they have to pay back these marks, I have no wish to keep them.' Fernando González said: 'We have no ready money.' Then Count Raymond answered them: 'As you have spent all the gold and silver, we pronounce this sentence in the presence of King Alfonso; that the Infantes make a payment in kind which the Cid shall accept.' At this the Infantes of Carrión saw that they must comply with the verdict. You should have seen brought in all the swift horses and stout mules, all the palfreys

tanta gruessa mula,   tanto palafré de sazón,
tanta buena espada   con toda guarnizón;
rrecibiólo Mio Cid   como apreciaron en la cort.   [3245
Sobre los dozientos marcos   que tenié el rrey Alfonso,
pagaron los ifantes   al que en buen ora nasco,
enpréstanles de lo ageno,   que non les cumple lo suyo,
mal escapan jogados,   sabed, d'esta rrazón.

138
Estas apreciaduras   Mio Cid presas las ha,   [3250
sos omnes las tienen   e d'ellas pensarán,
mas quando esto ovo acabado   pensaron luego d'ál:
'¡Merced, *ya* rrey señor,   por amor de caridad!
La rrencura mayor   non se me puede olbidar.
Oídme toda la cort   e pésevos de mio mal: [3255
de los ifantes de Carrión,   quem' desondraron tan mal,
a menos de rriebtos   no los puedo dexar.

139
Dezid, ¿qué vos merecí,   ifantes [*de Carrión*],
en juego o en vero | o en alguna rrazón?   [3258b-59
Aquí lo mejoraré   a juvizio de la cort.   [3259b
¿A quém' descubriestes   las telas del coraçón?   [3260
A la salida de Valencia   mis fijas vos di yo
con muy grand ondra   e averes a nombre;
quando las non queriedes,   ya canes traidores,
¿por qué las sacávades   de Valencia sus honores?
¿A qué las firiestes   a cinchas e a espolones?   [3265
Solas las dexastes   en el rrobredo de Corpes
a las bestias fieras   e a las aves del mont;
por quanto les fiziestes   menos valedes vós.
65v   Si non rrecudedes,   véalo esta cort.'

140
El conde don García   en pie se levantava: [3270
'¡Merced, ya rrey,   el mejor de toda España!
Vezós' Mio Cid   a llas cortes pregonadas;
dexóla crecer   e luenga trae la barba,
los unos le han miedo   e los otros espanta.
Los de Carrión   son de natura tal   [3275
non ge las devién querer   sus fijas por varraganas,
o ¿quién ge las diera   por parejas o por veladas?
Derecho fizieron   por que las han dexadas.

in fine condition, the good swords and coats of mail. The Cid
received them according to the reckoning of the court. Over
and above the two hundred marks held by King Alfonso the
young men paid the Cid all they could. They borrowed from
other people when what they had did not suffice. The tables were
certainly turned against them that day.

138

The Cid accepted the payment in kind and handed over the
various items to the care of his followers. When this business
was finished, another point was brought forward (by the Cid):
'I beg a favour of my lord the King in God's name. I cannot
forget my greatest cause of complaint. Let the court hear me and
sympathise with me in the wrong I have suffered. I cannot allow
the Infantes of Carrión, who have done me such dishonour, to
escape without a challenge.'

139

(Then, addressing the Infantes directly, the Cid continued)
'Tell me, Infantes of Carrión, what injury, real or imaginary,
have I ever done you? I am willing here and now to make it
good as the court may decide. Why did you wound my deepest
feelings? When you left Valencia I entrusted my daughters to
you with all due honour and abundant wealth. If you had no
love for them, you treacherous dogs, why did you take them
from their estates in Valencia? Why did you strike them with
belts and spurs? You abandoned them in the oak forest of Corpes,
at the mercy of wild beasts and birds of prey. In doing this you
have incurred infamy. If you do not give satisfaction for this
crime, let the court pass judgement.'

140

Count García (Ordóñez) rose to his feet and said: 'Give me
leave to speak, O King, greatest in all Spain. The Cid is used to
attending meetings of this solemn court of justice; he allowed his
beard to grow long to strike terror in the hearts of all. The lords
of Carrión are of such noble lineage that they should not consider his daughters fit to be their concubines. Who gave them to
them as lawful wedded wives? They did right in deserting them.

Quanto él dize   non ge lo preciamos nada.'
Essora el Campeador   prisos' a la barba: [3280
'¡Grado a Dios   que cielo e tierra manda!
Por esso es lue[n]ga   que a delicio fue criada;
¿qué avedes vós, conde,   por rretraer la mi barba?
Ca de quando nasco   a delicio fue criada,
ca non me priso a ella   fijo de mugier nada,   [3285
nimbla messó   fijo de moro nin de cristiana,
como yo a vós, conde,   en el castiello de Cabra;
quando pris a Cabra   e a vós por la barba,
non í ovo rrapaz   que non messó su pulgada.
La que yo messé   aún non es eguada.'   [3290

141
Ferrán Go[n]çález   en pie se levantó,
a altas vozes   odredes qué fabló:
'Dexássedes vós, Cid,   de aquesta rrazón;
de vuestros averes   de todos pagado sodes.
Non creciés varaja   entre nós e vós.   [3295
66r De natura somos   de condes de Carrión,
deviemos casar con fijas   de rreyes o de enperadores,
ca non pertenecién   fijas de ifançones.
Por que las dexamos   derecho fiziemos nós;
más nos preciamos,   sabet, que menos no.'   [3300

142
Mio Cid Rruy Díaz   a Pero Vermúez cata:
'¡Fabla, Pero Mudo,   varón que tanto callas!
Yo las he fijas   e tú primas cormanas;
a mí lo dizen,   a ti dan las orejadas.
Si yo rrespondier,   tú non entrarás en armas.'   [3305

143
Pero Vermúez   conpeçó de fablar,
detiénes'le la lengua,   non puede delibrar,
mas quando enpieça,   sabed, nol' da vagar:
'¡Dirévos, Cid,   costu[m]bres avedes tales,
siempre en las cortes   "Pero Mudo" me llamades!   [3310
Bien lo sabedes   que yo non puedo más;
por lo que yo ovier a fer   por mí non mancará.
Mientes, Ferrando,   de quanto dicho has,
por el Campeador   mucho valiestes más.
Las tus mañas   yo te las sabré contar: [3315
¡miémbrat' quando lidiamos   cerca Valencia la grand!

We care nothing for his accusations. At this the Campeador grasped his beard and answered: 'Thanks be to almighty God, it is long because it has had much loving care lavished on it. What reproach can you cast on my beard? All my life it has been my chief delight. No woman's son has ever plucked it and no one, Moor or Christian, ever tore it—as happened to yours, Count, in the castle of Cabra. When I took Cabra and plucked your beard, there was not a lad but tore out his bit. The piece that I pulled out has still not grown even again.'

141

Fernando González stood up and shouted: 'Forbear to press this claim, Cid; now that you have your money's worth returned, you may be content. We have no wish to continue this mutual strife. We are of the family of the counts of Carrión and have a right to marry the daughters of kings and emperors, and the daughters of petty nobles are not our equals. We did right in deserting them, and in doing so we are raised, not lowered, in the esteem of the world.'

142

The Cid Ruy Díaz looked at Pedro Bermúdez and said: 'Speak, Pedro Mudo, you silent man! They are my daughters but they are also your cousins. They insult me but they aim to strike your cheek. If I take up the challenge, you will have no chance of defending their cause.'

143

Pedro Bermúdez spoke in his turn, a little tongue-tied at first, but once he started there was no stopping him. 'I declare, Cid, you have got into the habit in every assembly of calling me Pedro Mudo! You know very well that I cannot help my defect of speech, but I shall not fail where deeds are concerned.' (Turning to Fernando he said) 'You lie, Fernando, in all you have said. It was an honour for you to be connected with the Campeador. I could tell a few tales about you! Remember what happened when we were fighting near Valencia. You asked the Cid's

Pedist las feridas primeras   al Canpeador leal,
vist un moro,   fústel' ensayar,
antes fuxiste   que a'l te allegasses.   [3318b]
Si yo non uviás,   el moro te jugara mal;
passé por ti,   con el moro me of de ajuntar,   [3320]
de los primeros colpes   ofle de arrancar;
did' el cavallo,   tóveldo en poridat,
fasta este día   no lo descubrí a nadi.

66v   Delant Mio Cid e delante todos   ovístete de alabar
que mataras el moro   e que fizieras barnax;   [3325]
croviérontelo todos,   mas non saben la verdad.
¡E eres fermoso,   mas mal varragán!
Lengua sin manos,   ¿cuémo osas fablar?

144
Di, Ferrando,   otorga esta rrazón:
¿non te viene en miente   en Valencia lo del león,   [3330]
quando durmié Mio Cid   e el león se desató?
E tú, Ferrando,   ¿qué fizist con el pavor?
¡Metístet' tras el escaño   de Mio Cid el Campeador!
Metístet', Ferrando,   por ó menos vales oy.
Nós cercamos el escaño   por curiar nuestro señor,   [3335]
fasta dó despertó Mio Cid,   el que Valencia gañó;
levantós' del escaño   e fues' pora'l león.
El león premió la cabeça,   a Mio Cid esperó,
dexós'le prender al cuello   e a la rred le metió.
Quando se tornó   el buen Campeador,   [3340]
a sos vassallos   violos aderredor,
demandó por sus yernos,   ¡ninguno non falló!
Rriébtot' el cuerpo   por malo e por traidor,
éstot' lidiaré aquí   ant' el rrey don Alfonso
por fijas del Cid,   don Elvira e doña Sol,   [3345]
por quanto las dexastes   menos valedes vós;
ellas son mugieres   e vós sodes varones,
en todas guisas   más valen que vós.
Quando fuere la lid,   si ploguiere al Criador,
67r   tú lo otorgarás   a guisa de traidor;   [3350]
de quanto he dicho   verdadero seré yo.'
D'aquestos amos   aquí quedó la rrazón.

145
Diego Gonçález   odredes lo que dixo:
'De natura somos   de los condes más li[m]pios,

permission to deal the first blows. You caught sight of a Moor and went forward to pit yourself against him, but you ran away instead, before you came up to him. If I had not gone to your aid, that Moor would have got the better of you. I outstripped you, engaged the Moor and defeated him at once. I gave you his horse and kept quiet about it, and have not told it to a soul until now. You were able to boast to the Cid and everyone else that you had killed the Moor and won your spurs. They all believed you but they do not know the truth. You are a handsome fellow, but a coward. You empty braggart, how dare you talk?

144

Tell me, Fernando, confess it now. Do you remember about the lion in Valencia—when the Cid was asleep and the lion got loose? What did you do, Fernando, in your fright? You got behind the Cid's couch—and showed yourself a coward. We stood round the couch to protect our lord until he, the conqueror of Valencia, woke up. He got up and went towards the lion. The lion bent down his head and waited for the Cid. Then he let himself be caught by the neck and put back in the net. When the good Campeador rejoined his vassals he looked round and asked for his sons-in-law, but could see no sign of them. I therefore challenge you in person as an evildoer and traitor. I shall maintain this in combat with you here in the presence of King Alfonso—on behalf of the Cid's daughters, Doña Elvira and Doña Sol. By deserting them you incurred infamy. They are women and you are a man, but they are your superiors in every way. When—God willing—it comes to fighting you will confess yourself a traitor, and I shall prove myself right in all I have said.' Here the altercation ended between these two.

145

Then Diego González spoke: 'We are high-born nobles and

estos casamientos   non fuessen aparecidos,   [3355
por consagrar   con Mio Cid don Rrodrigo.
Porque dexamos sus fijas   aún no nos rrepentimos,
mientra que bivan   pueden aver sospiros;
lo que les fiziemos   ser les ha rretraído,
esto lidiaré   a tod' el más ardido,   [3359b
que porque las dexamos   ondrados somos nós.'   [3360

146
Martín Antolínez   en pie se levantava:
'¡Calla, alevoso,   boca sin verdad!
Lo del león   non se te deve olbidar,
saliste por la puerta,   metístet' al corral,
fústed' meter   tras la viga lagar,   [3365
¡más non vestist   el manto nin el brial!
Yo llo lidiaré,   non passará por ál,
fijas del Cid   porque las vós dexastes;
en todas guisas, sabed,   que más valen que vós.
Al partir de la lid   por tu boca lo dirás   [3370
que eres traidor   e mintist de quanto dicho has.'
D'estos amos   la rrazón fincó.

147
Assur Gonçález   entrava por el palacio,
manto armiño   e un brial rrastrando,
vermejo viene,   ca era almorzado,   [3375
67v en lo que fabló   avié poco rrecabdo:

148
'Ya varones,   ¿quién vio nunca tal mal?
¿Quién nos darié nuevas   de Mio Cid el de Bivar?
¡Fuesse a Rrío d'Ovirna   los molinos picar
e prender maquilas,   como lo suele far!   [3380
¿Quíl' darié   con los de Carrión a casar?'

149
Essora Muño Gustioz   en pie se levantó:
'¡Calla, alevoso,   malo e traidor!
Antes almuerzas   que vayas a oración,
a los que das paz   fártaslos aderredor.   [3385
Non dizes verdad   [a] amigo ni a señor,
falso a todos   e más al Criador;
en tu amistad   non quiero aver rración.
Fazer te lo [é] dezir   que tal eres qual digo yo.'

we should not have made these marriages or entered into any
kind of relationship with the Cid, Don Rodrigo (of Vivar).
We do not repent of deserting his daughters, but they will
regret it, for as long as they live what we did will be cast up to
them. I shall defend this against the best champion: that by
deserting them we gained honour.'

146

Martín Antolínez rose to his feet and said: 'Hold your tongue,
traitor and liar that you are. Do not forget what happened with
the lion. You ran out by the door and got into the yard. You
hid behind the wine press, and your cloak and tunic were never
fit to wear again. I am bound to fight you on this point—that,
because you deserted them, the Cid's daughters are superior to
you in every respect. When the fight is over you will confess
yourself a traitor and that everything you have said is a lie.'
When the challenge to the two brothers was completed (the
third appeared),

147

Ansur González entered the hall, dragging his ermine cloak
and his tunic. Red-faced, he came straight from the table, and
there was little sense in what he said:

148

'Gentlemen, who ever saw such a thing? Who ever heard of
the Cid, that fellow from Vivar? Let him be off to the river
Ubierna to dress his millstones and collect his miller's tolls as
usual. Who gave him the right to marry into the Carrión family?'

149

Then Muño Gustioz stood up and said: 'Hold your tongue,
you wicked and deceitful traitor! You always breakfast before
going to say your prayers, and when you give the kiss of peace
you belch in people's faces. You lie to friend and lord—false to
them all and still more to God. I want no part in your friendship.
I shall make you confess that you are such a man as I say.' Then

Dixo el rrey Alfonso: 'Calle ya esta rrazón.   [3390
Los que an rrebtado   lidiarán, ¡sín' salve Dios!'
Assí como acaban   esta rrazón,
afé dos cavalleros   entraron por la cort,
al uno dizen Ojarra   e al otro Yéñego Siménez,
el uno es [del] ifante de Navarra | e el otro [del]
                              ifante de Aragón.   [3395-96
Besan las manos   al rrey don Alfonso,
piden sus fijas   a Mio Cid el Campeador
por ser rreínas   de Navarra e de Aragón
e que ge las diessen   a ondra e a bendición.   [3400

68r   A esto callaron   e ascuchó toda la cort.
Levantós' en pie   Mio Cid el Campeador:
'¡Merced, rrey Alfonso,   vós sodes mio señor!
Esto gradesco yo   al Criador,
quando me las demandan   de Navarra e de Aragón.   [3405
Vós las casastes antes,   ca yo non,
afé mis fijas   en vuestras manos son;
sin vuestro mandado   nada non feré yo.'
Levantós' el rrey,   fizo callar la cort:
'Rruégovos, Cid,   caboso Campeador,   [3410
que plega a vós   e atorgar lo he yo,
este casamiento   oy se otorgue en esta cort,
ca crece vos í ondra   e tierra e onor.'
Levantós' Mio Cid,   al rrey las manos le besó:
'Quando a vós plaze,   otórgolo yo, señor.'   [3415
Essora dixo el rrey: '¡Dios vos dé dén buen galardón!
A vós, Ojarra,   e a vós, Yéñego Ximénez,
este casamiento   otórgovosle yo
de fijas de Mio Cid,   don Elvira e doña Sol,
pora los ifantes   de Navarra e de Aragón,   [3420
que vos las den   a ondra e a bendición.'
Levantós' en pie   Ojarra e Íñego Ximénez,
besaron las manos   del rrey don Alfonso
e después de Mio Cid   el Campeador,
metieron las fes   e los omenajes dados son   [3425
que cuemo es dicho   assí sea, o mejor.

68v   A muchos plaze   de tod' esta cort,
mas non plaze   a los ifantes de Carrión.
Minaya Álba[r] Fáñez   en pie se levantó:
'¡Merced vos pido   como a rrey e a señor   [3430
e que non pese esto   al Cid Campeador:
bien vos di vagar   en toda esta cort,

King Alfonso spoke: 'That is enough. Those who have challenged shall proceed to combat, in God's name.' Just as this exchange of words ended, two knights entered the hall. One, called Ojarra, represented the Prince of Navarre and the other, Íñigo Jiménez, the Prince of Aragon. They kissed King Alfonso's hands, asking him to grant permission for the daughters of the Cid to be married with all due ceremony to these princes and so become Queens of Navarre and Aragon. They ceased speaking and the assembly waited to hear the answer. The Cid rose and said: 'I beg a favour of you, King Alfonso, as my liege lord. I am thankful to God that the Princes of Navarre and Aragon should ask for the hands of my daughters. You gave them in marriage before—for I had no part in making the match. Here are my daughters, I give them to you. I shall act according to your decision.' The King rose and begged for silence in the hall: 'I ask you, illustrious Cid' (he said) 'to give your consent to this marriage, which I authorise before this court. It will bring you honour, consideration and wealth.' The Cid rose and kissed the King's hands, saying: 'As you desire it, I give my consent.' The King replied: 'God reward you for this! To you, Ojarra, and to you, Íñigo Jiménez, I give authority for this marriage of the daughters of the Cid, Doña Elvira and Doña Sol, with the Princes of Navarre and Aragon to be celebrated with all due ceremony.' Ojarra and Íñigo Jiménez stood up and kissed the King's hands, and then those of the Cid Campeador. Homage was done and a solemn oath was sworn that the contract should be duly carried out. Many were pleased at this event, but not the Infantes of Carrión, who found nothing pleasing in it. Then Minaya Álvar Fáñez rose to his feet and said: 'I beg leave to speak, my king and lord, with all due respect to the Cid Campeador. I have kept silent through all these proceedings but now I wish

dezir querría   yaquanto de lo mío.'
Dixo el rrey: 'Plazme de coraçón;
dezid, Minaya,   lo que oviéredes sabor.'   [3435
'Yo vos rruego   que me oyades toda la cort,
ca grand rrencura he   de ifantes de Carrión.
Yo les di mis primas   por mandado del rrey Alfonso,
ellos las prisieron   a ondra e a bendición;
grandes averes les dio   Mio Cid el Campeador,   [3440
ellos las han dexadas   a pesar de nós.
Rriébtoles los cuerpos   por malos e por traidores.
De natura sodes   de los de Vanigómez
onde salién condes   de prez e de valor;
mas bien sabemos   las mañas que ellos han.   [3445
Esto gradesco yo   al Criador
quando piden mis primas   don Elvira e doña Sol
los ifantes de Navarra   e de Aragón.
Antes las aviedes parejas   pora en braços las tener,
agora besaredes sus manos   e llamar las hedes señoras,   [3450
aver las hedes a servir,   mal que vos pese a vós.
¡Grado a Dios del cielo   e [a] aquel rrey don Alfonso
69r   assil' crece la ondra   a Mio Cid el Campeador!
En todas guisas   tales sodes quales digo yo:
si ay qui rresponda   o dize de no,   [3455
yo só Álbar Fáñez   pora tod' el mejor.'
Gómez Peláyet   en pie se levantó:
'¿Qué val, Minaya,   toda essa rrazón?
Ca en esta cort   afarto[s] ha pora vós
e qui ál quisiesse   serié su ocasión.   [3460
Si Dios quisiere   que d'ésta bien salgamos nós,
después veredes   qué dixiestes o qué no.'
Dixo el rrey: 'Fine esta rrazón,
non diga ninguno   d'ella más una entención.
Cras sea la lid,   quando saliere el sol,   [3465
d'estos *tres* por tres   que rrebtaron en la cort.'
Luego fablaron   ifantes de Carrión:
'Dandos, rrey, plazo,   ca cras ser non puede,
armas e cavallos tienen   los del Canpeador,
nós antes abremos a ir   a tierras de Carrión.'   [3470
Fabló el rrey   contra'l Campeador:
'Sea esta lid   ó mandáredes vós.'
En essora dixo Mio Cid: 'No lo faré, señor;
más quiero a Valencia   que tierras de Carrión.'
En essora dixo el rrey: 'A osadas, Campeador.   [3475

to have my say in the matter.' The King replied: 'You have my permission to speak. Say what you wish, Minaya.' Minaya continued: 'I ask all here in this court to listen to me, for I have a great complaint to make against the Infantes of Carrión. I gave them my cousins in marriage on behalf of King Alfonso, and the marriage was celebrated. The Cid gave them great wealth but they, in defiance of us, abandoned their wives. I challenge them as wicked traitors. You belong to the family of the Beni-Gómez, which has produced counts of valour and worth. But well we know the evil manners of these young men today. I thank God that the Princes of Navarre and Aragon have asked for the hands of my cousins, Doña Elvira and Doña Sol. Once you had them as wives and equals, but now you will kiss their hands and acknowledge them as your superiors. You will have to do them service, however unwillingly. I thank God and good King Alfonso, for thus is the honour of the Cid enhanced. In every respect you are such men as I say. If anyone should answer or contradict me, I am Álvar Fáñez and will uphold my statement.' Gómez Peláez rose and said: 'What is the use of all this talk, Minaya? For in this court there are more than enough to take you on, and he who said otherwise would do so at his peril. If God wills that we should come off best in this affair, we shall then see what there was in your claim.' The King said: 'Enough of this. Let no one make any further allegations. The combat shall take place tomorrow at sunrise between the three on each side who took part in the challenge before the court.' At this the Infantes put in a plea, saying: 'Give us more time to prepare, King Alfonso, for we shall not be ready tomorrow. We have given up our arms and horses to the Campeador and we shall have to go to Carrión before we can fight.' The King, addressing the Cid, said: 'Let the combat take place where you decide.' The Cid replied: 'I shall not decide, for I prefer (to go to) Valencia (than) to Carrión.' The King then continued: 'As you

Dadme vuestros cavalleros   con todas vuestras guarnizones,
vayan comigo,   yo seré el curiador,
yo vos lo sobrelievo   como a buen vassallo faze señor
que non prendan fuerça   de conde nin de ifançón.

69v Aquí les pongo plazo   de dentro en mi cort,   [3480
a cabo de tres semanas   en begas de Carrión
que fagan esta lid   delant estando yo:
quien non viniere al plazo   pierda la rrazón,
desí sea vencido   e escape por traidor.'
Prisieron el juizio   ifantes de Carrión.   [3485
Mio Cid al rrey   las manos le besó
e dixo: 'Plazme, [señor].   [3486b
Estos mis tres cavalleros   en vuestra mano son,
d'aquí vos los acomiendo   como a rrey e a señor;
ellos son adobados   pora cumplir todo lo so,
¡ondrados me los enbiad a Valencia,   por amor
del Criador!'   [3490
Essora rrespuso el rrey: '¡Assí lo mande Dios!'
Allí se tollió el capiello   el Cid Campeador,
la cofia de rrançal,   que blanca era como el sol,
e soltava la barba   e sacóla del cordón.
Nos' fartan de catarle   quantos ha en la cort;   [3495
adeliñó a él el conde don Anrich   e el conde don Rremond.
Abraçólos tan bien   e rruégalos de coraçón
que prendan de sus averes   quanto ovieren sabor.
A éssos e a los otros   que de buena parte son,
a todos los rrogava   assí como han sabor,
tales í á que prenden,   tales í á que non.   [3500
Los *dozientos* marcos   al rrey los soltó,
de lo ál tanto priso   quant ovo sabor.
'¡Merced vos pido, rrey,   por amor del Criador!
Quando todas estas nuevas   assí puestas son,   [3505
beso vuestras manos   con vuestra gracia, señor,
e irme quiero pora Valencia,   con afán la gané yo.'

[*Lacuna of about fifty lines: one folio missing*]

150
70r   El rrey alçó la mano,   la cara se sanctigó:
'¡Yo lo juro par Sant Esidro   el de León
que en todas nuestras tierras   non ha tan buen varón!'   [3510
Mio Cid en el cavallo   adelant se llegó,
fue besar la mano   a Alfonso so señor:

like, Campeador, but hand over your champions fully armed and let them go with me. I shall act as their protector and guarantor, as a lord does for a good vassal, against any hurt or harm from anyone, whatever his rank. Here and now I appoint a fixed time in my court, that within three weeks they undertake this combat in my presence on the plain of Carrión. Any man who does not appear within the time appointed shall lose his suit. He shall be declared vanquished and be branded as a traitor.' The Infantes accepted this decision. The Cid kissed the King's hands and said: 'I agree. My knights are now under your protection. I commend them to you from this time on as their king and lord. They are prepared to fulfil their duty. In God's name, send them back to me in Valencia covered with honour.' The King replied: 'God grant it may be so.' Thereupon the Cid took off his hood of mail, displaying his pure white linen coif, and he loosened his beard from the cord that bound it. None of those assembled at the court could keep their eyes off him. Counts Henry and Raymond approached him; he embraced them warmly and begged them to take what they wished of his belongings. He besought all who sided with him to help themselves freely. Some did so and some did not. He remitted the two hundred marks to the King, who took what he wanted of the rest. (Addressing the King, the Cid said) 'I beg as a favour in God's name that, as all this business is now settled, you give me permission to return to Valencia, which I won at such cost.'

[*Lacuna of about fifty lines: one folio missing*]

150

The King raised his hand and, making the sign of the cross, (he said) 'I swear by St Isidore, whom we venerate in León, that there is not such a man as you in all our land.' The Cid rode up and kissed the hand of his lord, King Alfonso. 'You ordered

'Mandástesme mover   a Bavieca el corredor,
en moros ni en cristianos   otro tal non ha oy,
y[o] vos le do en don,   mandédesle tomar, señor.'   [3515
Essora dixo el rrey: 'D'esto non he sabor;
si a vós le tolliés   el cavallo no havrié tan bue[n] señor.
Mas atal cavallo cum ést   pora tal como vós
pora arrancar moros del canpo   e ser segudador,
quien vos lo toller quisiere   nol' vala el Criador,   [3520
ca por vós e por el cavallo   ondrados somo[s] nós.'
Essora se espidieron   e luegos' partió la cort.
El Campeador a los que han lidiar   tan bien los castigó:
'Ya Martín Antolínez   e vós, Pero Vermúez | e
                            Muño Gustioz,   [3524-25
firmes sed en campo   a guisa de varones;   [3525b
buenos mandados me vayan   a Valencia de vós.'
Dixo Martín Antolínez: '¿Por qué lo dezides, señor?
Preso avemos el debdo   e a passar es por nós,
podedes oír de muertos,   ca de vencidos no.'
Alegre fue d'aquesto   el que en buen ora nació,   [3530
espidiós' de todos   los que sos amigos son;
Mio Cid pora Valencia   e el rrey pora Carrión.

70v   Las tres semanas de plazo   todas complidas son.
Felos al plazo   los del Campeador,
cunplir quieren el debdo   que les mandó so señor,   [3535
ellos son en p[o]der   del rrey don Alfonso el de León;
dos días atendieron   a ifantes de Carrión.
Mucho vienen bien adobados   de cavallos e de guarnizones
e todos sus parientes   con ellos son,
que si los pudiessen apartar   a los del Campeador   [3540
que los matassen en campo   por desondra de so señor.
El cometer fue malo,   que lo ál nos' enpeçó,
ca grand miedo ovieron   a Alfonso el de León.
De noche belaron las armas   e rrogaron al Criador.
Trocida es la noche,   ya quiebran los albores,   [3545
muchos se juntaron   de buenos rricos omnes
por ver esta lid,   ca avién ende sabor;
demás sobre todos   í es el rrey don Alfonso
por querer el derecho   e non consentir el tuerto.
Yas' metién en armas   los del buen Campeador,   [3550
todos tres se acuerdan,   ca son de un señor.
En otro logar se arman   los ifantes de Carrión,
sediélos castigando   el conde Garcí Ordóñez:
andidieron en pleito,   dixiéronlo al rrey Alfonso,

me' (he said) 'to show the paces of my swift horse, Babieca, who has no peer in the world today. I give him to you as a present, my lord; order him to be led away.' The King answered: 'I will not accept your gift. If I took this horse from you he would not have so good a master. Such a horse is fit for such a man as you—to defeat Moors in battle and follow them in pursuit. May anyone who takes him from you be deprived of God's aid! You with your horse gain great honour for us.' Then they said farewell, and the court broke up. The Campeador gave wise advice to those who were to take part in the combat: 'Martín Antolínez and you, Pedro Bermúdez' (he said), 'and you, Muño Gustioz, hold firm in the field like brave men, so that in Valencia I may hear good reports of your conduct.' Martín Antolínez answered: 'Why do you say this? We have undertaken this duty and it is for us to see it through. You may hear of us as dead but not as defeated.' The Cid was glad to hear him speak like that, and he took leave of all his friends there. The Cid then set out for Valencia, and the King for Carrión. The three weeks of grace came to an end, and the Cid's followers arrived punctually to fulfil the duty laid on them by their lord. They were under the protection of Alfonso as king of León. After a delay of two days the Infantes of Carrión came, well equipped with arms and horses. All their relatives had plotted with them that, if they could find the Campeador's men unprotected in the field, they would kill them and so dishonour their lord. It was a wicked plot but it was not carried out for fear of King Alfonso of León. That night they all held vigil beside their arms and prayed to God for victory. The night had passed and dawn was about to break, when a great crowd of nobles assembled to witness the combat, which they were eager to behold. Above all, King Alfonso was there to see that justice was done and no wrong. The Cid's three men donned their armour, ready for the fray as champions of one lord. In another place the Infantes were arming while Count García Ordóñez plied them with advice. They then approached the King with the request that the swords,

que non fuessen en la batalla   las espadas tajadores |
                                  Colada e Tizón,   *[3555-56*
que non lidiassen con ellas   los del Canpeador,   *[3556b*
mucho eran rrepentidos los ifantes   por quanto dadas son,
dixiérongelo al rrey,   mas non ge lo conloyó:
'Non sacastes ninguna   quando oviemos la cort;

71r   si buenas las tenedes,   pro abrán a vós,   *[3560*
otros[s]í farán   a los del Canpeador.
Levad e salid al campo,   ifantes de Carrión,
huebos vos es que lidiedes   a guisa de varones,·
que nada non mancará   por los del Campeador.
Si del campo bien salides,   grand ondra avredes vós,   *[3565*
e si fuére[de]s vencidos,   non rrebtedes a nós,
ca todos lo saben   que lo buscastes vós.'
Ya se van rrepintiendo   ifantes de Carrión,
de lo que avién fecho   mucho rrepisos son;
no lo querrién aver fecho   por quanto ha en Carrión.   *[3570*
Todos tres son armados   los del Campeador,
ívalos ver   el rrey don Alfonso;
dixieron   los del Campeador:
'Besámosvos las manos   como a rrey e a señor
que fiel seades oy   d'ellos e de nós;   *[3575*
a derecho nos valed,   a ningún tuerto no.
Aquí tienen su vando   los ifantes de Carrión,
non sabemos   qués' comidrán ellos o qué non;
en vuestra mano   nos metió nuestro señor:
¡tenendos a derecho,   por amor del Criador!'   *[3580*
Essora dixo el rrey: '¡D'alma e de coraçón!'
Adúzenles los cavallos   buenos e corredores,
santiguaron las siellas   e cavalgan a vigor,
los escudos a los cuellos   que bien blocados son,

71v   e[n] mano prenden las astas   de los fierros tajadores,   *[3585*
estas tres lanças   traen seños pendones,
e derredor d'ellos   muchos buenos varones.
Ya salieron al campo   dó eran los mojones.
Todos tres son acordados   los del Campeador
que cada uno d'ellos   bien fos ferir el so.   *[3590*
Fevos de la otra part   los ifantes de Carrión,
muy bien aconpañados,   ca muchos parientes son.
El rrey dioles fieles   por dezir el derecho e ál non,
que non varajen con ellos   de sí o de non.
Dó sedién en el campo   fabló el rrey don Alfonso: *[3595*
'Oíd qué vos digo,   ifantes de Carrión:

Colada and Tizón, should not be used in the fight by the Campeador's champions. They deeply regretted having handed them over. The King, however, refused to grant their request, saying: 'When we held our court you made no objection to their use. If you have good swords they will prove to your advantage, and the same applies to the Cid's men. Rise and enter the field, Infantes of Carrión; it is your obligation to fight like men. The Campeador's champions will not be found wanting. If you are successful in the combat you will gain great honour, and if you are defeated do not blame us, for everyone knows that you brought this on yourselves.' The Infantes began to repent bitterly of what they had done. They would rather for all Carrión that it had been left undone. All three champions of the Campeador were armed and ready when King Alfonso went to inspect them. They said to him: 'We kiss your hands as our king and lord, asking that you should see justice done between them and us. Protect us in right but not in wrong. The Infantes of Carrión are here surrounded by their henchmen, and we do not know what plots they may be hatching. Our liege lord gave us into your care. Keep us from unjust attack for the love of God.' The King replied: 'This I shall assuredly do.' When their fine swift horses were led forward they made the sign of the cross over their saddles and swung into their seats. Their bucklers with strong bosses hung from their necks and they grasped in their hands the shafts of their lances from which three pennons fluttered. Around them stood a crowd of sturdy fighters. Then they rode out into the lists, and all three of the Cid's men were determined that each and every one of them would strike his adversary a hard blow. On the other side were the Infantes of Carrión, accompanied by many members of their family. The King appointed umpires to decide all points of dispute, so that there might be no argument. As they all stood ready in the field, King Alfonso spoke as follows: Hear what I say to you, Infantes

esta lid en Toledo la fiziérades,   mas non quisiestes vós.
Estos tres cavalleros   de Mio Cid el Campeador
yo los adux a salvo   a tierras de Carrión;
aved vuestro derecho,   tuerto non querades vós,   [3600
ca qui tuerto quisiere fazer,   mal ge lo vedaré yo,
en todo mio rreino   non avrá buena sabor.'
Ya les va pesando   a los ifantes de Carrión.
Los fieles e el rrey   enseñaron los mojones,
librávanse del campo   todos aderredor;   [3605
bien ge lo demostraron   a todos *seis* cómo son,
que por í serié vencido   qui saliesse del mojón.
Todas las yentes   esconbraron aderredor,
más de *seis* astas de lanças   que non llegassen al mojón.
Sorteávanles el campo,   ya les partién el sol,   [3610
salién los fieles de medio,   ellos cara por cara son,
72r   desí vinién los de Mio Cid   a los ifantes de Carrión
e llos ifantes de Carrión   a los del Campeador,
cada uno d'ellos   mientes tiene al so.
Abraçan los escudos   delant los coraçones,   [3615
abaxan las lanças   abueltas con los pendones,
enclinavan las caras   sobre los arzones,
batién los cavallos   con los espolones,
tembrar querié la tierra   do[n]d eran movedores.
Cada uno d'ellos   mientes tiene al so,   [3620
todos tres por tres   ya juntados son;
cuédanse que essora cadrán muertos   los que están aderredor.
Pero Vermúez,   el que antes rrebtó,
con Ferrá[n] Gonçález   de cara se juntó,
firiénse en los escudos   sin todo pavor.   [3625
Ferrán Go[n]çález a Pero Vermúez   el escúdol' passó,
prísol' en vazío,   en carne nol' tomó,
bien en dos logares   el astil le quebró.
Firme estido Pero Vermúez,   por esso nos' encamó,
un colpe rrecibiera   mas otro firió: [3630
quebrantó la b[l]oca del escudo,   apart ge la echó,
passógelo todo,   que nada nol' valió,
metiól' la lança por los pechos,   que nada nol' valió.
Tres dobles de loriga tenié Fernando,   aquéstol' prestó,
las dos le desmanchan   e la tercera fincó: [3635
el belmez con la camisa   e con la guarnizón
de dentro en la carne   una mano ge la metió,
por la boca afuera   la sángrel' salió,
72v   quebráronle las cinchas,   ninguna nol' ovo pro,

of Carrión. You might have fought this combat in Toledo, but you refused to do so. These three knights, followers of the Cid Campeador, I have brought under safe-conduct to the lands of Carrión. Do what is right and attempt no wrong. I shall take severe measures against any man who proposes to do wrong, and he will find no refuge in all my territory.' His words struck unpleasantly on the young men's ears. The umpires and the King marked out the bounds, the bystanders were cleared from the field. It was explained to all six combatants that any one of them who crossed the bounds would be considered beaten. The bystanders were ordered not to approach within six lance-lengths of the boundary. They drew lots for position and it was arranged that neither party should have the sun against them. The umpires then left the two parties facing each other. The Cid's champions approached the Infantes of Carrión, and they also advanced, each man intent on his own special adversary. They clasped their shields against their breasts, lowered their pennoned lances, bent down their heads over their saddle-bows and set spurs to their horses; the earth trembled as they galloped forward. Each one was intent on his man; three against three were joined in battle. The onlookers thought they would all fall dead at the same time. Pedro Bermúdez, the first to challenge, met Fernando González face to face, each striking the other's shield fearlessly. Fernando pierced Don Pedro's shield, but not deeply enough to reach the flesh, and his spear broke in two places with the shock. Pedro Bermúdez held firm and did not topple over. He received one blow but gave another in return, which broke off the boss of Fernando's shield and pierced the shield itself, which proved no protection. The lance struck through the breast near to the heart. His three layers of mail saved him, for two were pierced, but the third held. The lance drove it with the padded tunic and shirt a hand's breadth into the flesh, and the blood poured from his mouth. Every strap of the horse's caparison snapped, and his rider was knocked to the

por la copla del cavallo   en tierra lo echó.   *[3640*
Assí lo tenién las yentes   que mal ferido es de muert.
Él dexó la lança   e al espada mano metió,
quando lo vio Ferrán Go[n]çález   conuvo a Tizón,
antes que el colpe esperasse   dixo: 'Vençudo só.'
Atorgárongelo los fieles,   Pero Vermúez le dexó.   *[3645*

151

Martín Antolínez e Diego Gonçález   firiéronse de las lanças,
tales fueron los colpes   que les quebraron amas.
Martín Antolínez   mano metió al espada,
rrelumbra tod' el campo,   tanto es linpia e clara;
diol' un colpe,   de traviéssol' tomava,   *[3650*
el casco de somo   apart ge lo echava,
las moncluras del yelmo   todas ge las cortava,
allá levó el almófar,   fata la cofia llegava,
la cofia e el almófar   todo ge lo levava,
rráxol' los pelos de la cabeça,   bien a la carne llegava,   *[3655*
lo uno cayó en el campo   e lo ál suso fincava.
Quando este colpe á ferido   Colada la preciada,
vio Diego Gonçález   que no escaparié con el alma,
bolvió la rrienda al cavallo   por tornasse de cara.
Essora Martín Antolínez   rrecibiól' con el espada,   *[3660*
un cólpel' dio de llano,   con lo agudo nol' tomava.
Diago [Go]nçález espada tiene en mano,   mas no
                                   la | ensayava,   *[3662-63*
73r essora el ifante   tan grandes vozes dava:
'¡Valme, Dios, glorioso señor,   e cúriam' d'este espada!'   *[3665*
El cavallo asorrienda   e mesurándol' del espada
sacól' del mojón;   Martín Antolínez en el campo fincava.
Essora dixo el rrey: 'Venid vós a mi compaña,
por quanto avedes fecho   vencida avedes esta batalla.'
Otórgangelo los fieles   que dize verdadera palabra.   *[3670*

152

Los dos han arrancado,   dirévos de Muño Gustioz,
con Assur Gonçález   cómo se adobó.
Firiénse en los escudos   unos tan grandes colpes;
Assur Gonçález,   furçudo e de valor,
firió en el escudo   a don Muño Gustioz,   *[3675*
tras el escudo   falsóge la guarnizón,
en vazío fue la lança   ca en carne nol' tomó.
Este colpe fecho,   otro dio Muño Gustioz,

ground over his croup. The onlookers thought he had received his death wound. Pedro Bermúdez laid aside his lance and seized his sword. When Fernando González saw the sword he recognised Tizón and, before the blow fell, he cried: 'I am defeated.' The umpires acknowledged the admission, and Pedro Bermúdez stayed his hand.

151

Martín Antolínez and Diego González attacked each other with their lances so fiercely that both these were broken. When Martín Antolínez put hand to his sword, the whole field flashed— so clear and bright it was. With a side blow he struck away the top of Diego's helmet, cutting all the straps which held it on to the mailed hood; reaching the coif, he carried coif and hood away and, shaving the hair, touched the flesh. One part of the helmet fell to the ground and the rest remained in place. When the great sword, Colada, struck this blow, Diego González saw that he would be doomed to die and he pulled his horse's rein to turn his face away. Martín Antolínez was ready with his sword, but he struck with the flat and not with the sharp edge. Diego González held a sword in his hand but did not use it, and then he shouted out: 'Help me, great God! Protect me from this sword!' He reined in his horse, guiding it away from the sword, and drew it over the boundary line. Martín Antolínez remained victorious in the field. Then the King said: 'Come to my side; you have won this battle in fair fight.' The umpires confirmed the King's words.

152

Two of the challengers had vanquished their opponents, and now you will hear how Muño Gustioz made out with Ansur González. They too exchanged mighty blows. Strong and valiant, Ansur González struck Muño Gustioz's shield and pierced his armour beyond it, but the lance failed to reach the flesh. After this first blow, Muño Gustioz struck another, which pierced the

tras el escudo   falsóge la guarnizón:
por medio de la bloca   el escúdol' quebrantó,   [3680
nol' pudo guarir,   falsóge la guarnizón;
apart le priso,   que non cab' el coraçón,
metiól' por la carne adentro   la lança con el pendón,
de la otra part   una braça ge la echó;
con él dio una tuerta,   de la siella lo encamó,   [3685
al tirar de la lança   en tierra lo echó,
vermejo salió el astil   e la lança e el pendón.
Todos se cuedan   que ferido es de muert.
La lança rrecombró   e sobr'él se paró,

73v   dixo Gonçalo Assúrez: '¡Nol' firgades, por Dios!'   [3690
Vençudo es el campo   quando esto se acabó,
dixieron los fieles: 'Esto oímos nós.'
Mandó librar el canpo   el buen rrey don Alfonso,
las armas que í rrastaron   él se las tomó.
Por ondrados se parten   los del buen Campeador,   [3695
vencieron esta lid,   grado al Criador.
Grandes son los pesares   por tierras de Carrión.
El rrey a los de Mio Cid   de noche los enbió
que no les diessen salto   nin oviessen pavor.
A guisa de menbrados   andan días e noches,   [3700
felos en Valencia   con Mio Cid el Campeador;
por malos los dexaron   a los ifantes de Carrión,
conplido han el debdo   que les mandó so señor,
alegre fue d'aquesto   Mio Cid el Campeador.
Grant es la biltança   de ifantes de Carrión: [3705
qui buena dueña escarnece   e la dexa después
atal le contesca   o siquier peor.
Dexémosnos de pleitos   de ifantes de Carrión,
de lo que an preso   mucho an mal sabor;
fablémosnos d'aqueste   que en buen ora nació.   [3710
Grandes son los gozos   en Valencia la mayor
porque tan ondrados fueron   los del Canpeador.
Prisos' a la barba   Rruy Díaz so señor:

74r   '¡Grado al rrey del cielo,   mis fijas vengadas son!
Agora las ayan quitas   heredades de Carrión.   [3715
Sin vergüença las casaré   o a qui pese o a qui non.'
Andidieron en pleitos   los de Navarra e de Aragón,
ovieron su ajunta   con Alfonso el de León,
fizieron sus casamientos   con don Elvira e con doña Sol.
Los primeros fueron grandes,   mas aquéstos son mijores,   [3720
a mayor ondra las casa   que lo que primero fue.

shield and penetrated the armour through the boss; Ansur could not ward it off, and the lance pierced his armour. Muño struck him on one side, not near the heart, but he thrust his lance and pennon through the flesh an arm's length out on the other side; he gave him a twist and removed Ansur from the saddle. Then, withdrawing his lance, he cast him to the ground. The shaft, blade and pennon came out stained red with blood. All thought he had received his death blow. When Muño had recovered his lance he stood over Ansur González. Gonzalo Ansúrez cried: 'Do not strike him, for God's sake!' The fight was ended when this was done. The umpires said: 'We confirm the admission.' King Alfonso ordered the field to be cleared. The arms of the vanquished which were left there became his property. The Campeador's champions departed with honour, for they had, by God's grace, won the fight. There was great sorrow throughout the lands of Carrión. The King dispatched the Cid's followers by night so that they might have no fear of an attack. Like prudent men they travelled day and night and arrived safely in Valencia, where they joined the Cid. They had proved the Infantes of Carrión traitors and so fulfilled the obligation laid on them by their lord, who was greatly rejoiced to hear it. The Infantes of Carrión had suffered deep disgrace. May such a fate or worse befall anyone who treats a noble lady shamefully and then abandons her! We shall now leave the subject of the Infantes of Carrión, hard hit by the punishment they have received, and speak about the Cid. There was great rejoicing in Valencia over the honour won by the Cid's followers. Their lord, Ruy Díaz, grasped his beard and said: 'I thank God in His Heaven that my daughters are avenged! Let them now be considered quit of the estates of Carrión. I can give them in marriage without let or hindrance.' The Princes of Navarre and Aragon began negotiations and arranged a meeting for that purpose with King Alfonso of León. The marriages with Doña Elvira and Doña Sol were duly solemnised. Their first marriages brought them honour, but these were better still. See what

¡Ved quál ondra crece   al que en buen ora nació
quando señoras son sus fijas   de Navarra e de Aragón!
Oy los rreyes d'España   sos parientes son,
a todos alcança ondra   por el que en buen ora nació.   *[3725*
Passado es d'este sieglo   el día de cinquaesma;
. . . .   ¡de Christus aya perdón!
¡Assí fagamos nós todos   justos e pecadores!
Éstas son las nuevas   de Mio Cid el Canpeador,
en este logar   se acaba esta rrazón.   *[3730*

[*Explicit*]

Quien escrivió este libro, ¡dél' Dios paraíso, amen!
Per Abbat le escrivió en el mes de mayo
en era de mill ɔ.C.C   xL.v. años.   [el (el) rromanz
[E]s leído, datnos del vino;   si non tenedes dineros, echad
[A*l*]lá unos peños, que bien vos lo dar(ar)án sobr'el[*l*]os.]   *[3735*

honour accrued to the Cid when his daughters became Queens of Navarre and Aragon. Today the Kings of Spain are related to him and all gain lustre from the fame of the fortunate Campeador. He passed from this life on the day of Pentecost. May Christ pardon him as He may pardon us all, righteous and sinners alike. These are the exploits of the Cid Campeador, and here our story ends.

[*Explicit*]

    To the writer of this book may God give His Paradise, Amen! Per Abbat wrote it down in the month of May, in the year of Our Lord 1207. [The poem has been read out, give us some wine; if you have no pennies, throw down some pledges there, for you will get a good return on them.]

Abbreviations

Alex: *El libro de Alexandre. Texts of the Paris and the Madrid Manuscripts*, ed. Raymond S. Willis, Jr. (Elliott Monographs No. 32, Princeton and Paris, 1934, repr. New York, 1965).

Apol: *El libro de Apolonio*, ed. C. Carroll Marden, 2 vols (Elliott Monographs Nos. 6 and 11-12, Baltimore, 1917, corr. reissue 1937, Princeton and Paris, 1922; repr. New York, 1965).

Bello: Andrés Bello, *Obras completas*, vol. II, *Poema del Cid* (Santiago de Chile, 1881).

Berceo: see *Milagros, Sacrificio, San Lorenzo* and *Santo Domingo*.

Chanson de Roland: F. Whitehead (ed.), *La Chanson de Roland* (Oxford, 1942, 2nd edn. 1946).

Coplas de Yoçef: Ignacio González Llubera, *Coplas de Yoçef. A medieval Spanish poem in Hebrew characters* (Cambridge, 1935).

Cornu, *Etudes*: Jules Cornu, 'Etudes sur le *Poème du Cid*', *Romania*, X (1881), 75-99, and in *Etudes romanes dédiées à Gaston Paris . . .* (Paris, 1891), pp. 419-58.

Cornu, *R* XXII: Jules Cornu, 'Revision des études sur le *Poème du Cid*', *Romania*, XXII (1883), 533-36.

Cornu, *ZfrPh*: Jules Cornu, 'Beiträge zu einer künftigen Ausgabe des Poema del Cid', *Zeitschrift für romanische Philologie*, XXI (1897), 461-528.

Coromines, *DCELC*: Joan Coromines, *Diccionario crítico etimológico de la lengua castellana*, 4 vols (Berne, 1954-57, repr. 1970).

Criado de Val: Manuel Criado de Val, 'Geografía, toponimia e itinerarios del *CMC*', *Zeitschrift für romanische Philologie*, LXXXVI (1970), 83-107.

Fuero juzgo: *El Fuero juzgo* (Madrid, 1815).

Hinard: J. J. S. A. Damas Hinard (ed.), *Poëme du Cid . . . accompagné d'une traduction française, de notes, d'un vocabulaire et d'une introduction* (Paris, 1858).

Historia Roderici: ed. in Pidal, *España del Cid* (Madrid, 1969), II, pp. 921-71.

Huntington: Archer M. Huntington, *Poem of the Cid. Text reprinted from the unique manuscript at Madrid*, 3 vols (New York, 1897-1903, 2nd edn. 1907-08, 3rd edn. 1921).

Lang: H. R. Lang, 'Contributions to the restoration of the *PMC*', *Revue Hispanique*, LXVI (1926), 1-509.

Lba: Juan Ruiz, *El libro de buen amor*, ed. M. Criado de Val and E. W. Naylor (Madrid, 1965).

H

Lidforss: Volter Edvard Lidforss, *Los Cantares de Myo Cid, con una introducción y notas* (Lund, 1895).

Milagros: Gonzalo de Berceo, *Los milagros de Nuestra Señora*, ed. Brian Dutton (London, 1971); ed. A. G. Solalinde (Clás. Cast., Madrid, 1952 repr.).

PCG: *Primera crónica general de España que mandó componer Alfonso el Sabio . . .*, ed. R. Menéndez Pidal (Madrid, 1906, 2nd edn., 2 vols, 1955).

Pidal, CC: Ramón Menéndez Pidal, *Poema de Mio Cid* (Madrid, Clás. Cast., 1913, 2nd edn. 1923, 3rd edn. 1929, frequently repr.).

Pidal, *ed. crít.*: Ramón Menéndez Pidal, *Cantar de Mio Cid: texto, gramática y vocabulario*, 3 vols (Madrid, 1908–11; revised edn. 1944–46, repr. 1954–56).

Pidal, *ed. pal.*: *Cantar de Mio Cid*, vol. III: Texto (see above), and *Poema de Mio Cid. Facsímil de la edición paleográfica* (Madrid, 1961).

PMC: *Poema de Mio Cid*.

Poema de Yúçuf: Ramón Menéndez Pidal, *Poema de Yúçuf. Materiales para su estudio* (Granada, 1952).

Restori: Antonio Restori, 'Osservazioni sul metro, sulle assonanze e sul testo del *Poema del Cid*', *Il Propugnatore*, XX (1887), 97–159, 430–39; and *Le Gesta del Cid* (Milan, 1890).

Sacrificio: Gonzalo de Berceo, *El sacrificio de la misa*, ed. A. G. Solalinde (Madrid, 1913).

San Lorenzo: C. Carroll Marden (ed.), 'Berceo's *Martirio de San Lorenzo*', *PMLA*, XLV (1930), 501–15.

Sánchez: Tomás Antonio Sánchez, *Colección de poesías castellanas anteriores al siglo XV*, 4 vols (Madrid, 1779–90).

Santo Domingo: Gonzalo de Berceo, *Vida de Santo Domingo de Silos*, ed. Fr. Alonso Andrés, O.S.B. (Madrid, 1958).

Santob: Sem Tob de Carrión, *Proverbios morales*, ed. Ignacio González Llubera (Cambridge, 1947).

Siete partidas: Alfonso X, el Sabio, *Las siete partidas*, 3 vols (Madrid, 1807, repr. 1972).

Smith: *Poema de mio Cid*, ed. with introduction and notes by Colin Smith (Oxford, 1972).

Staaff: E. S. Staaff, 'Contribution à la syntaxe du pronom personnel dans le Poème du Cid', *Romanische Forschungen*, XXIII (1907), 621–35.

Tercera crónica general: Florián de Ocampo, *Las quatro partes enteras de la Crónica de España que mandó componer el . . . rey don Alonso . . .* (Zamora, 1541).

Veinte reyes: *Crónica de once o veinte Reyes*, see Pidal, *ed. crít.*, pp. 134–36, and Diego Catalán Menéndez Pidal, *De Alfonso X al conde de Barcelos* (Madrid, 1962), pp. 178–88.

Vollmöller: Karl Vollmöller, *Poema del Cid, nach der einzigen Madrider Handschrift* (Halle, 1879).

Notes

In these notes I have tried to achieve, at least in part, the following aims: to point out the principal divergences of interpretation from other editions of the Spanish text (though lack of space has prevented the inclusion of a detailed *apparatus criticus*), to give, on occasion, the literal meaning where the translation, for reasons of English style, has departed to some extent from the original, and to provide brief explanatory notes concerning the personages of the poem and some of the places mentioned. In the latter cases explanation is limited to those toponyms about which there is special difficulty or which cannot be easily identified on the map; I have also tried to offer some elucidation of historical events, customs and dress. Unless otherwise indicated, the numerical references are to the lines of the poem. A useful guide in English to works of criticism and a selective bibliography are to be found in Smith's edition; I am preparing a much fuller critical bibliography for the series 'Research Bibliographies and Checklists' (London, Grant & Cutler). Since the quotations from the MS are printed here in italics, the upright long *s* is given as the curved long *s* throughout.

Possible lacuna of up to fifty lines. The first folio of the extant MS is missing, and it is generally assumed that the first fifty lines of the poem are lost. They may have contained the reason for the Cid's banishment: an allegation by his enemies at court that he had embezzled part of the tributes Alfonso VI had sent him to collect from the Moorish *taifa* kingdoms of Seville and Cordova.

1   This epic formula recurs in shorter variants in 18, 277, 370, 374, etc. It was not at all unusual for warriors to weep in epic poems, cf. *Chanson de Roland* 2415, 2418-19, 4001, etc. Whatever details the lines presumed missing may have contained, it is difficult in artistic terms to imagine a more effective opening of the poem than this.

2   It is not altogether clear what the Cid was looking back at, but it is likely that his house and estates at Vivar are meant, cf. 115.

8-9   The Cid's laconic comment on his ill fortune and his thanks to God may be seen both as Christian resignation and as righteous determination to recover his position, cf. his happy mood in 14, and his identical reaction in 2830-31 (see also notes to 1933 and 2830-31).

11-12   When they see the crow to the right of their path on the way out of Vivar, it is a favourable sign for their general success in the future, but the crow they see to their left on entering Burgos is an ill omen for their reception there. The Cid's faith in omens is seen again in 859 and 2615, and the *Historia Roderici* confirms that the historical Cid was well versed in them.

13   The Cid wards off the ill omen, cf. 'nec maximus omen abnuit Aeneas', Virgil, *Aeneid*, V, 530-1.

14   The Cid's rejoicing may be interpreted as joyful acceptance of the challenge provided by adverse fortune to demonstrate his superior qualities in action. Álvar Fáñez, apparently a nephew of the Cid, becomes in the poem his chief companion and right-hand man, but there is no historical record of his accompanying him into exile; on the contrary, he was an important figure at Alfonso VI's court.

20   The syntax has been the subject of much controversy in that *si* may be optative (*sí* = *así*, 'would that') or conditional ('if only'); Smith inclines to the former (Amado Alonso's) view, but like Pidal, *ed. crít.*, Adiciones, p. 1221, I incline to the latter. See A. Badía Margarit, *Archivum*, IV (1954), 149-65.

22   **avié la** Pidal, CC, alters to *avie le* without indication, though he retains the MS reading in his *ed. crít.* (Smith likewise); *aviéle* would be preferable for the syntax.

24   There is no historical evidence of this decree. The reference is probably to a *mandato real*, an order usually of only a few lines, commonly dwarfed by its pendant wax seal, but these seals did not come into use in Spain until the twelfth century (see P. E. Russell, *Modern Language Review*, XLVII, 1952, 340-9).

27-28 The sanction for disobeying a *mandato real*, Russell points out, was usually no more than a heavy fine; the poet here uses an archaic form of the malediction used in Spanish donations and *acta*, which was in reality a pious hope, not a prescribed penalty.

31   **Campeador** lit. 'Campaigner', 'Battler', the epic epithet for the Cid used most frequently in the poem.

37-39 The rapid changes of tense between preterite, imperfect and present are characteristic of the epic style and occur frequently throughout. They cannot be followed in translation without producing a stilted effect.

52   Alfonso VI completed the building of Burgos cathedral, dedicated to St Mary, by 1095, but it was demolished in the thirteenth century and rebuilt by Ferdinand III.

55   MS τ *en Arlançon poſaua*, the *en* and *çon* written in above the line; with Smith I follow Bello and Pidal, *ed. crít.*, in regarding *en* as a mistaken correction and *posava* as an error for *passava* (cf. 2876); Lidforss retains the MS reading, and it is just possible to interpret 'he encamped on (the river) Arlanzón'. (The village of Arlanzón lies some 18 km east of Burgos and is too distant for the action that follows.)

62   A number of medieval Spanish legal codes tried to curb this excessive royal sanction on banished nobles.

65   Martín Antolínez acts as the Cid's majordomo throughout the poem and distinguishes himself in combat, but there is no record of his historical existence—he is probably an artistic creation.

82   The Cid's penury demonstrates, of course, his innocence of the accusation

of embezzlement which led to his exile; ironically, that exile will make him rich and powerful.

89 The names of the Jewish moneylenders are probably both masculine: Rrachel may be a form of Raguel, and Vidas a translation of *Hayyim*, the Hebrew word for life.

97 Many editors suppress the line, since it is identical to 99; I am with Huntington and Smith in thinking that the repetition may be intentional.

98 The *aljama* or ghetto was usually located within the fortified part of medieval Spanish towns, since Jews as aliens were under direct royal control.

153 The kissing of hands as token of vassalage was already regarded as 'the ancient custom of Spain' in the thirteenth-century *Siete partidas*, IV, 25, 4.

161 Each mark was worth eight ounces of silver or gold and was equivalent to 160 old pence; thus the 600 marks might tentatively be considered equivalent to £400 sterling, an extraordinarily large sum for the medieval period.

178 The over-tunic was usually short-sleeved, of ermine, coney or even sheepskin, with the fur lining the inside and the skin faced with red silk on the outside, sometimes with golden tabs, cf. 3092.

181 It seems that there must be at least a brief lacuna in the text after this line, because the scene shifts from the Cid's tent on the river bed to the Jews' apartment in the city (cf. 200).

182 I follow Sánchez and Bello in admitting *almofalla* ('army, host') in the sense of 'rug' (see Corominas, *DCELC*, s.v. *almozalla*); Pidal, *ed. crít.*, alters to *almoçalla*, and Smith thinks Pidal's arguments 'substantial', but retains the MS reading.

187 It is unlikely that five squires would have been required to carry 600 coins, but numerals are used poetically, or even symbolically; by far the commonest numerals are multiples of three, and the next commonest are multiples of five.

204 Pidal, *ed. crít.*, and Smith take these greetings to be interrogative throughout the poem, but the tone may rather be exclamatory.

209 The monastery lies 8 km south-east of Burgos and was one of the most important Benedictine houses in Castile from the ninth century. The Cid was certainly buried there in 1102 (three years after his death), but Doña Jimena was probably buried at San Juan de la Peña (see P. E. Russell, *Medium Aevum*, XXVII, 1958, 57-79, at 64).

212 The Cid is allowed only nine days to quit the kingdom (cf. 306-7), the same number as Bernardo del Carpio in the *PCG* 372a—again a multiple of 3. The thirteenth-century *Siete partidas* allow thirty days (IV, 25, 10).

225 **debdo** is a religious duty here, a bond of vassalage in 708, a promise to a liege lord in 3528, and filial duty in 2598.

237 The abbot of Cardeña from *c.* 1060 to *c.* 1086 was Sisebuto, assisted by Sebastián from 1082. There is no record of an abbot called Sancho, but the names of Sisebuto's immediate successors are not well documented.

239 Jimena Díaz, the Cid's wife, was the daughter of Diego Rodríguez, count of Oviedo, and sister of Froila Díaz (mentioned in 3004). She was

the first cousin of Alfonso VI, but the poet does not reveal any knowledge of the relationship except for a vague hint of her importance in 3039-40.

245   'the fortunate Cid': lit. 'he who was born in a good hour'.

256   **aquí vos llas** MS *Aq̃llas uos*, which Smith accepts, but it is a strange use of the demonstrative; although *aquí llas vos* would be attractive, the poem has no example of a direct weak object pronoun preceding an indirect one; I therefore adopt Pidal's solution.

319   This mass was often preferred to the mass prescribed for the day—a practice criticised in the *Siete partidas*, I, 4, 107.

330 *et seq.*   A deliverance prayer is commonly found in thirteenth-century Spanish narrative poems and in the French epics (cf. *Chanson de Roland* 2384-88), but this one is remarkable for its length and composite form.

337   The belief that the names of the Magi were unknown in Western Christendom until late in the twelfth century has been used as a criterion for dating the poem, but in fact the names are used on an Epiphany fresco in Tahull which dates from 1123 or slightly later (see Walter W. S. Cook, *La pintura mural en Cataluña*, Madrid, 1956, p. 39), and I have seen them partly obliterated on a twelfth-century fresco from Navasa (Huesca) now preserved in the museum at Jaca cathedral. Much earlier Rudolf Beer reported the names scribbled on a Ripoll codex about the year 1000 (see his *Die Handschriften des Klosters Santa Maria de Ripoll*, Vienna, 1907, I, p. 8). See also R. B. Donovan, *The Liturgical Drama in Medieval Spain* (Toronto, 1958) pp. 94-5, for a tenth-century example of the names in an Aragonese document.

358-60 The poet erroneously places the Resurrection before the descent into hell. 360 refers to the doctrine of the just.

375   One of the few similes in the poem, its rarity heightening its violent effect, cf. 2642.

393   **Spinaz de Can** Unknown place, which perhaps lay in the mountains south of Silos (see map). The name (lit. 'Houndsback') is common in Spain and Portugal.

394-95 For a discussion of the inversion of these lines see my 'Geographical problems in the *PMC*: I. The exile route', in *Medieval Hispanic Studies presented to Rita Hamilton* (London, forthcoming).

397   I am in agreement with J. Montero Padilla, *Pasado y presente de Riaza* (Segovia, 1963), p. 23, and M. Criado de Val that the Cid passes to the right of San Esteban (see map), not to the left as Pidal, *ed. crít.*, interprets (apparently with Smith's concurrence).

398   If *Alilón* is the present Ayllón, it could not be seen from the Cid's route, but Criado de Val suggests that it refers to one of the watch-towers in the area. There is in any case a geographical inexactitude at this point (see my article cited in the note to 394-95).

399   The poet regards Alcubilla (see map) as the end of Castile proper, because the lands to the south as far as Miedes were held by Moors under Alfonso VI's protection.

400   This ancient Roman causeway ran north-east to south-west from Osma to Tiermes.

402 **la Figueruela** Unknown place, which may have been within the 4 km between Navapalos and Fresno de Caracena.

406 The archangel Gabriel is usually the messenger or foreteller of events in medieval poems, cf. *Chanson de Roland* 2525-31. Apart from omens (see note to 11-12), this is the only supernatural event in the poem and, even so, it occurs in a dream. Pidal, *ed. crít.*, and Smith alter *sueño* to *visión*.

415 The range now called the Sierra de Pela is probably meant (see map). Before 1085 it marked the southern frontier of the Moorish lands under Alfonso VI's protection, but by 1091 he was able to extend the frontier much farther south, as far as the Guadiana at one point (Alarcos).

420 **¡sí el Criador vos salve!** lit. 'as the Creator may save you!'

422 Throughout the poem we find the typical medieval view that natural places are alien and frightening.

435 The attack on Castejón de Henares marks the opening of the Cid's campaign against the Moorish towns along the Henares, which were under the protection of the emir of Toledo until 1085.

440 **ciento** MS *.C*, followed by an erased letter of which I saw possible faint ink traces under the ultra-violet lamp (it could have been a second C, the scribe's eye possibly having been caught by the *C.C.* in 442), cf. a similar, but not identical, problem in 3733.

441 There is a fairly brief lacuna after this line, in which Álvar Fáñez must have ended his advice, since the Cid is giving the orders in 442.

442b Álvar Álvarez was apparently a nephew of the Cid, and Álvar Salvadórez was one of the Cid's vassals (there is historical record of both).

443b Galín García, a lord of Estada, was a vassal of Peter I of Aragon.

453 'Spain': *España* here, and in 1021 and 1591, may have the restricted meaning of 'Moorish Spain', cf. Juan Menéndez Pidal, *Sellos españoles de la edad media* (Madrid, 1921), p. 14.

492 The custom whereby the fifth share of any booty was reserved for the king was generally practised in Christian Spain and had its counterpart in Muslim law (cf. Qur'ān, sūra VIII, 42). Since the Cid is outlawed, the fifth falls to him as leader, but Álvar Fáñez, to whom he offers it as a special reward, instead broaches the idea of sending it to Alfonso.

501 This epic formula is used once for the Cid (1724), and twice for Álvar Fáñez (781, where he fulfils the vow he makes here, and 2453).

505 lit. 'there is all the other (i.e. the offered fifth) in your hand', spoken with a symbolic gesture, cf. 2088 and 2097-98 for the legal proxy or symbolic presence.

507-09 **el rrey** MS *Al Rey*, which, if we accept it (with Lang, p. 143, Pidal, *ed. crít.*, and Smith), would imply that the Cid feared his men would range afield (northwards!) into conflict with the king. By changing *al* to *el* (with Bello, and Pidal, CC—a change of mind?), we create a form of anacoluthon common in the poem which provides a much better meaning, cf. 528 and 532. Smith notes Bello's emendation and the meaning it gives, but retains *al rey* without revealing what sense he thinks it could have.

513-21 The poet does not mention the total value of the booty, but on the basis of line 674 we might put it at over 56,250 silver marks, and the Cid's fifth at over 11,250 silver marks in the form of Moorish slaves. From the ransom he actually receives 3,000 silver marks, slightly over a quarter of the value. The sums mentioned are certain to be poetic exaggeration.

529   **escuelas** lit. 'schools (of vassals)'.

Minyaya see note to 1418.

542-47 The Cid ends his campaign along the Henares and turns eastward, across the valley of the Tajuña, to the banks of the Jalón (see map), where he begins his second major campaign against the Moorish towns which were under the protection of the emir of Saragossa, although the poet mistakenly thinks them under the protection of the emir of Valencia (cf. 627). These campaigns are not attested historically.

551-52 Pidal, *ed. crít.*, assumes, probably mistakenly, that the Cid crossed to the north bank of the Jalón at this point (see my article cited in note to 394-95 for a full discussion of this section of the poem).

553   Alcocer probably represents Castejón de las Armas, as Criado de Val has suggested.

571   **Terrer** MS *Teruel*, probable scribal misreading of an abbreviation sign whereby the better known place was inserted, as Bello and Pidal point out.

607   **los delant** 'those in front', cf. *Alex* 74c; see Ramsden, 'The taking of Alcocer', *Bulletin of Hispanic Studies*, XXXVI (1959), 129-34, for a clear explanation of this passage.

611   Pedro Vermúdez is listed as a *potestad* in a document of *c.* 1069, but we cannot be sure that he was a nephew of the Cid (cf. 2351) or his standard-bearer.

627   Their historical protector was Muᶜtaman, emir of Saragossa, whom the Cid served during the years 1081-86.

636   There was no emir of Valencia called Tamín; the governor of the city at the time of the Cid's exile was Abu Bekr ibn Abd al-Aziz. As well as mistaking the city (cf. 627), the poet appears to have confused Abu Bekr with Tamim, the Almoravid governor of Spain from 1107.

637   **Tres reyes** Two of them were Fáriz and Galve (cf. 654), but it is not clear who the third was meant to be (perhaps a symbolic number).

654   Fáriz and Galve are fictitious, but they may be based on historical figures: Hariz, a Moor killed by the Cid in single combat at Medinaceli; Ghalid, the father-in-law of the Muslim general al-Mansur.

699   The line is long, and Lidforss and Pidal, *ed. crít.*, alter *peones* to *pendones* and omit *fizieron dos azes*, altering the sense—the mixed infantry refers to the Moors from the frontier incorporated in the armies of Fáriz and Galve; like Smith, I retain the MS reading.

708   **debdo** See note to 225.

715   lit. 'They place their shields over their arms'.

721   MS *Yo ſo Ruy Diaz el Çid Campeador de Biuar*; Pidal, *ed. crít.*, confusedly alters: *Yo so Roy Díaz, el Çid   de Bivar Campeador*, Smith ¡*Yo so Ruy*

Diaz el Çid   Campeador de Bivar! I follow Cornu, *R* XXII, in transposing *de Bivar* to end the first hemistich.

725 **[muertos]** I follow Pidal, *ed. crít.*, in this addition for the sense; Cornu, *ZfrPh*, adds [*moros*]; the other editors accept the MS reading.

737 Muño Gustioz was Doña Jimena's brother-in-law, and continued in her service after the Cid's death.

738 Martín Muñoz was governor of Montemayor (Montemor-o-Velho), and was Count of Coimbra from 1091-94.

741 There is no historical record of Félez Muñoz.

781 See note to 501.

784 Faulty assonance: Restori and Pidal, *ed. crít.*, alter *vencida* to *arrancado*; Smith, who does not object to the assonance, alters to [*arrancada*] for grammatical reasons he does not explain. There are other examples of the phrase: *venciemos la lid*, 831 (and cf. 1008, 1011, etc.).

816-18 The Cid here takes up the hint made by Álvar Fáñez in 495, and this is the first of three presents of horses he will send to Alfonso: thirty here, 100 in 1274 and 200 in 1813.

837 **[fincó]** Smith accepts the MS reading, but the sense requires some addition; Pidal, *ed. crít.*, inserts *fincó y* before *con*.

863-64 This marks the beginning of the Cid's third campaign in the poem, against the Moorish towns along the river Jiloca (see map), which were historically under the protection of the emir of Saragossa.

876 **aquesta** refers to the battle recently described, unfamiliar to the king, but, of course, familiar to the audience; Pidal, *ed. crít.*, unnecessarily assumes a lacuna.

883 **a cabo de tres semanas** lit. 'after three weeks', but it can mean no more than 'after such a short time', since, even in the vague time scale of the poem, five months or more have passed, cf. 573 and 664 (which themselves may be only notional references).

896 lit. 'this you do now, you will do otherwise hereafter'.

901 **e la** MS *ɀ dela*, which the other editors accept; I take the *de* to be scribal repetition.

902 In fact until recently the place was known only as El Poyo, although the twelfth- to thirteenth-century *Fuero de Molina* refers to 'Poyo de Mio Çit'.

904 MS *El de rio Martī*: a noun appears to be missing after *el*, as Lidforss noted; Pidal, *ed. crít.*, and Smith insert [*val*]; but the *Fuero de Daroca* (*c.* 1142) mentions 'rio de Martin', which I adopt by a simple transposition.

911-12 **allén de Teruel** 'beyond Teruel' must in fact mean to the north-east of that town, and the poet's geographical knowledge seems to be faulty here (see my article cited in note to 394-95).

Tévar Probably in the *término* of Monroyo, south of Alcañiz on the road to Morella (see map).

940 **Huesca** could be scribal error for *Huesa* as in 952 and 1089, as Huntington suggests, but *Pidal, ed. crít.*, p. 896, defends the MS reading here, since Huesca is only some 60 km north-west of Monzón (see map).

951 **Aluca[n]t** MS *Alucāt*, but the tilde is late; Pidal and Smith *Alucat*. The

pass in the mountains north-east of the village of Gallocanta is most probably meant, as Criado de Val points out.

952   **Huesa** MS *Huefca*, scribal error whereby the better known place is inserted. As Pidal, *ed. crít.*, p. 896, points out, Huesa is only some 25 km from Montalbán, while Huesca is 160 km away.

957   This count of Barcelona was Berenguer Ramón II the Fratricide, whom the Cid took prisoner on two occasions, in 1082 and in 1090; it is the second imprisonment which provided the basis for this episode, and some of the details are close to the account in the *Historia Roderici*.

962   This refers to some unknown quarrel during the Cid's first exile when he spent some time in Barcelona.

963   **non'** Pidal, *ed. crít.*, proposes that it be read = *no[m']*.

972   MS *Afi viene ef forçado q̃ el 9de amanos fele cuydo tomar*, which Smith preserves, but the sense is not good; with Lidforss I follow Restori's simple solution of transposing *que*; Bello and Pidal, *ed. crít.*, make more complex changes.

973   MS *trae grand ganançia*: Bello reorders *gr. ga. tr.*; Restori, Pidal, *ed. crít.*, and Smith *tr. ga. gr.*; I follow the order of 944 (cf. 988).

1002   **francos** i.e. Catalans; Catalonia had once been one of the marches of the Carolingian empire, hence 'Franks'.

1010   **Colada** The name probably derives from *acero colado* ('cast steel'). The *Colada* allegedly possessed by the Armería Real, Madrid, in modern times is certainly false; the original disappeared in 1503.

1011   lit. 'whereby he honoured his beard'; the Cid's beard is the chief symbol of his honour and virility, cf. 268, 789, etc.

1021   See note to 453.

1043   MS *Mas q̃anto auedes perdido non uos lo dare*, which appears to be scribal repetition (with variants) of the first hemistichs of 1041 and 1042; I follow Bello, Restori, Lidforss and Pidal, *ed. crít.*, in suppressing the line, which is not good syntactically (especially not the repeated *Mas*); Smith defends the MS reading.

1045   After *lazrados* the MS reads *z nō uos lo dare*, a further (inopportune) repetition, probably scribal, of the first hemistich of 1042, which I suppress with most other editors (Smith again preserves).

1072-73   There is certainly scribal confusion here, since *o me dexaredes* must be transposed into 1073 if *enjambement* is to be avoided; Pidal, *ed. crít.*, suppresses *e si non -edes buscar*, running the rest of 1072-73 together. Smith retains the MS reading, though recognising the problem of *enjambement*; he rightly points to 2522-23, but his examples in 347-48 and 3666-67 are not quite so severe.

1083   **conpeçós' de pagar** MS *conpeçolas de legar*, which, if it is interpreted 'He began to collect them together' (or 'gather them'), places the next line in limbo; Smith admits the MS reading, but in a note suggests *conpeçol[e]s*, which does not solve the lack of syntactical connexion with 1084. Pidal, *ed. crít.*, sensibly alters to *conpeçós de alegrar*, but I prefer *pagar*, both on the basis of 1201 and because *alegrarse* is usually followed by *en*, while *pagarse* is always followed by *de* and therefore fits better with 1084. It would be possible to read *conpeçólas de pagar*, since *pagar* may take *de* before the object of payment, but the presence of *que an fecha* makes this too forced.

1085 This line provides the only basis for beginning a second *Cantar* here, but Huntington was doubtful about the necessity to divide.

1086 Many editors relocate this line after 1084 at the end of the first *Cantar*, but it makes sense here if we take it as a reminder to the audience of the Cid's achievements to date (Smith takes the same view).

1087 **Alucant** MS *Alucāt*; Pidal, *ed. crít., Alucat,* Smith *Aluca(n)t.* If *Poblado ha* means 'he has occupied', then the place is probably Olocau, near Liria, as in 1108; but if it means 'he has left a garrison in' (less likely), it probably means the pass near Gallocanta referred to in 951.

1089 **Huesa** MS *Huesca* (see note to 952).

1090 The Cid moves south-eastward to begin his fourth campaign in the poem, against the lands of the emir of Lérida.

1092-95 The historical Cid was in Burriana *c.* A.D. 1091, but not until the year 1098 did he capture Almenara and Murviedro (Sagunto), four years after the capture of Valencia.

1145-53 The order of lines is certainly confused unless we are to take most of them as having different subjects; Lidforss and Pidal reorder radically (and differently), but Bello and Smith retain the MS order, the latter on the grounds of the abrupt and elliptical style; Criado de Val defends the MS order as interlaced narration. I have made sufficient reordering to follow the poet's usual sequence in battle descriptions (cf. 785-803).

1151 **de pies de cavallo** 'at full gallop', but it may mean 'from under the horses' hooves', cf. *Alex* 505ab [*P* MS].

1181 Apparently a reference to Yúçuf (cf. 1621, 1850), i.e. Yusuf ibn Tešufin, first Almoravid caliph of Morocco (A.D. 1059-1106).

1182 **Montes Claros** the Atlas mountains; the reference to a war is probably anachronistic in that it seems to refer to that waged by the Almohades, who conquered the Atlas *c.* 1122, against Yusuf's grandson, Tešufin.

1185-86 An impossibly long night's march, since it is 140 km from Murviedro (Sagunto) to Celfa (Cella).

1200 In the MS *en* is written above the line by an early corrector, perhaps by the copyist himself, and there is a letter erased after *Riqza* which Pidal, *ed. pal.*, claims to have been an *a*, thus in *ed. crít.* he reads *creçiendo va riqueza a mio Çid*, etc. (cf. 296, 1977, 2316); Smith follows him without comment. I follow Huntington and other editors in admitting the early correction, cf. *creçremos en rrictad* 688 (and cf. 1883, 1905, 1929, 2198).

1208 The respite was a common procedure which had had biblical authority (cf. Samuel, 1, 11, 3) and may have been of up to thirty days' duration; it was twice adopted by Alfonso VII, at Oreja in 1139 and at Coria *c.* 1142.

1222 Probably a reference to the Almoravid governor of Seville, the general Sir ibn Abu Bekr, who conquered that city in 1091. There is no record that he ever tried to recapture Valencia from the Cid (cf. note to 2314).

1229 Cf. the Saracens' fate in the Ebro in *Chanson de Roland* 2471-74.

1230 Pidal, *ed. crít.*, and Smith alter *Marruecos* to *Sevilla* (cf. 1222), the latter considering it a distraction of the copyist; but the Almoravid general probably referred to came originally from Morocco, and from 1091, Seville belonged to the Almoravid empire of Morocco; thus, as Pidal *ed. crít.*, p. 851, himself points out, the reference is curiously accurate, if we interpret 'That king from Morocco'.

1238 Leaving the beard untrimmed was a sign of grief from biblical and Roman times, and the practice continued into the seventeenth century in Spain.

1240-42 Smith follows Vollmöller and Lidforss in continuing the direct speech of 1240 into 1241-42, but *entrarié* and *avrié* can hardly be first person forms. I follow Pidal in taking this to be a switch from direct to indirect speech, which is commoner in the poem than the reverse (contrast 526-27).

1274 This is the Cid's second present to the king (see note to 816-18).

1285-86 The Cid here fulfils the promise made in 258-60 (cf. 386).

 los diesse Bello and Pidal, *ed. crít.*, insert *quinientos* after *los* in view of 1422-23, arguing that *diesse* may be haplography for [.*d*.] *diesse* (Smith adopts this form); it could, however, be another example of poetic licence (or forgetfulness, cf. note to 1719-20).

1288 **de parte de orient** lit. 'from the east', i.e. from France, as viewed from Old Castile, not from Valencia.

1289 Jérôme de Périgord, brought to Spain *c.* 1096 by Bernard de Sédirac, the first archbishop of Toledo, to take part in the Cluniac reform, was consecrated bishop of Valencia by Bernard in 1098, four years after the Cid's capture of Valencia (see C. J. Socarrás, *Iberoromania*, III, 1971-72, 101-11).

1299-1300 The Cid wants to make a bishopric, but there had been a Mozarabic bishopric there prior to 1094. The historical Cid refounded the mosque as a cathedral dedicated to St Mary in 1098.

1333 The Cid has fought only two pitched battles (cf. 1111 and 1225), and Pidal, CC, takes this line to be a lapse, or possibly a scribal misreading of II as U (= 5), but the 'lapse' is also in the *Veinte reyes*. The motif of the five pitched battles may have been ancient and familiar to the poet, otherwise we should have to suppose two scribal errors and emend: 'e fizo *dos* lides campales e *amas* las arrancó.'

1342 St Isidore, author of the famous *Etymologiae*, was bishop of Seville from 599 to 636; his remains were translated to León by Alfonso's father, Ferdinand I, in 1063.

1345 Count García Ordóñez, lord of Pancorbo and governor of Nájera, was an important figure at Alfonso's court; the reprimand in 1348-49 is likely to be unhistorical.

1371 **otra** may mean no more than 'ninguna', see note to 2866.

1372-73 Diego and Fernando González were grandsons and, later, nephews of counts of Carrión (they had no right to the title *infante*) and belonged to Alfonso VI's *schola regis*. There is no record of their betrothal or marriage to the Cid's daughters.

1418 **Mianaya** Most editors alter to *Minaya*, but Pidal, *ed. crít.*, Adiciones, p. 1211, notes that it is probably *mi* + Basque *anai* ('brother'); in the form

Minyaya in 529 *ny* may well be a graph for *nn*, with which the title was often spelt.

1424 **Ximina** The MS is clear; most editors alter to *Ximena*, but the form is found in notarial documents.

1435-36 This promise might have been a sufficient undertaking to a contemporary audience, for the affair is not mentioned again, but in any case a medieval public would probably have rejoiced to see the Jews tricked.

1464 The *alcaide* or governor of Molina in the Cid's time appears to have been Ibn Ghalbûn (Avengalbón), who in the poem becomes a close ally of the Cid.

1475 **Frontael** Pidal, *ed. crít.*, and Smith alter to *Fronchales*, a form of Bronchales (province of Teruel), but this may be an earlier form of the toponym.

1486 In the right outer margin between this line and 1492 there is a rough drawing of a woman's head, and there is a similar, but fainter, drawing in the same margin of folio 31*r* opposite 1500-07.

1492 Campo Taranz is a flat scrub between Luzón and Medinaceli, which in medieval times was probably more wooded (*mata* = 'thicket').

1495*b* **sopiesse** Cornu, *Etudes*, Pidal, *ed. crít.*, and Smith alter to *sopiessen*, but this is unnecessary and alters the sense.

1496 **detard[an]** MS *de tardo*, but a later hand changed the *o* into an *a* and added a tilde (not a correction of Pidal's, as Smith appears to think).

1508-09 MS *En buenos cauallos a petrales τ a cafcaueles / E a cuberturas de çendales τ efcudos alos cuellos*, which Smith retains; but since it is unlikely that the shields were worn by the horses, I follow Pidal, *ed. crít.*, in reordering the hemistichs (but not in his other changes).

1519 This oriental habit is also found in *Chanson de Roland* 601 and *Alex* 1880*d*.

1530 This promise, like the one to the Jews in 1436, is not seen to be fulfilled.

1565 **Mianaya** See note to 1418.

1577 **e sus** MS *τ de fus*; Pidal and Smith retain the *de*, but it is clumsy syntax.

1581 **acordaran** MS *acordaron*. The phrase *acordarse con oras* is not found elsewhere; Bello suggests 'juntarse a rezarlas'—similar to the present translation; alternatively, Lang, p. 238, proposes 'with as many of the clergy as could go with him, that had made arrangements regarding their [canonical] hours', to which Pidal, *ed. crít.*, Adiciones, p. 1224, inclined.

1584-90 The scribe appears to have dislocated the line order; Lidforss places 1589 after 1590; Smith reorders 1589, 1588, 1590; I follow the more radical reordering of Pidal, *ed. crít.*

1591 **España** See note to 453.

1596 Another case of unexpected historical accuracy, since Alfonso imprisoned Jimena and her children in December 1089, but the poem implies that they were well looked after at Cardeña.

1601 **deleite** Corrected in the MS; Huntington and Pidal, *ed. pal.*, read *delent*, *ed. crít.*, *deleyt*, Smith *dele[i]t*.

1621 Yusuf (see note to 1181) did not come himself to try to recover Valencia, but sent his nephew Muhammad ibn 'Ayiša, who was defeated by the Cid *c.* 1095.

1652 Bello, Restori and Pidal, *ed. crít.*, suppress *e si quisieredes*; Smith retains, interpreting 'stay in this hall, or if you wish go up to the tower'; I take the *e* to be pleonastic as in 248, 255, 1749: lit. 'stay in this apartment, if you wish, in the fortress'.

1672 **ent[r]an** MS *estā*; Lidforss and Smith preserve *estan*, but the syntax is not good, as Bello and Pidal point out.

1681 We are not told of his release, and he turns up in 1719 without explanation.

1688-89 **dezir nos ha** Restori and Lidforss take *nos* = *nos* [*se*], but the pronoun order would be curious; Pidal, *ed. crít.*, and Smith invert these lines, but since the absolution clearly follows the mass in 1703 the emendation is not good. It may be a case of delayed expression of the subject, cf. 1340; Bello and Lidforss also retain the MS order.

1719-20 In the MS a later hand cancelled *τ Aluar Saluadorez*—no doubt a reader who remembered he had been captured in 1681; Bello, Restori, Lidforss and Pidal, *ed. crít.*, suppress these words and *Alvar Fañez* and run the lines together; Smith suppresses *e Alvar Salvadorez*, keeping the lines separate. Pidal admits that the poet never mentions any release yet refers to Alvar Salvadórez again in 1994 and 3067 (Smith accepts that as forgetfulness), but thinks it doubtful he would have forgotten so soon (he mentions, however, Cervantes' forgetfulness over Sancho's stolen ass in *Quixote*, I, chs. 23 and 25). I am with Huntington in ignoring the later cancellation.

1752 Pidal, *ed. pal.*, punctuates interrogatively but in *ed. crít.*, as a statement (Huntington and Smith same).

1754 **Rrogand** Perhaps apocope of present participle, but Sánchez, Hinard, Lidforss, Pidal, *ed. crít.*, and Smith suppress the *n* to make it imperative.

1761 **En buelta con él** lit. 'Together with him'.

1763 **daña** Thus the MS, and it could be a dialectal form; all the editors save Huntington alter to *doña*.

1778 **arrad[í]os** MS *arriados*, probable scribal error, as Cornu, *Etudes*, and Lang, pp. 245-46, point out; cf. 'andavan erradíos', *PCG* 354*a* 2, 'andando erradíos por esos montes', *PCG* 335*b* 13 (and cf. *Milagros* 646*c* and 884*d*, and *Santo Domingo* 469*a*) = 'run wild'; while the not very common *erradíos* does not appear to occur with *a-*, there are a number of examples of *desarrados, desarrar*, etc. *arrear* ('to equip') does not appear to have occurred as **arriar*, but the other editors assume it here, though it does not suit the meaning so well. For a similar description of loose horses after a battle in the poem, cf. 2406.

1780 **al** MS *el*; I follow Hinard, Cornu, *Etudes*, and Restori in this emendation, cf. 1782; Pidal, *ed. crít.*, objects to it, maintaining that we have a case of anacoluthon; if so, it is particularly violent; Smith retains *el* without comment.

1785 The tent description was a literary theme, cf. *Alex* 2539-95, *Lba* 1266-1301.

1796 **caye** can be read as imperfect *cayé*, or as present indicative with antihiatic yod.

1813 This is the Cid's third present to the king, cf. 816-18 and 1274.

1820 Pidal, *ed. crít.*, and Smith place all this line in direct speech yet retain *ovisse* (one would expect **oviere*); Bello alters *he* to *hia* (**ie* would be better) making it all indirect speech; but cf. 1240-42.

1823-24 Contrast the vague description of this journey with 1473-93 and 1542-59. The sierra is probably the eastern part of the Guadarrama, since the travellers reach Valladolid (see map).

1839 Although Smith sees a difficulty in that they had earlier sent a message to herald their arrival in 1828, *mandado* here may have the sense of sending immediate outriders.

1848 **ondra** i.e. the favour of releasing Jimena and the daughters.

1863 **biltadamientre** 'basely', he being an *infanzón* and they kings, albeit Moorish (Pidal and Smith interpret as 'effortlessly').

1874 It is not clear whether they are given three horses between them or three each; the latter makes better sense: presumably, a destrier, a palfrey and a pack-horse.

1889 This formula is used for the receipt of bad news, cf. 1932, 2828, 2953.

1899b There were three kinds of gathering, in ascending order of importance: *juntas* ('meeting'), *vistas* ('assembly'), *cortes* ('the royal court or *curia regia*'); the last is sometimes in the singular in this sense.

1929 **creç[r]ié** I follow Restori and Pidal, *ed. crít.*, taking the king as the subject of *connoscié* but the Cid as the subject of *creç[r]ié*; Nyrop, *Romania*, XVIII (1889), and Lidforss admit the imperfect as a case of *imperfectum futuri*; Smith also admits it without comment on the difficulty.

1933 The Cid's reaction of gratitude to this unwelcome proposal is somewhat similar to his reactions in 8-9 and 2830-31.

1948-49 The intercalation of the introductory clause is most unusual, but one cannot repunctuate 1948 as part of the Cid's statement in 1947, on grounds of either syntax or meaning; one could, however, invert the line order here to ease the construction.

1951 **ir[i]emos** I follow Restori and Pidal in this alteration, necessary for the syntax; Smith retains *iremos*, but glosses 'we would gladly go'.

1958 Pidal, *ed. crít.*, and Smith regard the line as being in indirect speech.

1971 **A[n]dria** O. Schultz-Gora, *Zeitschrift für romanische Philologie*, XXVI, 718, related it to the French *cendal d'Andrie*; the isle of Andros was once famous for its silks.

1980 The ranks of Spanish nobility were basically three: in descending order, *ricos omnes* (consisting of *condes* and *podestades*), *yfançones*, and the vague *fijos d'algo*, which could include *caballeros* and even *escuderos*, and, more widely, all men of good lineage. The complex English ranks make it difficult to find exactly corresponding terms.

1999 Although these two vassals prepare for the journey (cf. 1994 and 1996), the Cid now orders them to stay; it is possible that the poet reeled them off in the formal list (cf. 735-41) without considering their special task (Smith makes the same point); for a similar lapse within a few lines, see 1719-20.

2001b I follow Bello and Pidal, *ed. crít.*, in inserting [*otros*] because of the difficulty of finding the caesura, which Smith awkwardly places after *que*.

2021 This form of prostration or kow-tow was Persian, Indian and Oriental in origin.

2022 As well as the Germanic, Italic and Slav custom of taking grass into the mouth as a sign of total submission (see G. L. Hamilton, *Romanic Review*, IV, 1913, 226-27), there may be an echo of Nebuchadnezzar's banishment (Daniel, 4, 25). Duncan McMillan, in *Coloquios de Roncesvalles* (Saragossa, 1956), pp. 253-61, suggests that *a dientes* = 'lying face down' (cf. O. Fr. *adenz*), but the only other examples I know in O. Sp. = 'with (their) teeth' (cf. *Alex* 407*ab* and 824*cd*).

2035 lit. 'and I give you a position in the whole of my kingdom'.

2039-40 The Cid kisses hands on accepting vassalage and gives the kiss of fealty; kissing hands was the ancient Spanish ceremony of vassalage, and since the Cid is apparently not receiving lands in fief he does not perform the usual European ceremony of paying homage (*postura*).

2042 Álvar Díaz was lord of Oca and brother-in-law of García Ordóñez.

2060 The Cid's appearance has the same effect on the court in 3099-100, 3123-24.

2115-16 With Hinard, Lidforss and Pidal, *ed. crít.*, I invert these lines for the sense; Smith retains the MS order.

2121-25 This repeats the end of the betrothal ceremony (2101, 2106-07, 2109), and the Cid's remarks in 2132 and 2134 fill out his reply in 2110. It is not clear whether it is consecutive narration, with the anxious king informally repeating part of the ceremony to smooth over a difficult situation, or a form of 'double narration', with two accounts of the same ceremony, the second filled in with more detail about the *manero* or sponsor.

2126 Pidal, *ed. crít.*, and Smith alter *dem'* to *devos*, thus destroying the irony in the Cid's remark. J. Horrent, in *Mélanges . . . M. Delbouille* (Gembloux, 1964), II, p. 285, well defends the MS reading; Smith argues on the basis of the same formula in 2855 and 3416, but he fails to allow for the poet's ability to vary a formula for a higher artistic purpose.

2144-45 These fifty horses are additional to the sixty in 2118 if the narration is consecutive, or they may be counted in those sixty if this is double narration (see note to 2121-25).

2199 The Cid does not tell his daughters who their husbands are to be; because the audience knows, the poet assumes Elvira and Sol know, cf. 876.

2230 **amos sodes ermanos** lit. 'you are truly brothers'; this formulaic phrase will later be used pejoratively of the Infantes.

2240 We are not told which Infante married which daughter.

2275 [*ovo a algo*] The words have been repeatedly subjected to chemical reagents; under the ultra-violet lamp one can faintly see *algo*, as well as *ouo* written above the line; like Smith, I follow Pidal's reading (in a note he suggested *lo ovo* [*por*] *voz* [*tratado*] as an alternative).

2278 There is nothing in the MS to indicate the beginning of the third *Cantar* save a large capital letter and the sense of 2276.

2283 '. . . seized them', probably the Infantes, since the new subject is expressed in the next line.

2297 This implies that the Cid is so brave he does not bother to cover his arm.

2314 Búcar may be a recollection of the Almoravid general Sir ibn Abu Bekr (see note to 1222), or of Abu Bekr ibn Abd al-Aziz, the historical emir of Valencia (called *Tamín* in 636).

ouyestes possible dialectal form of *oyestes* (cf. *Poema de Yúçuf* 67d); Pidal takes the *u* to be antihiatic *v*; Lidforss alters to *oyiestes*, Smith to *oyestes*.

2327 **por** 'instead of'; thus F. Hanssen interprets, in *Anales de la Universidad de Chile* (Santiago de Chile, 1911), pp. 44-45, but Pidal, *ed. crít.*, p. 1113 n., takes *por* to be causal, expressing the motive.

2333 **tan blancas como el sol** lit. 'as white as the sun'.

2337 *Lacuna of about fifty lines*: we are fortunate in having a summary of some of the missing section in 3316-25. Out of bravado the Infantes have requested the first blows in the battle. Fernando flees when a Moor he has begun to attack turns on him and he is aided by Pedro Bermúdez, who kills the Moor and takes his captured horse to Fernando, offering to keep silent about his cowardice. The text picks up when Fernando is thanking him for this generous offer.

2338 A famous line, unnecessarily emended to *aun vea el ora que vos merescades tanto* by J. H. Frere, British Minister in Madrid during the Peninsular War, who suggested the emendation to the Marqués de la Romana; later, when the latter was in Denmark, Frere sent as secret emissary for the British government a Roman Catholic priest known as Mr Robertson, whose sole credential was the emended line from the poem, at once recognised by Romana (see Robert Southey, *History of the Peninsular War*, London, 1823, I, p. 657).

2369 **delant al** Very rare use of *a*; it could be scribal error for *el*.

2373 **orden** The Order of Cluny, which began the reform of the Spanish Church in the eleventh century (see note to 1289).

2375 **corças** MS *corcas*. Stags or harts were often used for personal or family arms, cf. those of Pope Victor II (1055-57): 'Gold, a standing stag sable with but one antler gules' (see D. L. Galbreath, *A Treatise on Ecclesiastical Heraldry*: I. *Papal Heraldry*, Cambridge, 1930, p. 69).

2398 The general fighting has not been described; almost cinematographically, the poet closes on to the actions of the two leading participants.

2420 **braça** lit. a fathom, a measure of 6 ft (originally, the length of the outstretched arms).

2422 *et seq.* This description is close to the *Chanson de Roland* 1324-30.

2426 **Tizón** (post-medieval form *Tizona*) probably meant 'the burning sword' (cf. Eng. *brand* and O. Norse *brander*; O. Fr. *brant* = 'blade'); it seems to have been in the possession of the kings of Aragon and, according to Pidal, may still exist in the Armería Real in Madrid.

2430-32 I interpret that the Cid's men strip the battlefield, while he, after chasing Búcar, returns to the Moorish tents, where they rejoin him.

2439 **esteva** Thus the MS, which I follow Huntington in admitting (cf. *Fuero juzgo* 113*a*); the other editors alter to *estava*.

2455 The line is clearly misplaced; Pidal, *ed. crít.*, relocates it between 2437 and 2438; I relocate it after the arrival of the Infantes, who can hardly be counted among the Cid's vassals. Smith defends the MS order on the grounds that the line is a typical introduction to a speech; it is not, however, the vassals who speak, but Minaya, last mentioned in 2449.

2465-67 Assonance in *á-a*, which could support a *laisse* division between 2463 and 2464 (faulty assonance in the latter line), and between 2467 and 2468; Huntington divides thus, and Smith, who renumbers these sections 119*b*, 119*c*.

2483 Pidal, *ed. crít.*, ends the Cid's speech at 2481 and is thus forced to change *nuestro* to *dellos*. Smith interprets 'part of the booty is already divided among us, part is in the safe-keeping of the *quiñoneros* (who will divide it later)'. I interpret 'part of it belongs to me and my vassals, part of it is in the Infantes' possession', cf. the Infantes' large share in 2509 and Fernando's further reference in 2531 to the Cid's statement here.

2487 **olbidado** would be better for the grammar if it were corrected to *olbidada* (against the assonance).

2500 **abrán** MS *abram*, which Pidal and Smith admit, the former thinking it reminiscent of Galician and Leonese forms; it may, however, be scribal error by anticipation of *de mí* (the scribe thinking erroneously of a dative construction **abrá[n]m'*); for the normal construction, cf. 754, 1899.

2505-06 Pidal, *ed. crít.*, and Smith insert *la mayor* after Valencia and make the remainder of 2505 the second hemistich of 2506, altering *con* to *de* and suppressing *e de todos sus vassallos* (thus losing the distinction between companions and vassals). Other editors make different changes. These emendations seem excessive in the face of one long line and one faulty assonance.

2508 Lidforss and Pidal, *ed. crít.*, relocate this line between 2506 and 2507, considering it should refer not to the Infantes but to the Cid's vassals; this places an enormous strain on the syntax of 2506-07, and *de coraçón* might be ironic (Smith defends the MS order on very similar grounds).

2509 The Infantes have each received more than four times the share paid to each knight, cf. 2467, probably by virtue of their kinship with the leader.

2522-23 Faulty assonance and *enjambement*: I follow Restori and Lidforss in inverting the MS word order *traidor provado*. Pidal, *ed. crít.*, relocates the lines between 2530 and 2531, where they fit the new assonance in Fernando's speech; but they make perfectly good sense in the MS line order. Smith follows Pidal, claiming that in the MS order the lines interrupt what the Cid is saying about the Infantes' marriages; but, on the contrary, his mistaken belief that they have fought bravely in his army reinforces his assurance that they will receive estate as a result of the marriages (2525); nor does Smith explain how 2526 fits his reordering, since the Cid's mention of the messages that will go to Carrión otherwise refer to the Infantes' assumed prowess, cf. 2444-45, 2479-81. The serious problem here is the rare case of *enjambement* (cf. my emendation to 1072-73).

2525 Pidal, *ed. crít.*, and Smith alter *nuestros* to *vuestros* without comment; I interpret 'by marrying into our family'.

2539 The poet pretends to use the rhetorical device of *occultatio*, while proceeding to divulge the evil plan.

2543 Although pairs usually speak together in the poem, Pidal, *ed. crít.*, assumes that the second Infante begins to speak here.

2552 Lidforss and Pidal, *ed. crít.*, assume that there is a change of speaker (the other Infante) here, apparently approved by Smith in a note.

2568-69 The MS is confused: *Dixo el Campeador daruos he mys fijas τ algo delo myo | El Çid q̃ nos curiaua de aſſi ſer afontado*; I follow Coester, *Revue Hispanique*, xv (1906), 98-211, Restori and Pidal, *ed. crít.*, in placing 2569 first, suppressing *Dixo el*, *q̃* and *aſſi*, and rearranging *Cid* and *Campeador* (but not in their other changes); Smith retains the MS reading.

2574 Huntington and Pidal, *ed. pal.*, read τ after *paños*, but the sign, now very faint, was added; the editors *de paños e de ciclatones*, but Jesusa Alfau de Solalinde, *Nomenclatura de los tejidos españoles del siglo XIII* (Madrid, 1969), pp. 140-41, points out that *paño* was a generic term for all cloth.

2598 See note to 225.

2600 Smith in a note wonders whether *ayades* should be *ayamos* or *mandedes* and points out that no editor has alluded to the possibility. But if we take *mensajes* to be 'messengers' (cf. 1834), we might interpret literally 'that you have your messengers in the lands of Carrión, i.e. '. . . send your messengers to . . .'

2602 **lo doblava** 'did the same', or possibly 'kissed them twice over'.

2657 **el Ansarera** Unknown place, but the name implies that geese were kept there; it is likely to have been just below Medinaceli, on the north bank of the Jalón (cf. 2687).

2676 MS τ *uos cõſſeiaſtes pora mi muert*; Pidal, *ed. crít.*, suppresses *pora* for syntactical reasons and relocates this line and 2675 before 2681 for the assonance; Smith retains the MS reading (and line order) but admits the unusual syntax.   *consejar muert* occurs in 2670 and in *Fuero juzgo*, prologue 12a, p. xi b, thus one can consider *mi* as a disjunctive pronoun, and reorder for the assonance.

2687 **iva** MS *yuan*, which cannot properly be maintained unless the order of 2687-88 is inverted, and that would locate El Ansarera on the south bank of the Jalón; I follow Pidal, *ed. crít.*, in suppressing the *n*; Smith *ivan*.

2691 **Atienza** MS *Atineza*, which may be scribal error.

2693 **Montes Claros** The mountains still known by this name, where the Jarama rises (see map), lie too far to the south-west to fit the itinerary described; see my 'Geographical problems in the *PMC*: II. The Corpes route', in *Mio Cid Studies* (London, forthcoming).

2694 **Griza** Unknown place, perhaps Riaza (see map). Nothing is known of Álamos, which may refer to a person rather than to a place, unless it is a garbled reference to the poplar groves on the river Riaza near the town of the same name.

2695 **Elpha** Pidal, *En torno al Poema del Cid* (Barcelona and Buenos Aires, 1963), pp. 181-86, suggests that the word may refer to an elf or wood nymph, thought to inhabit river banks or caverns.

2697 The problem of the location of the oak wood of Corpes has generated much controversy (see my article cited in note to 2693). It may have been at El Páramo, near Castillejo de Robledo, where there is a tradition that the Cid's daughters were abandoned nearby.

2719 MS *Nos vengaremos aq̃ſta por la del Leon*; Pidal, *ed. crít.*, takes *aquesta . . . la* to have the function of a neuter with the noun unexpressed (cf. *desondra* 2762) and he retains the MS reading (Smith likewise, without discussion). It is curious that no editor has noticed that the syntax of the first hemistich is impossible (though Bello showed his unease by putting a colon after *vengaremos*): it must be *vengar*+ direct object (cf. 1070 and 2868), or *vengarse de* (cf. 2894 and the passive in 2758); thus *la del león* must be the direct object of transitive *vengaremos*, and *Nós* the subject pronoun (it could not in any case be a weak object pronoun because of its colocation, see H. Ramsden, *Weak-pronoun Position in the early Romance languages*, Manchester, 1963, pp. 99-103). The omission of the noun is less serious and *desondra* need not be supplied.

2728 Above all it is the method of their ill treatment which produces the outrage and sense of shock, and which increases the dishonour.

2731 lit. 'Do not commit such cruelties upon us', or 'Do not expose us to such ignominy'; the phrase was connected with martyrdom, cf. Berceo, *San Lorenzo* 26, and biblical Latin EXEMPLARE (see Corominas, *DCELC*, s.v. *ejemplo*).

2743 **que sin cosimente son** Perhaps lit. 'that they (the daughters) are without feeling', i.e. 'benumbed'. Pidal, CC, interprets 'without strength', but admits that in other texts *sin cosimente* means 'mercilessly'. If, with Cirot, *Revista de Filología Española*, IX (1922), 164, we take this latter meaning with the Infantes as subject, we destroy the correlation of *tanto . . . que*.

2783 **Valas tornando** Possibly 'he turns them over'. Pidal, CC, and Smith interpret 'gradually he brings them round', but for that meaning *tornar* is usually followed by *en*+ *recuerdo* or *sentido* (cf. *Apol* 113*c*, 315*a*); for a physical direct object, cf. 'ouo . . . el braço a tornar' (*Apol* 528*b*).

2812 **la torre de don Urraca** Now La Torre, 7 km west by south-west of San Esteban de Gormaz; the hill has no tower on it today. The detour taken here provides the second possible example of faulty geography in this area, cf. 398, and see my article cited in note to 2693.

2814 **Diego Téllez** Probably a reference to the person of this name who was governor of Sepúlveda in 1086, but there is no documentary evidence that clearly connects him with Álvar Fáñez's household or with San Esteban.

2828 This is the formula used on the receipt of bad news, cf. 1889, 1932, 2953.

2830-31 The Cid is similarly grateful for misfortune in 8-9 and 1933.

2843 **Gormaz** MS *SantEſteuan de Gormaz*; scribal confusion of the castle of

Gormaz with the town of San Esteban de Gormaz, as 2845 makes clear (Bello, Pidal, *ed. crít.*, and Smith all make this suppression); Criado de Val defends the MS by taking 2845 *et seq.* to be a repetition in fuller form of 2843-44; but 2844 makes this hard to accept, since *por verdad* there is concessive: 'though they had been ordered to ride by night and day (2839), they did, in truth, spend one night at Gormaz'.

2849 **enfurción** lit. 'tributes or rents paid to a landlord in kind'.

2853 For the symbolic presence, cf. 505, 2088 and 2097-98.

2864 **otro tanto las ha** The phrase is otherwise unknown. Restori suggests *conortado las ha* ('he has comforted them'). It seems to refer to what follows, and like Pidal and Smith I preserve it ('also encourages them'?).

2866 **sin otro mal** *otro* here (and perhaps in 1371) is a reinforcing negative complement, equivalent to *ninguno*. The usage is not common but is sufficiently authenticated, cf. *PCG* 389*a* 44 and 626*a* 16, Berceo, *Sacrificio* 167*d*, *Apol* 513*a*.

2875 **Alcoceva** Possibly a gully which enters the Duero on the north bank at the most northerly point of the large bend between San Esteban and Gormaz.

      dexan Gormaz MS *de SantEſteuan de Gormaz*, which is certainly erroneous, since the party set out from San Esteban; Pidal suggests a scribal misreading of an earlier **desan* (or **dessan*) *Gormaz* (Smith emends likewise).

2876 **Bado de Rrey** Vadorrey, a fort which stood near the old ford across the Duero, near Morales (see map).

2911 The lesser dishonour is that indirectly touching the Cid (cf. 2910); the greater dishonour is the actual outrage (cf. 2909). The king is responsible both for arranging the marriages and for ordering the Cid to acquiesce in them. For the legal phrase *rancuras paucas vel grandes*, see A. Ubieto Arteta, *Colección diplomática de Pedro I . . .*, doc. No. 105, p. 358.

2924 **San Çalvador** Oviedo, where the cathedral is called St Saviour's.

2934 Pidal, *ed. crít.*, and Smith reorder to *los inojos fincó*, and, in company with Bello, Restori and Lidforss, suppress *aquel Muño Gustioz* as scribal anticipation of 2935, but the repetition may be deliberate.

2951 **sabidor** 'wise', perhaps 'wise in legal matters', cf. 3005.

2953 Cf. 2828.

2969 Thirty days was the more usual respite; the number may well be symbolic.

2993 **ir a** MS *yr a*; Pidal, *ed. crít.*, reads *irâ*, Smith *ira [a]*, and the future indicative is a possible reading; but the infinitive depending on *quisiesse* can stand despite the repeated negative.

3002-03 **Anrrich** Henry, grandson of Robert I, Duke of Burgundy and nephew of Queen Constanza, Alfonso VI's wife; by 1095 he had married Alfonso's bastard daughter Teresa and was made governor of Portugal. **Rremond** Raymond, Count of Amous in Burgundy, Henry's cousin and rival. He was the fourth son of William I, 'Têtehardie', and by 1087 had married Alfonso's legitimate daughter, Urraca, and was made governor of Galicia; their son became Alfonso VII, the emperor (*r.* 1127-57).

3004 **Fruella** In the MS the word is much affected by reagents; even under the ultra-violet lamp the *F* is not certain and the *r* very doubtful. Froila Díaz was Jimena's brother (see note to 239).

Beltrán Eighteen years after the Cid's death he became Count of Carrión (anachronistic reference).

3008 Assur González was the Infantes' brother, and Gonzalo Assúrez their father.

3009 Probably an emphatic reminder to the audience of the Infantes' presence.

3014 Perhaps a vague memory of the Cid's failure to arrive in time to help Alfonso to raise the siege of Aledo in 1089 (the reason for his second banishment); the Cid sent one of his vassals to reason with the king (cf. the parallel in 3016-17), but he only secured the release of Jimena and the children. Alfonso actually held a court in Toledo in March 1088, which the Cid attended, but the reason for it was a donation to the Papacy and the adoption of a new style for Alfonso (reflected in 2923-26 and 2936).

3027 **oyó** Bello, Milá, *De la poesía heroico-popular castellana* (Barcelona, repr. 1959), Restori, Cornu, *Etudes*, and Lidforss alter to *vyo*, Pidal, *ed. crít.*, to *vido*, Smith to [*vio*], but the MS reading can be defended as catachresis (cf. the opposite change in 1662 and 2347), or as reported speech (i.e. 'when the king heard that he was to do that . . .').

3039-41 The Cid reminds the king of Doña Jimena's importance (see note to 239).

3047 **San Serván** The castle of San Servando, across the Tagus gorge from Toledo, above the bridge of Alcántara; Alfonso VI rebuilt it as a monastery and it formed part of his donation to the Papacy in 1088 (see note to 3014).

3080 **desobra** Pidal interprets as 'demasía, desmán' and Smith as 'outrage' but the word is otherwise unknown; perhaps it should be read 'de sobra' (cf. *Poema de Yúçuf* 18d, where *sobras* seems to mean 'ill treatment'). It may, however, be a scribal error for *desonra*, 'dishonour', or for *desabor*, 'displeasure, unpleasantness' (cf. *Calila e Dimna*, ed. Keller and Linker, ch. II, 4 (p. 31), etc.).

3099-100 Pidal and Smith punctuate with a comma after *valor*, making the cloak the object of admiration, instead of the Cid, but cf. 2060 and 3123-24.

3115 The gift of this bench or throne has not been mentioned before.

3188 The nephew is not named here, but it is Pedro Bermúdez, cf. 3301 and 3623. Supposing a scribal omission, Lidforss inserts [*Pero Vermuez*] and Pidal, *ed. crít.*, and Smith insert *don Pero*; it may be an error, but it is not unknown in other medieval works for names to be withheld to a later point in the narration.

3215 In the MS the first hemistich reads *Dixo Albarfanez leuantados en pie*; scribal confusion. Most editors suppress *Dixo Albarfanez* and alter *leuantados* to *Levantós'*; it would be possible to retain more of the MS reading by repunctuating 3214-16 thus (with minor changes): *Dixo el buen rrey: 'Assí lo otorgo yo.' | Dixo Álbar Fáñez: '¡Levantados en pie, ya Cid Campeador!' | [Dixo el Cid:] 'D'estos averes que vos di yo . . .' etc.,* especially since 2027 is almost identical to 3215 and contains one of the three other examples of *os* as a weak object pronoun in the poem.

3216b The Cid here addresses the defendants directly, whereas earlier he had put his case to the judges; E. de Hinojosa, *Estudios sobre la historia del derecho español* (Madrid, 1903), pp. 90 *et seq.*, sees this as a mixture of the old Germanic law of direct confrontation and the later procedure of greater judicial intervention.

3220 **señor** MS *fabor*, which all the editors accept, Pidal, *ed. crít.*, p. 834, taking the phrase to mean 'hablan a su gusto', but this does not make good sense. I take *sabor* to be scribal anticipation of the last word of 3222, and *a so sabor* was common enough for the scribe to turn to (cf. 234, 1381, etc.); the commonest construction was *fablar con*+ object but *fablar* takes a direct pronoun object in 154 and a direct expressed noun object in 2229 (cf. *Coplas de Yoçef* 289a).

3277 Smith punctuates the line with exclamation marks.

3302 **Pero Mudo** lit. 'Peter the Dumb'—a pun on his name (he is noted for his taciturnity and stutter in the poem). We need not assume a memory of the form **Vermúdoz* here, as Smith (note to 611) suggests, since the audience would be aware that *Vermúez* meant 'son of Vermudo'.

3304 Perhaps 'they insult me, they slap your face' (metaphorically speaking). Pidal and Smith interpret the second hemistich as 'it is you they are getting at indirectly', without convincing supporting evidence. *Veinte reyes* has a similar passage: 'E como quier qu'ellos me digan esto, a ti dan las orejadas'. Cf. 'Sabed que dueña que haze cavallero non da orejada, mas [el caballero] bésala a todo su plazer tres vezes', *Enrique Fi de Oliva* (1425, ed. 1498), ed. Gayangos (1871), p. 65. There are two O. Fr. examples of *donner une oreilliee* = 'to slap', and, without mentioning our examples of *orejadas*, Corominas (*DCELC*, s.v. *oreja*) refers to *pestorejada* in *Cavallero Zifar* [but in Wagner's edition it is given as *prestorejada*], which was replaced in the first printed edition with *palmada* and which meant 'slap on the cheek'. The presence of the definite article in *dar las orejadas* could imply that such an action usually accompanied a challenge (though the slaps may not actually have been delivered).

3310 A further obscure reference to their earlier attendance in court, cf. 3272.

3316 **¡miémbrat'** Bello, Cornu, *Etudes*, Lidforss and Smith take this to be interrogative, as though it read *¿miémbra[s]te?* Pidal, *ed. crít.*, does not punctuate, but it must be imperative, as he notes in his Vocabulary.

3325 'won your spurs'; lit. 'done a noble deed'.

3366 **vestist** MS *veftid*; Cornu, *Etudes*, Lidforss, Staaff and Smith alter to *vesti[ste]d*, but, as Pidal points out, in that case the object pronoun would have to precede the verb (**non te vestiste*); Ramsden, *Weak-pronoun Position*, pp. 64-66, finds no example in his texts of postposition after a negative adverb but cites Gessner's solitary example from the *Fuero juzgo*; it is therefore not the same case as *fusted* in 3365 as Smith maintains, and *vestir* is reflexive only in 1587 (contrast 991, 1871, 3087, 3093).

3379 **Rrío d'Ovirna** The river Ubierna, on which Vivar stands; a more recent mill is still working there. *Infanzones* commonly owned mills, but they did not work them themselves. There may be a faint aspersion on the Cid's parentage here, since a late ballad suggests that the Cid's father Diego Laínez begot him by a peasant woman (by a mill girl in a seventeenth century reference); the legend of the bastardy may be older, because the *Tercera crónica general* goes out of its way to deny it. In folk-lore bastards were commonly thought to be stronger than sons born in wedlock.

3385　When the celebrant said the *Pax Domini* it was formerly the custom of the Church for the communicants to kiss one another.

3394　**Ojarra** Unknown personage; the name is from Basque *otso*, 'a wolf', cf. the form *Ochoa*.

　　　Íñigo Jiménez A person of this name was governor of Meltria *c.* 1106-07 and favourite of Alfonso the Battler, king of Aragon.

3399　**rreínas** Contrast 3448. Neither daughter in fact became queen; Cristina (Elvira) married (*c.* 1098-99) a prince of Navarre, Ramiro, lord of Monzón, who was grandson of King García de Atapuerca; their son, García Ramírez, became king of Navarre in 1134. María (Sol) married Ramón Berenguer III the Great, Count of Barcelona (nephew of the count in the poem); they had two daughters, but María died in 1105 when she was about 25; she may have had a first marriage, or merely a betrothal, to Pedro Pedrez, son of Peter I of Aragon.

3457　**Gómez Peláyet** A Leonese noble, who may have been the son of Pelayo Gómez (the third son of Count Gómez Díaz).

3496　Pidal, *ed. crít.*, and Smith alter the sense: *Adeliño al c. don A. e* [*a*]*l c. don R.*, but I cannot think with Smith that the counts must still be on the judges' bench here—the lawsuit is over by 3491.

3507　A folio was removed from the MS after f. 69; we may therefore assume a lacuna of about fifty lines. The chronicle versions give an account here of how the Cid raced Babieca to demonstrate the horse's excellence to the king, *Veinte reyes* stating that this demonstration took place in the Zocodover, or market-place, of Toledo. There was no need for Pidal, *ed. crít.*, to start a new *laisse* in 3508.

3528　See note to 225.

3532　The Cid does not appear again until 3710, almost at the end of the poem.

3623　Although the duels are fought simultaneously, the poet describes them consecutively, according to the order in which the challenges were issued.

3662-63 MS *Diagonçalez*: haplography; Smith admits *Dia Gonçalez*; Pidal, *ed. crít.*, suppresses the name and relocates the line between 3659 and 3660, thus losing the effect of 3664, where the mention of Diego's rank makes his cowardice appear more shameful.

3666-67 With Hinard and Pidal I take Diego to be the subject of *asorrienda*, *mesurando* and *sacó* and his horse to be the object of each of these verbs (Smith likewise). Diego admits defeat by fleeing from the field, cf. 3607.

3679　Bello, Pidal, *ed. crít.*, and Smith suppress this line as scribal repetition of 3676—it prevents one seeing 3680-81 as strict narrative succession; but 3680-81 may be poetic detailing of the blow struck in 3678-79.

3690　Assur's father shouts out to admit defeat on his son's behalf.

3691 Pidal and Smith take this line to be in the direct speech of 3690, while Huntington ends the direct speech after *campo*; but 'The field is won!' (cf. 1740) would sound strange on the lips of the defeated man's father. I take *acabarse* to mean 'to be carried out' (cf. 1771, 3205), *esto* in 3691 being the same as *Esto* in 3692, i.e. the father's surrender on the son's behalf. (Contrast the passive use of *vençer*, when the words *campo*, *lid* or *batalla* are not present, = 'to be defeated', cf. 3484, 3607, 3644.)

3694 The weapons of defeated traitors were the perquisite of the monarch.

3715 Pun on the legal phrase *heredad quita*, 'land free from encumbrance'.

3723 **señoras** lit. 'ladies' of Navarre and Aragon, but cf. 3399.

3724-25 Pidal argues that there was sufficient connexion between the Cid's descendants and the kings of Castile and Aragon by 1140 for that year to be the *terminus a quo* of the poem. The connexion by then was still extremely tenuous, however, and A. Ubieto Arteta, *Arbor*, XXXVII (1957), 145-170, points out that on a strict interpretation of these lines the earliest possible date of composition is 1201. Line 3725 was inscribed on the Cid's new tomb in Burgos cathedral at Menéndez Pidal's suggestion; this was probably the last line written by the poet (see next note).

3726 In 1099, the year of the Cid's death, Whit Sunday fell on 29 May, but the more reliable *Historia Roderici* says that he died in July of that year. P. E. Russell, *Medium Aevum*, XXVII (1958), 57-79, at 74, was the first to point out the 'suddenness and crudity of this ending' and suggested that the lines from 3726-30 were an alteration by the copyist to truncate the end of the poem, which may have clashed with the now lost *Estoria del Cid* (*c.* 1238-60?), a vernacular prose legend mentioning the Cid's embalmed body being displayed for ten years by the monks at Cardeña until the nose fell off.

3727 This faulty line supports Russell's argument that it is part of a scribal interpolation (see previous note).

3731 **escrivió** 'wrote out', 'copied down', see Alarcos Llorach, *Investigaciones sobre el Libro de Alexandre* (Madrid, 1948), pp. 47-50, and J. Horrent, in *Mélanges . . . M. Delbouille* (Gembloux, 1964), II pp. 275-89, at p. 276. **libro** 'book', i.e. 'manuscript copy', see Horrent, *loc. cit.*

3732 **Per Abbat** The name of a scribe, either of the extant MS or, more probably, of an earlier MS copied in 1207 but now lost.

3733 After the second C there is a space large enough to have contained another letter which coincides with a crease in the parchment (the crease runs from just above this point to the bottom of the folio). Pidal mentions the crease (probably the result of earlier application of reagents), which disappeared temporarily when he applied further reagents; he found no trace of ink in the controversial space. Under the ultra-violet lamp I too saw no ink traces whatever. We cannot even be sure that there were signs of an erasure (i.e. there may have been nothing written in the space, a view to which Huntington inclined). If there had been anything there it could have been another C, or the conjunction *τ*, which is sometimes found in dates in that form. It is not clear why anyone should have wanted to erase the conjunction, but the erasure of a third

C might have been done to correct an automatic error made by the fourteenth-century copyist (this is Ubieto's view), or by someone later to pass off the MS as being older than it is. As it stands, the date is 1245 *Era* [*de Julio César*], in fact, counting from the foundation of the Roman provinces in Spain, thirty-eight years ahead of the Christian era; this cannot be the date of the extant MS, thus it may refer to its predecessor, made in A.D. 1207.

3733-35 The words after *años* are in a different, but fourteenth-century, hand, and are badly affected by the repeated use of reagents; they provide evidence of the extant MS being used in actual performance.

Addenda

While the edition has been with the publishers, new studies have appeared on various aspects of the poem; I include the most important of them below.

page 3, line 3 On the Cid's campaigns in the east of the Peninsula, see David Hook, 'The conquest of Valencia in the *CMC*', *Bulletin of Hispanic Studies*, L (1973), 120-26.

page 6, lines 14-16 L. P. Harvey ('The metrical irregularity of the *CMC*', *Bulletin of Hispanic Studies*, XL, 1963, 137-43) was the first to suggest that the faulty metre of the poem might be the result of dictation to a scribe, and his view has been supported recently by Stephen Gilman, who admits none the less that the formulae show that the original 'chanted' version must itself have been metrically irregular (see 'The poetry of the *Poema* and the music of the *Cantar*', *Philological Quarterly*, LI, 1972, 1-11); see also Kenneth Adams, *BHS*, XLIX (1972), 109-19.

page 10, line 30 For an interesting account of gradation and contrast in the poem, see A. D. Deyermond, 'Structural and stylistic patterns in the *CMC*', in *Medieval Studies in honor of Robert White Linker* (Madrid, 1973), pp. 55-71.

page 12, last line A similar view is expressed by Ruth H. Webber, who has carried out a useful analysis of the thematic structure of the poem from the 'oralist' or Lordian viewpoint; see 'Narrative organization of the *CMC*', *Olifant*, I, No. 2 (December 1973), 21-34, at 29.

page 13, note 26 Colin Smith also suggests that Per Abbat could have been the author or at least the 'reworker' of the poem (see 'Per Abbat and the *PMC*', *Medium Aevum*, XLII, 1973, 1-17); he refers to the Per Abbat connected with a diploma forged in Cordobilla (province of Palencia) *c.* 1223, which lists among its alleged witnesses the Cid and nine other personages from the Cid legend. Interesting as this investigation is, it is fairly otiose if *escrivió* in *PMC* 3731 means no more than 'copied'.

page 16, note 29 For a revised statement of Ubieto's views and a long account of the historical and geographical problems, see *El 'CMC' y algunos problemas históricos* (Valencia, 1973).

page 17, line 19 Shortage of space has enabled me to include, for the most part, only the annotations of my disagreement with Colin Smith's critical text; the reader should bear in mind, however, the very many occasions when our readings coincide.

page 217 (Abbreviations) [insert] *CMC: Cantar de Mio Cid.*

page 236, note to 2731 A valuable investigation of the possible connexion between the sufferings of Elvira and Sol and the martyrdom of female saints has been carried out by John K. Walsh, 'Religious motifs in the early Spanish epic', *Revista Hispánica Moderna*, XXXVI (1970-71), 165-72 [appeared 1974].